To MY FRIEN
RUTH

Tommy Wilson

I AM
TOMMY
ON STAGE AND BACKSTAGE

TOM WILSON

◆ FriesenPress

Suite 300 - 990 Fort St
Victoria, BC, V8V 3K2
Canada

www.friesenpress.com

ISBN
978-1-5255-2907-8 (Hardcover)
978-1-5255-2908-5 (Paperback)
978-1-5255-2909-2 (eBook)

1. BIOGRAPHY & AUTOBIOGRAPHY

Distributed to the trade by The Ingram Book Company

INTRODUCTION

I wrote this book with the thought that people will enjoy my stories as much as I do remembering them. I have included my early years to give some insight into who Tommy Wilson is and how he got that way. Then came the music business. There is name dropping. I was in a unique position. I was a musician who recorded hit songs and performed on stage in front of millions of fans and I was also an agent who met, booked and performed with many of Canada's and the world's rock stars.

The list is long; it includes Little Caesar and the Consuls, the Guess Who, the Rolling Stones, Gordon Lightfoot, David Clayton Thomas, Randy Bachman, the Lovin Spoonful, Bobby Curtola, Add to that Blood Sweat and Tears, Triumph, Steppenwolf, the Beach Boys, The Five Man Electrical Band, Johnny Cash,, Alice Cooper, Elton John, Burton Cummings and, well, you get the idea.

I was involved in a lot of firsts and had a backstage pass to most any concert anywhere. What's particularly wonderful about my life in the music industry is that I made so many friends along the way. Sadly I have also lost more than a few. "One wild roller coaster ride" is how I describe it. I went from being a fan to an unpaid roadie, a musician, and $30 a week booking agent and on to the top. It was like an acid trip up and down, up, down again and up.

That was my world from 1939 to 1980. Those years cover the most exciting era of my life in the business. Everything after that was tweaking to make it better (or sometimes worse). I travelled a lot. Mostly across Canada and the United States and also got to Europe. I flew to New York and Detroit sometimes weekly and throw in San Francisco, Nashville, and Chicago, Los Angeles, Boston and so many other American cities. I was on the road constantly. I was also fitting in trips across the Canadian west from Winnipeg to Vancouver as well as overseeing my offices in Ottawa, Montreal and Halifax. (Too bad this was all before Air Miles). While this book has many stories about musicians both famous and not so famous, I also focus on the ins and outs of the business side of music. I met, hung out with and worked with just as many fascinating behind the scenes people who controlled the business as those on the performing side. I hope you enjoy my journey.

PROLOUGE

It was early May the spring of 1979. One day I was sitting in Tim Horton's having a coffee facing the fact that I had finished my last project and that I had nothing else coming up. I was feeling burned out after over three decades of non-stop working. I was bone tired. Worst of all, thanks to booze, smoking, drugs and my personal and business life roller coaster ride, I was so stressed out I was bordering on a mental meltdown. I wondered how the hell I had ended up here. How did all this happen? The feeling continued to bother me day and night. I couldn't sleep and I finally made a decision. I had to make a change. I needed to get away and clear my head. I cleaned up all of my loose ends in Toronto, made sure my wife Lucy and my kids Lisa, Tom Jr. and Jeremy were all taken care of then, on May 19, grabbed a cab to the airport and boarded an Air Canada flight to Los Angeles. This meant leaving everything behind with no idea what I was going to do when I got there or how long I would be away. I just knew I had to be somewhere else. It was a five hour flight so I had a lot of time to let my mind wander and reflect back to when, where and why it had all started.

CHAPTER 1

Start Me Up

I was born at a very young age, as they say, in Toronto, on February 8, 1939, and lived most of my early year's downtown. According to my mom I came out of the womb looking for trouble. She used to tell me that my birth was what started World War II. I have one brother, Jimmy, who is four years older than me. I was a typical kid growing up in a working-class/middle-class neighbourhood that was predominantly Jewish.

My dad, James Skillen Wilson, was born in 1913 in Bangor, a seaside town in Northern Ireland. He immigrated to Canada when he was 16 years old, bringing along his 14-year-old brother Jack, and they decided to settle in Toronto. Family rumour has it that they left Ireland in a hurry. Something about the IRA and a bank robbery? My mom, Mary Helen Ryan, was French Canadian, born in 1910 in Saint-Eustache, Quebec. The second oldest in a family of seven children, she had to drop out of school in Grade 4 to take care of her younger siblings. When she was old enough to leave home she relocated to Toronto. There she met dad, who was three years younger than her.

He was a hard-drinking, racist, Irish Protestant and devout Orangeman. Mom was a naive, gentle, non-drinking, bilingual, French-Canadian Roman Catholic. A challenging and toxic combination. Both my parents worked, my dad at Dill Manufacturing, a metal-processing company at Bathurst and King Streets, my mom was right across the street at a textile company working the night shift. This was 1940s wartime, so women were needed in the workforce to replace the men who had gone overseas to fight Hitler and The Nazis. That made my brother and me "latchkey kids". In other words, we pretty well took care of ourselves. Parental guidance was not available.

I don't remember much until I was about three. I can remember we lived on Schollard St. Behind the house was the Rosedale Valley. A large wooded stretch between Yonge St and Bayview Ave. My brother told me there were ghosts living in the woods. Scared the hell out of me. I was three! Truth be known it was home for a lot of homeless people. My first girlfriend. A blonde girl the same age as me. She had a carriage with a doll in it. We would stroll up and down the street pushing the carriage together then sit on my front porch and talk. What the hell do 3 year olds talk about?

We moved to a three-storey rented house at 254 Harbord Street, just west of Bathurst, where the rent was $25 a month. We very seldom locked the front door—no need as we were bordering on poor. The house was a big problem at first. We didn't know until we moved in that it was infested with rats. Not the cute little ones, but big, ugly grey sewer rats that you could hear running through the walls and across the floor. Dad set six to eight traps every night, every morning there would be a rat in every one. He borrowed a terrier called Billy from a friend he worked with. Billy took his job seriously and usually caught as many rats as the traps. This went on for a couple of months—it was bad! One day I opened the oven door of the kitchen stove. There, staring back at me was one big mother of a rat. It scared the shit out me (I was only four). I slammed the oven door shut and climbed up on the kitchen table, which is where my brother found me about half an hour later. One night my mom was the butt of a joke that my dad thought was hilarious. He tied a dead rat to the string that you pulled to turn on the kitchen light. Mom reached up to pull it and screamed in terror as her hand encountered the rat. Dad was the only one who thought the prank was funny.

Before I came along, mom enrolled Jimmy in St. Peter's Catholic School on Bathurst Street near Bloor St. and she would converse with him in both French and English. That didn't last long. When the old man found out he told Mom not to speak that "frog" language and to get Jimmy out of that fuckin' mick school or else! She knew what that meant. She transferred Jimmy to King Edward Public School. I never learned to speak French.

At first, dad got drunk just on the weekends, but it gradually escalated to every day. He eventually lost his job at Dill and ended up as a window cleaner.

Sometimes he took me to work with him. I got to hang beside him in harness six or seven storeys above the ground, sometimes higher. I'm sure that was against the law but the view was great. Sometimes he would wake Jimmy and me in the middle of the night, when mom was at work, to meet his girlfriends. I had to sit on their laps. I liked the attention

Now a hardcore alcoholic, dad was getting more and more abusive to mom, my brother, and me. Jimmy and I would get out of the house as soon as we could every day. It was a 100-yard dash to Markham Street and around the corner to get out of sight. If we didn't make it the old man would order us back home. Jimmy and I learned to run very fast at an early age. It wasn't all bad though mostly, thanks to mom. She continually defended us and, more often than not, took the heat for us. Every year, just before Christmas, she would head out to the local Household Finance branch and borrow enough money to get us presents and a tree. Then she would spend the next year paying back the loan.

From the time I was about four until about twelve years old, we spent a good part of the summer weekends with my aunt and uncle, who worked as hired hands on a series of farms in the Simcoe, Ontario area. Sometimes our parents would leave us with them for a week or two. The drive from Toronto to the farm was insane. My mom would sit in the back seat with a mini sandwich bar. On dad's command, "Mary, make me a sandwich!" she would (usually tomato and lettuce with mayonnaise) and hand it to him. Sometimes he would take only one bite and then toss it out the window. He would stop for a beer or two (or more) in every town with a tavern. There were four or five along the route, and for some reason they were all called the Queen's Hotel. The normally two-hour drive would become four, so by the time we got to Simcoe the old man was flying pretty high. We had four country cousins. Bernice and Mervin, the two oldest, were the same age as me, Dorothy was a few years younger, and Barbara was the baby. Usually we worked on the farm from dawn to dusk, picking tobacco and strawberries, hoeing corn, baling hay, and other jobs as needed. My favourite was driving the hay wagon, which was pulled by two huge horses. Once they stampeded on me; I was hanging on for dear life on top of an eight-foot stack of hay bales as the horses raced down the path from the field to the barn. They finally ran out of steam after what seemed like a mile and I got them turned around and headed back to the field. I had to hang out with Mervin. I picked on him a lot. I taught him how to smoke, stealing the cigarettes from my dad's pack. One time I talked him into climbing up onto the rafters at the top of the barn, then pushed him off and jumped after him—we both made a soft landing in the hay. Mervin was not an adventurous guy. The best story about the farm is the Chicken Caper of 1947. One weekend we stopped in Simcoe on the way to the farm and dad went into a farm-supply store that sold baby chicks—you know those little yellow balls of feathers. I don't know what he was thinking, but he bought a hundred of them, packed into four boxes, that he loaded into the car with us. When we arrived at my uncle's farm, dad got us to unload the boxes and take the chicks into the house. Dad released them giving instructions to his brother Jack to take care of them making it clear that the chicks were dad's property. It doesn't take much imagination to picture the chaos of a hundred chicks running all over the place.

Within a couple of days my uncle had erected a wire fence and a chicken coop outside in the front yard and transferred the chicks to their new home. My brother, Jimmy, takes over the narrative from here:

> *"Times were tough for Uncle Jack and his family. They barely eked out a living, so sometimes when my old man wasn't around, they would chow down on a chicken. Dad would arrive at infrequent interludes to do—you guessed it—a chicken audit. He would sit on a chair and have the chickens paraded past him while he counted. Fortunately he was, by this time, heavily into the booze so the chickens and the scenery would start to get somewhat out of focus. At this point, as the chicken audit continued, Uncle Jack had his kids start recirculating the chickens around the back of the coop, so Dad was unknowingly counting the same fowl two or three times. From his point of view, the audit always indicated a nice increase in the chicken population, and Uncle Jack was a hero! "*

Life on the farm was seldom dull. When I was six, and showing off as usual, I fell off a fence I was climbing and smashed my left elbow on a flat rock. Uncle Jack drove mom and me to the local doctor, who diagnosed the injury as a bad sprain. He wrapped it tightly to control the swelling and sent us off. By the time we left to go home the next day, my arm was swollen to twice its size. My mom knew it was much worse than a sprain, while my dad was calling me a wimp because I was crying. When we reached home, she immediately called our family physician, Dr. Golden, whose office was a block away, and got an emergency appointment. The doc took one look at my arm and told Mom to get me to Sick Children's Hospital fast.

The hospital, located at the corner of Elizabeth and College Streets, just west of Bay Street at that time, was (and still is) famous for its innovative treatment of all types of children's medical problems. Dr. Golden had phoned ahead and he obviously had some pull, because I was immediately taken into X-ray. It turned out that all the bones in my elbow had been shattered and they were concerned that I might lose the arm. They promptly arranged to get me into surgery where the doctor opened up the elbow and wired everything back together. I now had a plaster cast from my armpit to my wrist. I spent the next week in bed in the hospital. Finally my mom was told that the operation had been successful, but I would need months of physiotherapy if the arm was ever going to function properly again.

When the cast came off, even trying to bend the stiff arm was very painful. Dad's idea of physio was me sparing with my brother to exercise the elbow. Poor Jimmy. We put on the boxing gloves and I learned to fight by using my injured left arm to jab and punch my brother. Jimmy had to fight on his knees because I was so short and that made him an easy target. I could whip around behind him and punch the hell out of his head. When he tried to retaliate the old man would cuff him on the ear and tell him to stop it but Jimmy did get in a couple of good shots that put me on my ass. The positives for me? I kept my arm and I learned how to box.

On Harbord Street we always had boarders living with us. A middle aged married couple in the upstairs front room, a single guy in the upstairs middle bedroom, and another in the room at the rear of the house. All were from the Maritimes. Downstairs mom and dad used the dining room as a bedroom, putting up drapes to separate it from the living room. We always ate in the kitchen. Jimmy and I had the third-floor attic, where we slept together in a double bed. There was only one bathroom for the whole house. Sometimes, rather than go all the way downstairs, Jimmy and I would just open our window to pee. Eventually the guy in the rear moved out and I got that room which was great because there was a porch roof outside where I could sneak out, shinny down the drainpipe, and go play with my friends. I never got caught.

I went to King Edward Public School, on Bathurst south of College Street, the same as Jimmy. The students were almost all Jewish, which was great for us kids because we got all the regular school holidays plus the bonus of all the Jewish holidays when the teachers would sometimes send us home early because of a lack of students. I was a tough and angry kid. I was also short in temper and height— a bad combination. I attended kindergarten for a few weeks, and then decided to take a pass. I wandered around outside the school until the other kids came out, and then I would corner one of them, take their artwork, and give it to mom as mine. I suppose that classifies me as a bully. It worked out great until Parent's Night, when mom asked the teacher how I was doing. Her reply was "Who?"—She thought we had moved. Bad news for me at home. Whenever Jimmy and I got caught doing anything wrong, dad would make us stand in front of him in the living room and drop our pants and underwear. Off would come his leather belt, we would turn around and bend over, and he would administer ten or more whacks to our butts. Sometimes this was even done in front of people who happened to be visiting—take that one to a shrink! One memory that always stands out for me is when we got our first TV set. It was a Sylvania Halo light, which had a lit-up frame around the screen. Friday night was Pabst Blue Ribbon Fight Night. Dad would be drunk and yelling at the boxers on the screen. "Kill the black bastard!" he would yell. We couldn't figure out who the hell he was talking about as both the fighters were black. Then there were the parties where friends and sometimes relatives would come mostly to drink their brains out. I remember one scary night when a lady named Rosie, a so-called friend of dad's, tried to get me alone and almost succeeded. Rosie was a heroin addict and in her drunken and drugged stupor she wanted to shoot me up with her needle. I dodged around her and told Jimmy who told my dad who disarmed Rosie and threw her out of the house. Whew!

When I was old enough, around ten I think, I lucked into a job going around the neighbourhood on Saturday mornings to turn off lights and other utilities for the religious Jews. They called me the *Shabbes goy* kid. I never knew what that meant until years later. A *Shabbes goy* is a non-Jew who performs certain types of chores like shutting off lights and others that Jewish religious law forbids Jews doing on the Sabbath. I took care of about 15 homes and picked up 25 cents, sometimes 50, from each one. The front door would be left unlocked so I could get in and the money was usually left either in a bowl by the door or on the kitchen table, because they couldn't touch money either. I also had a part-time job delivering prescriptions and other stuff on my bicycle for the local pharmacy.

One family thing we sometimes did on Sundays was to drive to Granma's small farm in Weston. If the old man couldn't or wouldn't drive we would ride the streetcar to the end of the line and then walk. Granma was my mom's mother, who had moved to Toronto when her first husband died. There she met and married Charlie Horner. The family—usually ten or more people—would get together and play guitars, sing country songs, have picnics on the lawn, and… oh yeah, drink.

I somehow managed to get through public school, though not without some challenges. I learned early on that the best defence was attack, and it worked most of the time. When I did lose, which wasn't often, my classic line was "You should see the other guy." Besides spending a lot of time in the principal's office, I got detentions, had to do the stand-in-the-corner-facing-the-wall thing, and got the strap fairly often, especially from my Grade 8 teacher, Mr. Gang who was an interesting character. He was even shorter than me, so he had to stand on a chair to properly apply the ten blows of the strap to my palms. I would never admit that it hurt. My dad hit a lot harder, and not on the hands.

Despite my issues, I did make it to high school. We had three choices. Central Tech was the trade school, Harbord Collegiate was for academics, doctors, and lawyers, and Central Commerce was for the commercial people. A lot of future secretaries were at Commerce, so it was a popular place for guys to hang around, trying to get lucky.

I chose Central Tech, where I made the junior basketball team and played for almost two years. I was pretty good; even though I was short, I was fast. That and I practised for hours every day. The Harlem Globetrotters were my heroes. Growing up, there weren't many sports I didn't play, and most of them I did well—except for hockey. How un-Canadian was that? I couldn't skate worth a damn, so I got the name the "Ankle Kid." I made up for my lack of mobility on skates with a busy stick that cleared the way in front of me. Funny thing though. I could do all kinds of tricks on roller skates and even waltz but not on ice skates.

There was always a lot to do in our neighbourhood: Honest Ed's Warehouse store at Bloor and Bathurst, Kresge's and Woolworth Five and Dime stores which were the forerunners of Wal-Mart type stores. They had everything you could imagine really cheap and you could hang out for an afternoon to enjoy some shoplifting. Wouldn't you know I got caught lifting a giant balloon? I hid it under my jacket and was walking out of the store when I felt a hand on my shoulder. Who knew they had security I lucked out. They didn't charge me or anything so I got to walk away. Whew! Jimmy and I would go to movie matinees at one of the four local theatres on Bloor Street. It cost a nickel to get in for which you got the news, a cartoon, and an intermission, so you could buy some popcorn, a soft drink, or a chocolate bar and then the feature film which was usually a series western that ran a different episode every week. Roy Rogers, Hopalong Cassidy, the Lone Ranger, and Gene Autry, as well as Superman and Batman, were favourites. At the end of the show you had to stand and wait while the national anthem, "God Save the King," was played. We would be almost blinded when we left the dark theatre and hit the daylight sun.

A lot of us joined the Midtown K Club, a community centre sponsored by the Kiwanis, in the basement of Bathurst Street United Church, at Bathurst and Lennox Streets. There you could play basketball, do gymnastics, and play all kinds of board games in the games room, as well as table tennis or darts. There was also a crafts room where you could make all kinds of gadgets out of wood and glass or other hobby stuff. It was a home away from home. Another regular activity was Friday nights at Knox Presbyterian Church at Harbord and Spadina. Happy Hour, which started at six p.m., we sang hymns and memorized Bible verses. If we stood up and recited the verses correctly, we got a pencil as a prize. Invariably on the way home, fights would start and turn into brawls in the middle of the street, so the hour was eventually cancelled. I usually held my own, but a couple of times big brother had to pitch in and help me out.

I was asked to leave Central Tech in Grade 10 because of my antisocial attitude and lack of interest in academics. I was only 14 but, thanks to Barb McWilliams, a friend from King Edward School, I managed to get a job first as a mail boy with the Ontario government, working in the Legislative Building in Queen's Park. I graduated from there to the printer's division. I learned to be a Queen's Printer. That didn't work out. I got into a difference of opinion with the foreman who was a bully and an asshole so I, having enough of his bullshit, dragged him over to my printing machine and put his tie in the roller. One of the guys stepped in and cut his tie of at the knot so I didn't get to see his face hit the rollers and do a black face. Too bad. I had to appear at a Civil Servant Disciplinary Hearing because you can't just fire a civil servant which was me. It was recommended that I resign. Good choice of words. Instead I was relocated to the main government warehouse at Keele St. and 401 Highway.

Because of my age I had to attend school at night. I chose Ryerson, where I managed to get through two courses in two years, economics and business administration until I was 16 and old enough to quit permanently. I also worked nights as a pin boy at the Brunswick Bowling Alley on Bloor Street, where I didn't last long. One night a drunk who was bowling thought it would be fun to heave a ball down the alley and try to hit me as I set up the pins. I went after him with a couple of pins and had almost got to him when my boss grabbed and held on to me. At least he threw the asshole out but that ended my career as a pin boy, as well as the extra income. As often as I could I played billiards at the pool hall at Dovercourt and Bloor and actually made money playing and betting on the games. I wasn't great at it, but, I was good enough.

As I got older I spent less and less time at home. I had three close friends, Gord McWilliams, Bill Williams, and Al Skorayko. I could hang out at their houses and, sometimes if I timed it right, would be able to get a free dinner. I was considered to be almost a part of their families.

Dad was getting progressively worse and I was now old enough to try to fight back, so things were getting pretty violent. We went from hair-pulling to fists, and one time even to knives. I'm certain now that he was just playing with me when it got to the knives, but it sure seemed serious to me. Finally, one day, fed up, Jimmy got into it with dad in the kitchen. He landed a punch that spun the old man around so that he smashed into the cast-iron stove. He broke his ankle in three places and ended up on crutches. Now he could play the sympathy card, which was almost as bad as the abuse. Even worse for me, he now had a crutch to hit me over the head and shoulders with. Fortunately, most of the time, he wasn't mobile enough or sober enough to reach me.

At this point our landlord decided to raise the rent from $25 a month to $75 (no rent controls in those days). Jimmy was working as a gas station attendant. Even though he was only 18, he figured it was better to pay a mortgage than rent. He managed to scrape together enough money to make a down payment on a house, so in 1954 we moved to 727 Lansdowne Street, just north of Bloor. My brother was always the quiet angry guy, but he grew up really quickly and had taken over running the family. Up till then Mom had done everything, but she was now taking Jimmy's advice.

Dad was getting worse having alcohol-induced hallucinations and staring to lose it. The cops showed up at our place on a regular basis because of noise violations and assault accusations. One incident that sticks in my mind was when dad was sure there was someone on our roof waiting for us to come outside so he could shoot us. Dad got out the .22 rifle we had for shooting groundhogs at the farm and stood outside waving the gun around, looking for a target. We managed to get him calmed down and back inside the house and hid the gun before the cops arrived.

After only one year Jimmy sold the Lansdowne house and we moved to a bungalow Jimmy had bought in Scarborough. It wasn't long before I left, moving to a rented room on Lee Avenue in the Beaches—nice landlady and the deal included room and board. I was still working for the government. Fed up with him Jimmy threw the old man out of the bungalow and dad moved to a flophouse somewhere around Jarvis and Shuter, a rough area of Toronto. Mom was the last to leave shortly after when Jimmy met a girl, Mary Ellen, at a party and announced that he was getting married.

We helped Mom get her own apartment, and she was happy with her new life. By then I think she was working at Parkers Dry Cleaning on Yonge Street and making enough money to take care of herself. Both Jimmy and I visited her a lot. She even started to smoke and drink (or at least pretended to) and got herself a boyfriend. Huey was a really nice guy who was devoted to her. She got to dominate that relationship, which also made her very happy.

In 1954 I was hanging out at Queen and Davenport with some bikers who had became friends. I was 15 years old. At first I was more like a mascot than a biker, since my wheels was a Raleigh three-speed racing bicycle. I'm not sure why they put up with me. Maybe it was the amusement I provided by following the guys on my bicycle from the restaurant on Queen Street West to our other hangout, the Evergreen Restaurant, on Bloor just east of Bathurst. When the bikes (mostly Harleys) were parked, they took up almost the whole block, and we packed the restaurant. Sometimes we went to Fran's Restaurant on Yonge

Street, north of Eglinton Avenue. I could usually keep up with the group but had to pedal my ass off and ended up breathless a lot. One night, on the downhill trip back to Bloor Street, I got stopped for speeding—40 miles an hour in a 30 mph zone. The cop, who had seen the big bikes go by, was laughing his head off and just gave me a warning.

Over the next couple of years I worked my way through some used motorcycles. First up, a Harley Hummer, which was one step up from the bicycle—not a lot of credibility other than it had a motor. Then a 1948 Indian Chief, the biggest bike I ever rode. At five foot five I looked like a midget sitting on it, my arms stretched to the limit just to reach the handlebars, but now I could go on out-of-town tours with the guys. Unfortunately the bike blew up under me. (Yes, Virginia, I quickly checked for damage to my lower parts—fortunately there was none.) Then came a Matchless, an English touring bike made by one of the world's oldest motorcycle manufacturers, dating back to 1899. It was really comfortable and very boring, boring, and more boring. Next was a Harley 45, a World War II army courier bike that was brutal to ride. With no springs to absorb the shock of the roads, it was continually attacking my kidneys, but now I was a fully fledged biker. Finally I got a Triumph Tiger 110, which made me very happy. That sucker could almost fly, and I loved it. In 1956 Johnny Sombrero started the Black Diamond Riders club in Toronto. I rode with them for just over a year. It was a lot of fun hanging out and travelling around southern Ontario with 20 or more bikes in a two-by-two line along the highway. We were drinking a lot and occasionally got into fights when we stopped at some of the bars along the highway. The parties were legendary: sometimes in a farmer's field or a bar, sometimes at different houses around the city and always the women. That's where I learned the true meaning of free love.

My favourite hang-out place was Sunnyside Beach, on Toronto's waterfront across the street from Sunnyside Amusement Park that had lot of rides and a roller coaster. My buddy Gord had a beautiful 1948 Ford Monarch car and used to follow the bikers to the beach. We would gather early in the evening a couple of times a week. Sometimes there were more than a hundred bikes, as well as cars with doors open, all with their radios turned on. It was early surround-sound. We would listen to the Hound, disc-jockey George Lorenz, on WKBW Radio, which came in loud and clear from Buffalo—the best R&B show ever. I was having the time of my life.

The first thing that made me think twice about what I was doing with my life was when my friend Hoppy, who rode a Harley K, rear ended a tractor-trailer on the Queen Elizabeth Highway and was decapitated. Very ugly. Then one night, in the summer of 1957, I dropped off my current lady friend, Myra, at a cottage northwest of Toronto. On the way out, daydreaming and, yes, drunk, I smashed into an eight-foot-tall stone pillar that marked the entrance to the property. I was travelling too fast and hit it head-on, literally. We didn't wear helmets. I was knocked out; I'm not sure for how long. When I woke up I could see some lights and not all of them were stars in the sky. I tried to start the bike. No luck and in the dark I couldn't tell what the problem was.

I gave up and staggered to a cottage across the road, and the source of some of the lights I had seen. I knocked on the door and when it opened explained what had happened. The man kept staring at me. I couldn't figure out why until I saw myself in the hall mirror. My head and face were covered with blood. Fortunately he let me in and his wife cleaned up the mess that was my head. They were good people. I thanked them and called Gord, who drove up and took me to the hospital. The doctor pleasantly informed me that I should be dead then stitched up my head and turned me loose.

Gord and I went back to pick up my bike. The entire front end was demolished, but we hooked it up to the back of Gord's car and he drove me home. The bike was a write-off. The front end had folded up like an accordion and just about crushed the engine. That was the end of my biker adventures. Some great and some not-so-great memories are all that's left.

CHAPTER 2

Little Caesar and the Consuls

Toronto, Ontario. The year was 1957. I was seventeen years old, considered to be good-looking, charged up on testosterone, and hooked on rock 'n' roll. I had no idea then that I would eventually spend most of my life in the music business. I was just hoping to get lucky and have a lot of fun. Rock and roll was hot and so were the young ladies who followed the bands and now I had special access. My buddy Wayne Connors, whom the ladies loved, played drums for an up-and-coming band called the Impacts. The group performed at community clubs, in church basements, movie theatres during the intermissions, dancehalls, and anywhere else somebody wanted to dance and could afford a band. I'd help carry the equipment, and with that came free access to the gigs and the ladies. I capitalized on all the opportunities that came my way.

Wayne was friends with the guys in the Consuls. During the fifties and sixties they were one of the hottest rock and roll bands in Toronto. No surprise. Bruce Morshead ran a very tight ship and was a good leader. A man of many talents, he sang, wrote hit songs, and played keyboards. Norm Sherratt, who also wrote tunes, was the group's lead singer, played the saxophone as well as most other instruments and worked with Morshead on the vocals and music. Everybody in the band worked on the arrangements. Ernest Stubbs was on stand-up bass, Pete DeRemigis on drums and Gene MacLellan, another songwriter, singer and played guitar.

From the minute we met Gene and I hit it off. He was easy to be around, lots of fun, and the girls adored him. Women were turned on by his vulnerable look and signature crooked grin. No question, Gene was a chick magnet. He was great onstage but those who hung out with him knew he didn't really enjoy performing. He didn't even like the music business. What he loved was writing and he had amazing talent. His songs include "Snowbird" and "Put Your Hand in the Hand" for Anne Murray as well as tunes for himself and several other artists. He won numerous awards for his writing and for his own records. Few realized it but Gene was battling a host of health issues including childhood polio, a heart condition and a string of car accidents that affected him both physically and emotionally, but he hid the pain with his self-deprecating sense of humour. Gene holds a special place in my heart. He was the guy who gave me my first opportunity to perform professionally. The fact that our trio was short-lived didn't matter. It featured Gene on guitar and a drummer whose name escapes me; I did vocals. No bass yet. This one gig group was formed after Gene left the Consuls and before he joined the Suedes. We rehearsed in Gene's garage and called ourselves the Trilites. Gene was the only real musician. Doomed before we started we played our first and only show at Metropolitan Hall, in the west end of Toronto, a popular weekend spot, where bands got the chance to find an audience. We were so bad it was comical. We just never jelled, and it showed. It was as if we had never rehearsed. That show was not a memorable one, and it couldn't end quickly enough for Gene or me! This is so embarrassing to admit. Gene and I swore never to talk about it again and laughed about it for years after.

Just about everybody played the Met. Bert Tyrala, with his sidekick Gary Alles and his partner Mike Fermante, had opened the joint. They set it up so they could have a place to hang out and have fun "away from the wives"! In the early days they paid each band $35 for the night, no matter how many members it had. The stage was the size of a postage stamp. It wasn't uncommon to be playing when all of a sudden there would be a huge crash because the drummer had fallen off the back of the stage. Everybody thought it was part of the show.

Gene was always good for loads of laughs and became a great friend. For years afterwards we only saw each other at TV shows we were appearing on, but the bond was always there. It was a sad day in 1995 when Gene took his own life, a humungous waste. His daughter, Catherine MacLellan, is a very busy performer today and who, like her dad, is a talented writer and singer (check out her website *www.catherinemaclellan.com/* and also on YouTube—she's great).

TID BITS

"Put Your Hand In The Hand" was recorded by more than 100 artists including Joan Baez, Bing Crosby and Elvis.

Robbie Robertson also played guitar with the Consuls, but he didn't stay long. Morshead wanted him to play bass instead of having two guitars in the band. *What?* He left. It is ironic that later, with Ronnie Hawkins, he did play bass for a while. At fourteen Robbie was already being noticed as an up-and-comer, and he went on to become one of the world's legendary guitar players. He grew up to be a respected songwriter, actor, record and film producer as well as writing books and scores for movies. Considered a music business icon, he has also received kudos for helping Canada's aboriginal community, of which he is a native son, to celebrate and build awareness of their history and culture.

By 1959 the Consuls were in freefall. Ernest was gone. Pete, Gene, and Robbie had left to form the Suedes, featuring Scott Cushnie on keyboards. Later Robbie went on to join Ronnie Hawkins and the Hawks then Levon Helm and the Hawks, same band different name who backed Bob Dylan and, eventually, formed that incomparable music phenomenon known as The Band!

Gene decided to go it on his own as a successful solo artist performing, writing hit after hit, and winning awards for his recordings. Scott Cushnie tried his hand at producing records as well as running Ronnie Hawkins's recording, management, and publishing companies. He produced Hawkins's single "Got My Mojo Working" and Robbie Lane's "Fannie Mae," both strong regional hits.

While this was happening I had left the government and taken a job as a record picker at CBS Records Canada located on downtown Toronto's Wellington Street. As a record picker my job was twofold. One goal was to stay awake. The other was to go through the racks of vinyl records while holding an order form in one hand then, with my other hand, to pick out the items on the invoice and put them into a cart. Boring! That's where I first met Eddie Colaro and football-star-turned-salesman Charlie Camilleri. Charlie played for the 1946 and '47 Grey Cup winning Toronto Argonauts and then went on to become one of the best-known artist reps and a legend in the record business. Eddie Colaro's career path was a lot bumpier first with CBS and later with Capitol Canada. These amazing guys both deserve to be in the Canadian Music Hall of Fame. They were at my first wedding, in 1961, and showed up again when I was working as an agent with artists on their labels. They were also a huge help in breaking the Consul's first hit single, "If," which was on the CBS label. Oops. Getting ahead of myself here.

In 1959 I got a promotion at CBS, which by then had moved north to Leslie Street in Don Mills. I had a new title. Warehouse Supervisor. Supervising packaging and shipping was about as dead-end as it gets but some awesome perks came with the job. Loads of free records and when recording artists on the label came and toured the building the warehouse was included. I met and got a chance to talk to Johnny Cash, Marty Robbins and Carl Perkins, three of my heroes. Plus Tony Bennett, Frank Sinatra, Johnny Mathis, Bob Dylan, Barbra Streisand, and Duke Ellington! One singer I never met but always wanted to be Billie Holiday. She died in 1959 of heart failure **caused** by cirrhosis of the liver all of it caused by drugs. What a waste. I had more than a thousand albums in my personal collection, along with a big pile of 45s. That was the good news. The bad news was a rumour that got to my boss at CBS, Ms. Dorie Edmonds, the branch manager. Fate went to work and she managed to get me fired for trying to take her job. I denied and protested to no avail. She was politically solid with the company so I was out. By the way the rumour was true. Ha! Two quotes come to mind. One: "Nothing ventured nothing gained". Two: "There is a reason for everything and everything always works out!" I was about to find out if they were true!

On a long shot I called Ron Scribner. He was a local 16 year old kid that was running some dances occasionally using live rock bands including one of which was the Consuls. Ron and I had crossed paths a few times at his dances and got to know each other pretty well. I knew he was looking for somebody to work with him because he was getting busy. We talked and he hired me as an agent for thirty dollars a week. It was like an internship. Now that took care of a lot of bills NOT!! It was all he could afford and I was desperate. Fortunately I was a quick study and learned how to do what I was supposed to be doing very quickly and the money improved.

Same year shortly after all this turmoil in my life my friend Wayne Conners called me. He had moved on from the Impacts and was now the drummer for the Consuls He told me the Consuls needed a bass player and, even though the only thing I had ever played was the radio, he thought I should try out.

I thought, "*I can do this!*" You know the feeling you get when you really want something? Wayne was instrumental in helping me get me into the band. Same year the Consuls got a name change. Bruce Morshead, the leader of the group, because of his attitude, got labelled with a stage name from the film Little Caesar, starring Edward G. Robinson, an actor famous for his roles as a control-freak gangster. Little Caesar & the Consuls was born! It didn't take long for everyone to short form that to Caesar

For some unknown reason my brother, not me, originally got guitar lessons when we were kids and he never really used them. That pissed me off so one day, fed up; I broke the guitar over his head. "Goodbye, Bobby Breen guitar," I said as it cracked into unfixable pieces. When my dad made Jimmy return the pieces to the Sutherland Music School Dr. Sutherland was not impressed, until Jimmy told him the story. So he got off without having to pay and I was the villain.

TID BITS

Bobby Breen was born in Montreal and achieved star status in the early 1930s through to the '60s. He first found fame as a child performer, then as a guitar player, and not long after as an actor. He's still alive and living in Florida. Sorry about the guitar, Bobby.

While I didn't get music lessons as a kid I did have an opportunity to sing onstage with the choir at Toronto's Knox Presbyterian Church. My big moment was a solo belting out as best as I could, "God Sees the Little Sparrow Fall." If you know the song, tell me how the hell do you belt that one out? My whole family came for the big moment, unfortunately on the wrong Sunday, so they didn't see me perform. Well, that's not entirely true. My brother had to be there with me every week and he brought mom with him so they heard me. Jimmy says I was great. Mom, a Roman Catholic, felt a little uncomfortable in a Presbyterian church, but anything for her baby. That would be me.

Back to Caesar. I was going to be the bass player for Caesar. My first move was to buy a Danelectro bass for $125 which required monthly payments of a whopping $12.50, no interest, to the Long & McQuade Music Store on Yonge Street. My next was to negotiate my way to securing an amp for free. It was homemade and was built by my favourite Uncle, Eddy Horner, who played guitar, sang and even made it onto the radio a couple of times performing live. He looked like Eddy Arnold, the legendary American country singer. Uncle Eddy was a carpenter and a very talented musician!

Kenny Pernokis, the new guitar player for Caesar, generously offered to teach me how to play bass and I spent hours learning where my fingers had to go. A few weeks later I was onstage in the Georgetown Arena's Rose Room, backing Danny and the Juniors a hit American rock and roll singing group. Imagine how I felt onstage, knowing I could play just enough notes, all at the bottom of my bass's neck, to get me through the night. I had no idea what to do higher up the neck so I played what I knew. All the guys were really supportive, and that helped me survive. Truth be told, it didn't hurt later on that I was also their agent.

At the Rose Room the low notes on the beat-up piano were really bad because some keys were missing and the whole thing was out of tune. Norm Sherratt, our lead singer and resident Mr. Fix It, would do a band-aid tune-up on the battered and scarred pianos the halls provided so you can imagine the shape they were in and what we had to face onstage. It was decided that the bass would have to fill in the holes. Bruce and I played some of the same bass runs on the low side of the piano. Somehow I managed to stumble through my debut night, filling the holes, trying new notes along the way and inventing some out of sheer desperation. I moved a lot on stage which helped cover my questionable playing. Nervous does not begin to describe how I felt. An out-of-body experience comes more to mind. "Am I really doing this?" I asked myself as I tried to hold it together.

I must have been doing something right, because I became a full-time member of the band. Soon enough I got over the nerves. I learned to play the bass better in the months and years that followed, but I was still no genius and that was evident. Ironically the reason I lasted so long was because I could sing, only played simple, and Norm, Kenny, and I worked together well on the front line. Wayne would sometimes come off the drums and Norm would take over while Wayne sang some Ray Charles tunes. He was a big hit with the crowd and soon became known as Chick Conners. With one more change to come we would be the group's nucleus for the next four years.

Being a member of the band was a lot better than being a roadie: it opened a whole new playground. Although I now had member status Peter DeRemigis, the former Consul drummer, always referred to me as "the roadie." I'm not sure if that was some kind of demeaning thing or just a nickname. Finally, years later, he came out to see us at a gig in Scarborough, Ontario—a first. After the show he walked up to me and said, "You're good, Tom." That was a major moment for me. It meant a lot, because Peter is a cool guy and one hell of a drummer.

The band's leader, Bruce Morshead who I thought was like a white Fats Domino, was a taskmaster and he became a big influence in my life in those early days. Little Caesar and The Consuls rocked both rock 'n' roll and r&b dance music, and over the years, I got to perform in front of millions of people. The formula was basic and always the same: it was the KISS Principle—Keep It Simple, Stupid. The "Caesar shuffle" referring to the simple rhythms that made it easy to dance to the music. You could be the worst klutz in the world, with two left feet, but you could still dance to Caesar. That was the secret of the band, along with its carefully chosen songs. KISS is what sustained us for more than 60 years.

However, maintaining that principle sometimes gave us problems. To convince musicians to play basic is never easy. You have no idea how hard it can be to make creative people understand that simplicity is often the mark of creative genius. Bruce kept the band simple, organized and disciplined. Everyone could sing lead which made the band unique. We would rehearse a song over and over, 40 times if necessary, until it was letter-perfect and God help you if you changed one note onstage. That rigidity was probably one of the reasons why Robby, Pete, and Gene left the Consuls.

Once I learned what I was doing, or thought I did, I occasionally ad-libbed. I finally felt like a real bass player, my fingers had graduated to relationship status with my guitar's note-rich neck, even if it was only via the dots. The guys in the band laughed at me a lot and my attitude constantly pissed off Bruce. We argued, but not so much about the music as about the bookings I was making for the band. I didn't care. I was having fun learning, the band usually worked three or more dates a week, and we were at the upper end of the money for local bands—as much as $250 and sometimes more. And, thanks to me, no management fee. It was a good thing I was a partner in the band and, oh yeah, the agent. That saved my butt many times in the early years.

I always tended to be a rebel, practically from birth. I disliked people telling me what to do, and that got me into a lot of tricky situations and even physical disagreements, but life was never dull. Somewhere during this period Norm Sherratt and I were living on Jackman Avenue, north of the Danforth near

Broadview, renting rooms from the family of Ted Warburton, a trumpet player/ friend of Norms. Those were rocky times but thankfully fun was never far away. I sold my car, a 1952 Ford Meteor sedan, to Sherratt because I needed the money. A short time after he went to go out in the car and it was gone. He asked me if I knew where it was but I honestly didn't know. I thought somebody had stolen it. As it turned out the bank had repossessed it because I was behind on the payments that I was supposed to be making. I thought it was funny, Norm not so much.

As I expanded my knowledge and experience of the business Morshead and I began to have major disagreements and confrontations. I was relentless; I knew what I wanted. That may sound egotistical to some but it was true. My dream was being in a hit band going on the road and working with the best. Sorry, Bruce. I could have been more diplomatic. For what it's worth Morshead was a far better musician and writer than I was and always beat my ass at tennis. Most important he was a good friend for a long time.

In June 1961, at 21 years old, I decided to get married. Joanne Catherine Stewart was a beautiful 19-year-old girl who I had chased off and on for three years until she caught me. She was very intelligent and also, with her Scottish heritage, very thrifty which helped us save for the future. We moved into a one-bedroom apartment on Woodington Avenue around the corner from the Bank of Nova Scotia at Woodbine and Danforth where Joanne worked as a teller. We hung out with a group of friends on Degrassi Street, where Joanne's best friend Betty Richards and a couple of our other friends lived. (The street became famous later because of the hit television series named after it.) We would all get together when we could. Some us would drink ourselves stupid. It was fun and the sexual advances were kept to a minimum which I found very frustrating!

Joanne's father was not a fan of mine but her mom and sisters, Judy and Jane were so he had to tolerate me and eventually, I won him over. Wayne Connors was my best man and two of the guests at the wedding were my old friends from CBS Eddy Colaro and Charlie Camellari. Unfortunately so was my father —uninvited. He was still living in a flophouse on Jarvis Street and panhandling on Yonge Street where Jimmy had seen him a couple of times. I had taken Joanne to meet him to tell him we were getting married. I don't know what I was thinking—he actually came on to her. It was not a pleasant experience and it came back to haunt me when he showed up at the church drunk, staggered through the door, and fell flat on his face in the aisle. My uncles got him out of there and drove him back to where he was living. My soon-to-be-new wife was mortified, but we went ahead with the ceremony and made it through the rest of the day. Not an auspicious beginning.

CHAPTER 3

Agents and Managers.
What the hell do they do?

This is where we start to get into the real reason for this book. THE BUSINESS! It's understood that I started in Toronto which was and is the music centre of the music business in Canada. First the obvious. Without the musicians and other performers there was no business. In the fledgling rock and roll business in Toronto, for the most part, there were no real agents that worked with the rock musicians other than in the bars. Some young people tried. They liked the music and wanted to either help their friends or hustle a buck. Not stupid, just inexperienced. The bands played at house parties or the matinees at the theatres between movies, church YPC dances usually held in the basements of the churches, high school dances, sometimes at the proms although that was still mainly reserved for the Glen Miller type bands. Let's understand the real agent's view. We were street urchin level, non-professionals, according to the old guys in the pro-agents world which were the agents that booked the bars, the big shows and had all the connections to make things happen. Also understand the agent was thought of as an entry level position except for those very few that actually decided to make it a profession. The rest moved on as quickly as possible to management and other careers in the business. Anything rather than being the agent. For the purpose of this discussion you didn't play in the bars without the agent. Same rule applied in the larger concert venues, radio, television, or film. It was a love hate relationship that had existed back since the beginning of time. Think about it. A couple of cavemen fighting over the kill of the day. Chances are an agent was there to negotiate the settlement on behalf of one side or the other. Agents could work for the musician or the employer. Another fine line. As a musician you depend on the agent for jobs and the manager for direction. You had to pay the commissions involved and, sometimes, resented being told what to do. Ditto on the agents that also managed. Wow! 10% to 15% for the agent, another 10% or more for management. Doesn't sound fair does it? Where was it written it had to be fair? Wait till we get to the lawyers. HA! I always wondered why some agent didn't step up and charge a fee no matter what happened sane as the lawyers did. Agents only got paid their commission if the job went off okay and often even then had to chase the artists and the bands for their commission until the agents caught on and got into upfront deposits held in trust just like the lawyers which was illegal according to The Toronto Musicians Union. You couldn't collect your commission up front. Like we cared! I don't know many agents that also made good managers. It was a blurred line between the two. Managers were supposed to be more personally involved with the artist or band and were picking up a fee for finding an agent to keep the artist working as well as arranging for recordings and promoting the artist's career. It more often than not didn't work out that way. There were a few in Canada. A lot of the agents, promoters, record company people, the radio Disc Jockeys (Let's call them djs) and others did take a shot, at being managers, for the most part, unsuccessfully. Some agents and managers were real and actually did something. Too many didn't. Point being. Some did do their job, did take care of the artists, sometimes for no money, sometimes for too much money. When you figure the average fee for a four to six piece band on the one-night circuit in the early 60's was $75 to $150, and we have all seen a lot that played for nothing just to play. It still happens today. The major problem with working the one night circuit was the lack of money. The top bands could make $200 to $250 a gig. In the bars the work was more consistent and so was the money. Do the math. Agents and managers were a creation of the inability, lack of knowledge or sometimes lack of interest of most artists/musicians to take care of their own careers. All we wanted to do is play. To a lot of them and that includes me, at first, it was all bewildering. Extend that to all the other support people required and there are a lot of them. Managers, lawyers, accountants, engineers, producers, equipment stores, road managers, road crews, sound technicians, publishers, writers, record companies, recording studios, publishing companies, television, radio djs/hosts, media reps, photographers and on and on and on and, oh yeh, agents! Also very important, the promoters and last but not least the fans who, along with the artists and bands, paid to keep the industry humming along. Sorry if I missed anybody. All had the same goal ideally. Take care of the artists; make them famous and successful (not necessarily the same thing.) All of these services cost money that, if they all do their job right, the fans and the artists get to pay and support a future multi- billion dollar industry. On behalf of the musicians I think Les Emerson from Five Man Electrical Band said it best. *"The only thing I hate about the music business is the business."* Wise words! Contrarily, a lot of musicians made the transition from musician to the business side or managed a combination of both. The one thing that a lot of people forgot was a very simple point. Without the musicians those of us that chose to be in the business side of music would have nothing to do. Sometimes that reality got lost in the shuffle.

When I started as an agent with Ron Scribner in 1959 there were not very many agents booking Canadian rock & roll bands anywhere in Canada other than in the bars or local 'who cares" gigs. We had to literally force Canadian rock and roll on the market. Sure there were promoters but they were doing the middle of the road and jazz bands, folk artists or country acts. If they did book rock and roll it was the U.S.A. artists. The local rock and roll bands mostly booked themselves. Some had managers. Usually a friend. To us the booking agents were the old guys like Harold Kudlets, The Harold Kudlets Agency in Hamilton, who was well connected with the right people legal and illegal in Toronto, Montreal and Vancouver and had influential contacts in the entertainment business in the U.S.A. Harold controlled most of the bars booking live talent in Ontario and a fair chunk of Canada. He is said to be the agent that introduced rock and roll to Canada. Quite true. Operative words here are "introduced to Canada" Not a lot of support for home grown talent. Granted, and good for Harold, there were a couple of bands in Hamilton that he worked with because the bars were asking for local talent. It was cheaper. Live music was a draw and profitable. One local group that he did work with was the Count Four whose drummer was Ed Preston future vice-president and general manager of RCA Records Canada and a huge supporter of Canadian talent and one of those musicians that made the leap to the business side. Ed and Harold became lifelong friends. Even when he was working with RCA Ed kept playing until, in 1976, he was appointed vice president at RCA and the rest is history. Great career.

Initially, it was more the country acts that were making the inroads on tours and in the bars than rock and roll. Harold brought the rockabilly, r and b and blues artists to Canada. Conway Twitty, Marty Robbins, Ronnie Hawkins, John Lee Hooker, Matt Lucas, Chuck Berry, Bo-Diddley, Fats Domino, Clarence Frogman Henry and many more U.S.A. artists. First to Hamilton and then on to the Yonge St. strip in Toronto as well as other bars around Ontario. He certainly deserves credit for being instrumental in getting Hawkins and The Hawks signed to Roulette Records in New York. Roulette was reported to be a Mafia funded label. It was. No surprise. It was pretty commonplace in the entertainment business in the U.S.A. Payola was a reality. Harold was also involved in the formation of Levon Helms & the Hawks forerunner of The Band and he managed them for a short time. Got to admit Harold was always available to talk with and free with his advice once I got into the agency business. He was very kind to Ron and I booking our bands into the bars and clubs he controlled although, with all due respect, it was good for him too. That's something an agent would say. We were so cynical. Truth be known it was good for all of us.

Then there was Bud Matton. A musician who was booking the Canadian bar circuit as well as bar tours in the U.S.A., especially in Las Vegas, with more of the dinner show type bands. With the exception of a Malton & Hamilton, a comedy team that he actually did manage, because they were popular on the bar circuit and friends of his. He had three solid agents that I remember. Jimmy Finch, Brian Ayers, who also performed with Grant Smith & the Power, one of Bud's top bands, and Dennis Matton, Bud's son. He also had Charley Mathers who worked out of his house in Las Vegas and had all the contacts needed to book all the major casinos. One of the major artists he worked with was Tom Jones who opened a lot of doors for Charley and Bud. Over the years a lot of other agents would pass through the revolving door at Matton's. Think of it as a rehab centre where when one who would falter, needed a job, or just got fucked up, would enter the Matton's rehab, talk to Bud, re-energize and then leave, refreshed, ready to face the challenges again. (That includes moi!) I did get to know Bud really well and later ended up visiting him a couple of times when he semi-retired to Florida. Got to ride around in his boat and pretend to enjoy deep sea fishing.

TID BITS

Bud was approached by Shania Twain early in her career to manage her. He turned her down. His reason? "I don't manage." Now that's an agent!"

Last, certainly not least, the agent for the stars, Billy O'Conner and he was a star in his own right. Besides being a very busy musician he also owned Billy O'Conner Enterprises which handled a lot of the entertainment going into the Canadian National Exhibition in Toronto, other fairs across the country plus a big business in conventions, television, radio, and live theatre. He was also the host and musical director for the very popular Billy O'Conner late show which was replaced by the award winning Juliet show starring Cavazz Juliette Augustina Sysak (There's a mouthful), shortened to Juliet, on CBC Television. The show was on right after the hockey games. Great for ratings. He also had a spot on CHUM Radio doing a half-hour of news in 1961. He introduced a lot of new artists to the business including Gordon Lightfoot. Bud had first worked for Billy as an agent before, with Billy's help, he opened The Bud Matton Agency. Billy was always helping somebody including me. He was one of my mentors. While visiting his home I met his family and his son Gary a very talented kid even then. Billy opened up the world of fairs, television and conventions business to me. At first he booked the dates for our artists but eventually left me to book direct. He continually allowed me to tag along as he met with different people in the business. He did know everybody and introduced me to all of them. Worth a million dollars!

We never considered any of the three "Oldies" as competition, nor they us for that matter. All of them were helpful in sharing their knowledge. They controlled, not only the bar business in Ontario, but just about everything else in entertainment except our niche with the new rock and roll business in high schools, parties and one night dance halls. Our key to penetrating this market? Live rock and roll music for the teenagers. Simple! Most of our bands were more interested in recording, playing the one night dances and concert style jobs. We used the bars as backup gigs. You have no idea how many underage non-union musicians were playing in the bars then! At first we booked most of our bar dates and convention dates through Harold, Bud and Billy, but that gradually stopped being necessary as we and home grown rock & roll grew. In time they started calling us to book our bands and not too long after that we were booking direct with a lot of the bars, restaurants, taverns, and television and entertainment venues heretofore unavailable to us without the big guys.

In the early 1960's other agents started showing up booking the "garage bands" that had not yet reached the level of visibility to make it on our circuit. These agents booked the smaller halls and other venues that couldn't afford our bands. Many of those people followed the road to more professional levels in the business. The goal for everyone was to record hit records and tour.

CHAPTER 4

IF

I n 1963 Caesar went into The Arc Studio and we recorded our first hit. A song called "IF" written and sung by Bruce Morshead. The flip side was "Two Bits" also written and sung by Bruce. If you can find an original copy of the 45 record you will note that the writer and publisher credits were Ron Scribner. What???? Scribner song writing? An oxymoron. Couldn't write, couldn't play an instrument, couldn't sing and had two left feet so couldn't dance either but he did love music. This happened because Bruce was working during the day and couldn't or wouldn't take the time off so Scribner was the only one available to go and register the tunes with BMI. The other guys weren't involved. What you may ask was the matter with me going? As far as I know Bruce told Scribner to take care of it which he did and neither one said anything to me. BMI Canada was formed by Broadcast Music of the U.S.A. in 1940 to represent its music repertoire. By 1947 it was the largest music licensing company in the country representing Canadian music composers, writers and publishers, protecting their performing rights administering the collection and distribution of their royalties from airplay, record sales, live performances and any other uses of the music. Who could forget the amazing BMI president Harold Moon and his dedication to Canadian music?

I finally took the rights for Bruce's music back from Scribner many years later. This is a blatant example of a writer not knowing the value of registering his or her own music. Here's the rub. By the time I got the rights back the royalties were down to around $300 a year and going down. I wrote it off as a manager's fee which was an extra almost $6 a week income to me. All the previous royalties when the record was a hit all went to Scribner. To my knowledge we never saw a dime. There were many other Canadian artists doing the same thing with the same result. I had now taken over all the booking and promotion for the band. Morshead, assisted by Norm Sherratt, ran the rehearsals and picked the music and everybody pitched in on the arrangements. We all made the decisions when it came to recording. We were one of those bands without a manager. I was acting like one. Stupid me. I probably should have been charging the usual 10%. I can't count the people that have told me how dumb they thought I was for not charging the band for the work I was doing over and above being an agent. It never occurred to me to do so. I was in the band. They did have a manager in the early years before I joined. His name was Roger Kennedy. I don't remember him but Norm Sherratt tells me he was the guy that made the connection with Able Records in New York for the band.

When I first started with Caesar they had Peter Harrington a rotund, fast talking, sweaty man, as their manager and who was the person that hooked up the band and our agency with Marie Martel and the Hurdon brothers who were Bobby Curtola's managers. The Hurdons owned a record label, Tartan Records that Bobby was signed to. The Hurdons wrote and recorded Bobby singing their songs and Marie took care of business. Over the next couple of years we backed Bobby on shows often and we became good friends and remained so for many years.

At one point Marie asked if we would like to become Bobby's full time backup band. We declined. Day jobs were one reason but it was also that we didn't want to be a backup band preferring to have our own career. Bobby Curtola was the number one teen heart throb in Canada. When he was on a show with Bob Hope in Winnipeg, and with support of Red Robinson Mr. Radio in Vancouver, his records, starting with "Fortune Teller", went ballistic in The States

TID BITS

Bobby got to know Elvis Presley really well and when Elvis died he left Bobby the special ring that he always wore when he performed at the Las Vegas Hilton.

Back to Peter Harrington manager. Unfortunately, he was a little too distracted by and overly interested in the younger girls that were around Curtola and the band to a point of touching inappropriately at first then getting more aggressive. A great concern to all of us. So after a couple of incidents we fired the asshole. Personally I would have liked to have charged him as a criminal. Little Caesar and The Consuls, the Mid-Knights, Chad Allen and The Expressions, Wes Dakus and the Rebels, Crowbar, or at least members of Crowbar, all ended up backing Curtola occasionally on gigs. Interesting sidelight. Curtola was very instrumental in helping our agency set up the first national tour circuit in Canada. He was the hot pop star in the country so working with him was great for the image and recognition. Surprisingly Curtola, despite all the awards he has received over the years including The Order of Canada, is not in The Canadian Music Hall of Fame which is mind boggling. He died in 2016 of a heart attack but I am not alone in thinking it was from a broken heart when his lady, the love of his life, died in a tragic car crash in December, 2015

With our single "IF" I used every trick in my book to get airplay and sales including driving all over Ontario with boxes of records in my trunk. In most places I was really well received just because I had taken the time to show up in person. I had signed the band to CBS Canada for a one record deal. Two guys from the past, Charlie Camilleri and Eddie Colaro who were salesmen for CBS when I worked there in 1956 to 1959. Remember? Both had become good friends of mine. Charlie and Eddie arranged to have "IF" included in virtually every shipment of records that went out of the CBS warehouse to clients like Sam The Record Man, A&A Records, Hal Waggoner in Hamilton all huge retail outlets. Sam Sniderman also had Roblin wholesale distributors. Other wholesalers were Handleman Drugs, Sherman's and Bud Farquinson's Pindoff Records. Between Charlie, Eddy, myself, and the guys in Caesar, we covered all the radio, television stations and other media. Thanks Eddie & Charlie. By phone and sometimes in person we contacted every station across the country cajoling and begging for airplay. I did most of the interviews and television appearances because, remember, the guys couldn't or wouldn't take the time off from their day jobs. Through everything that Caesar accomplished we were always only part time. I have often wondered what we would have done if we had been full time. Different headset.

I remember once doing an interview on the way to Greenhurst a dance pavilion in Stroud near Lindsay, Ontario where we were playing. I stopped off to say hi to Tex Bagshaw, the hot dj at CKLY Radio in Lindsay the top station in the area. He put me on the air and it was going great until I spotted a red button on the sound board and asked what it was for. Tex said "don't touch that" at the same time as I pushed it and POOF! The station was off the air! After some scrambling the engineer got everything turned back on. What the hell. I found out what the button did and we all had a good laugh.

We managed to gain enough attention to get the band national recognition and a great regional hit. It didn't hurt the image and made bookings and more money easier to get.

Scribner and I managed, through the bands and the agency, to make a lot of friends in radio, television and other media over the years. Alan Waters, Al Slaight, Dave Johnson, Chuck McCoy, Jay Nelson, Tom Rivers, John Sprague and pretty well everybody else at CHUM including the off air staff. My forever friends dj's Bob Laine, Bob MacAdorey, Duff Roman and Roger Ashby were the band's super supporters. Alan Trebek at CFTO, Don Daynard, CKFH, Toronto, Nevin Grant, CKOC, Hamilton, John Donaby, CKLB in Oshawa and later CHUM. Dave Charles, CJBQ Bellville and Q107 Toronto, Dave Mickie/ David Marsden CKEY, John Gilbert CKPT, Peterbourgh, Gary Parr CKLC Kingston, Rosalie Trombley CKLW Windsor, Paul Ski in St Thomas, Donnie and Bob Burns in Winnipeg, Roy Hennessey and Red Robinson in Vancouver and Joey Reynolds in Buffalo. Sorry if I missed anybody. I know I have. Oh yea. Little Keith Elshaw at CFOR in Orillia. The list is virtually endless. Everybody liked the guys in Caesar. I can say, without reservation, we knew everybody that was anybody in Top Forty radio in Ontario and me almost everybody across the country. Even more important they knew Caesar!

CHAPTER 5

Ron Scribner the Legend

Ron Scribner was only 16 when I first met him even at this early age he was a visionary into the future of the rock and roll entertainment business in Canada that ended up making him an icon and one of the top agents in the country. An interesting character that is worth a book of his own. He was "The Man" and I was fortunate to spend the time I did with him. He made my "there is a reason for everything and everything always works out" philosophy come true. We learned together. A very educational and sometimes hilarious journey. We were as close as anybody could be next to brothers. His family was the most important thing in his life. Scribner was a soft spoken mild mannered curmudgeon exuding charisma and you just had to trust him. Most everybody respected and liked him. Underneath it all a very shrewd businessman. The most organized/unorganized person I have ever met. He was great at almost everything he did except saving money, weight control and driving a car. Outwardly very under control. In reality very stressed out and always on the brink of disaster financially. The biggest challenge? He had a huge weight problem, going from 250 pounds down to 180 and back up more often than a toilet seat at a mixed party. He kept three full sets of clothing to handle the changes. The man exercised, dieted and starved himself until, just watching him, I lost weight! This was one of the demons in his life that he couldn't control. The other? He was the most distracted driver I ever met. To ride with him was, well, perilous comes to mind. He would be driving, talking, looking at me and writing notes to himself and apparently ignoring anything going on outside the car. Scary as hell! This was all before cell phones and texting. We would have never made it out of our teen years otherwise. The words distracted driver would be an understatement even then. He fully expected the other drivers to accommodate whatever the hell he was doing with his car. I got tired of yelling and gasping in terror. This is where I developed my poke and point directions. I'd poke him in the shoulder to get his attention and point in the direction we wanted to go or to note that the car in front of us had stopped or that we were driving so slow a transport truck behind us was climbing on our bumper and blasting the hell out of his horn. We spent a lot of time driving on the shoulders of roads. I can't count the number of highway off ramps or turns we missed before I created the poke and point system.

I'm sure he had every rock & roll and rhythm and blues record ever made. He was also the most intensely motivated person I had ever met. He devoured all of the self-improvement motivational and you can do it books, tapes, videos available. He attended as many of the live seminars of anyone who mentioned success training as he could. His bible was "Think and Grow Rich" by Napoleon Hill and was very much inspired by Andrew **Carnegie**, two gurus in the motivational game. Scribner would give copies of the book to individuals that he thought could use the inspiration. You would note the quizzical look on the face of the recipients. What the hell is this? Not exactly everybody's cup of tea. He talked me into taking The Dale Carnegie Power Sales Course. I got an award for "Being the one that did the most for the class". What the hell kind of award is that in sales? I did read all the books and listened to the tapes but they have never had the same impact on me that they did on Ron. He was constantly on my case to improve. Addicted comes to mind. He had a great sense of humour and never got mad. Ask anyone. Well except me. I loved pissing him off. It wasn't that hard. As far as I know I was the only one that could. Some kind of merit badge there. He was a good friend. One of the best. Even when, later on, when we became competitors, we always stayed friends although we did push that bond on more than one occasion.

Initially Caesar was being booked occasionally by Scribner, an aspiring promoter, for his dances at the Willowdale Community Centre in North Toronto. He was just starting to get more involved in booking bands in different halls around the city and then elsewhere in Southern Ontario sometimes promoting his own shows. As previously noted my new wife Joanne was working at a bank. I have to give her credit for putting up with me in those first years. Our social life was the music business. I did everything from booking to promotions, licking stamps, checking out bands in rehearsal during the day, clubs and other after hour places at night, getting home at 3am or just going direct to the office and also still playing with Caesar. I was operating on four or five hours sleep per night so my personal life was almost non-existent except for my more than occasional dalliances. My wife Joanne was very tolerant. Personally I would have divorced me.

Scribner and I both had a vision of what could happen if we put our minds to it. I know that sounds corny but fortunately, as it turned out, we were right. The Power of Positive Thinking and always love of the music. In 1960 The Ron Scribner Agency was created. The beginning of our dream. Turned out I was a very good agent. I actually was impressed with myself. At first we worked out of the basement in Ron's home at 6 Dalemy Court in Willowdale then later moved to 197 Maxome Ave around the corner. Bigger house. I was treated as one of the family. Our basement office was hardly awe inspiring. I didn't have a desk. Ron and I shared one so sometimes I sat on the hearth of the fireplace and used part of it as a desk to lay out my papers. I did have a phone. Later I got a kitchen table to use. Moving on up!

Scribner was already working with Ritchie Knight and The Mid-Knights when I came onboard. They were put together in 1958 by Leo Donahue and George Semkiw with Jim Gwilliams on drums, Roger Woods on bass and John McCanliss on guitar. In 1961 it had a wholesale change of members. Now it was George Semkiw (guitar), Rich Hubbard (vocal), Barry Stein (drums), Mike Brough (sax), Doug Chappell (bass), and Barry Lloyd on Hammond organ. They quickly became a hot band in the market and later, in 1964 were one of the first Canadian rock bands to have a number one hit record in Canada with "Oh Charlene". George Semkiw handled their bookings. He had turned all his contacts over to Scribner who was then booking the band exclusively. This was followed with Little Caesar and The Consuls. These two bands were key to building the agency. We started approaching other bands for representation. Simple formula. Book the bands anywhere and it was a hands down a re-book and most important taking care of business. Nobody else was doing it on the level we were. Prior to this the music was country or big band dance orchestras. We used the Mid-Knights and Caesar as the door openers. Worked like a charm. Then as our roster expanded the floodgates opened. The company grew very quickly. There was a constant flow of people showing up in our basement office. Upstairs Ron's mother Edna and two sisters Valeria and Brenda carried on family life as if nothing was happening in the basement. Everybody wanted to be booked with the Ron Scribner Agency. Within a very short time we were representing or working with most of the good rock and roll and rhythm and blues bands and artists in the area. I got a raise. Yeh! Joanne and I moved into our first penthouse at 20 Carluke Crescent in the Bayview Ave. and 401 hwy. area. We lived on the Penthouse Floor and our apartment was as Penthouse 4 because it was one of six apartments on the "thirteenth floor" which would have been unlucky. Superstition abounds.

TID BITS

George Semkiw, guitar player for The Mid-Knights, started as a roadie same as I did.

One of the first bands we worked with after the Mid-Knights and Caesar was The Beau Marks from Montreal. We first caught them at The Le Coq'dor Tavern on Yonge St. booked by Harold Kudlets who had the bar exclusive. They did play a lot of bars but we did some one-nighters for them which Kudlets couldn't or wouldn't do and where they did really well. We worked with the band over the next couple of years. Huge hit with "Clap Your Hands" on Quality Records. #1 in Canada and top 30 in the U.S.A. They also did American Bandstand in Los Angelis. They were unique in the respect that they were a Canadian rock band writing their own material, recording in local studios and getting international recognition. A sign of times to come. Let me repeat myself. Writing original material and that was what was missing in the Canadian bands. The Beau Marks were forerunners. That helped us considerably in getting the attention of everybody because of their success and our affiliation which we promoted the hell out of. Like almost any band, they preferred the one night jobs to bars but played more bars where the money was much better and more consistent as far as working and paying the bills. You will hear that a lot with musicians. "Paying the bills!"

I haven't discussed the Canadian record companies all working with Canadian rock and roll artists as far back as the 1950's and continuing to expand their

Canadian content into the sixties when the music became mainstream. Needless to say we worked closely with almost all the labels to promote our artists and bands on the live circuit as it made sense for all of us to co-operate. As we grew we had artists on virtually every major and some independent labels in the country and were getting a lot of support. It was a given that the U.S.A. was light years ahead of us when it came to the music business. Most of our bands were playing the American songs that we heard on the radio, watched on television or were played by the djs at the dances and in the bars. That's what the people wanted to hear. We bought their records at the limited number of record stores that carried them, most notably, Sam Sniderman's Sam the Record Man and Alice and Mac Kenner's A&A Records side by side on Yonge St. I used to mail order some great r&b and blues 45rpm records from a catalogue put out by Buckley's Music Store in Nashville, Tennessee. In the U.S.A. the djs were the voice of American Music. Alan Freed, Dick Clark, George Lorenz The Hound, Wolfman Jack, Murry The K and so many others. Tons of record companies recording virtually anybody and getting hits while our bands were playing second fiddle either opening for or backing the foreign artists when they came to Canada. A couple of the labels were pushing home grown but the best was yet to come.

Totally off topic. Scribner was the man that first introduced me to "Purple Jesus" a drink that he invented that became famous as the party drink. It contained vodka, lemon gin, rye, ginger ale, grape juice and other interchangeable liquors. It had to be made in an old fashioned galvanized wash tub. Nobody knew why. That was just the rule. A couple of drinks and your body went numb with your brain following shortly after. It became the drink of choice for those of us that were members of The Purple Candle Club, Scribner's name for the dances he ran with his partner dj Duff Roman. He had lifted the name from CKEY dj Ray Starr who called his nightly rhythm & blues show The Loyal Order of the Purple Candle. Scribner and Roman focused on tapping into the huge summer cottage country migration of students and young adults into the Muskokas in Northern Ontario. First choice Bala in 1962. The dance was in the Bala Community Hall. The only competition was Dunn's Pavilion that had a strict 40's orchestra type dance band policy as did all the dance pavilions across Canada. This was the beginning of the change over from the old dance bands to rock and roll. Virgin territory in Ontario for our bands. Scribner had been running other dances under the Purple Candle name, but nothing like the success in Bala. People came out of nowhere, and from everywhere. They jammed the place. Duff Roman was a disc jockey at CKEY Radio in the early 60s and then moved to CHUM in 1965. Over the years we did a lot of stuff together from the dances, recordings and working with artists he recorded including Caesar and other artists he managed, the Paupers and David Clayton Thomas. Obviously the on air promotion from Duff and the other djs was priceless for the bands and our agency.

At the dances Duff was the master of ceremonies/dj and spun records between the sets of the live bands that our agency booked. The parties there were legendary. All those pale rock and roll musicians frolicking in daylight, out on the beach, with the teen ladies from the city. It was a sight to behold. Sunburn became a common malady. One night when we played there Sherratt and I hooked up with two hot Willowdale ladies. Me with Nancy a great looking blond and Sherratt with the other, dark haired hottie, Laura. The four of us carried on our affairs for a few months. Meanwhile, with success of Bala in hand, Ron and Duff opened dances in Skeleton Lake and Torrance. Later, they took over the legendary Frankie's Surf Club in Port Carling. I remember one beautiful Saturday morning driving north with Scribner on Hwy 400 to Hwy 118, from Toronto to Port Carling, around 135 miles (222.3 kilometres) away towing a trailer with Scribner's famous Purple Candle Music Machine aboard. It resembled the control board in a recording studio. A lot of flashing lights, sliders and other bells and whistles. We were enjoying the drive with the radio pumping out great r&r and r&b music. We got off the 400 onto Hwy. #189, a two lane secondary road and then to Muskoka District Road# 118 that would lead us to Pt. Carling. Once we got off the busy 400 Highway, there wasn't much traffic. We were making good time at about 75 mph (120 kilometres) when suddenly the car lurched. I looked out my window and there was the trailer with Ron's music machine on it right beside me then gone in an instant. I poked and pointed Scribner and watched as the trailer flew 6 or 7 feet in the air over a wire fence into a field beside the highway. There were 5 or 6 cows standing around watching all this going on. No panic. Just chewing their cud and placidly enjoying the show. Would be a great commercial for something. We pulled over to the shoulder of the road and backed up to where the trailer was to assess the damage. Scribner's comment."Well." That was the comment. As it turned out not a scratch on the machine. The trailer frame was a little bent but the axel and wheels appeared to be okay so we carried the machine up and over the fence, then the trailer, hooked it up to the car again, loaded the machine on, and away we went got to Pt. Carling intact. Fortunately the Purple Jesus ingredients were safely stored away in the trunk.

Bob Burrows, lead vocalist with Bobby Kris & The Imperials, shared a short story with me

"And then there were those Purple Jesus parties. My goodness! (Only Bob would say that) Once I had a drinking competition with Scribner in Bala. We both drank half a 26er of lemon gin straight followed by Purple Jesus. For me instant oblivion. I not only forgot who I was I didn't care. Scribner was hardly fazed while the guys were carrying my unconscious body around on their shoulders."

That, in varying degrees, was not an uncommon story.

Where was I? Oh yeh. It was a huge plus as an agent that I was also a musician. It gave us certain credibility with the bands and we were friends with most of them. I still am. We started using Caesar, the Mid-Knights and as many of our other bands as we could to backup artists that we were bringing in from America as well as some co-booking through Kudlets and with local promoters. From there, remembering I was still "the needed the money agent", I made sure that the Consuls backed just about every act that came into Ontario; Danny and The Juniors, Carl Dobkins Jr., Del Shannon, the Vibrations, the Royal Teens, Little Anthony and The Imperials, The Charmaines, Bobby Vinton, Gene Chandler, Ray Stevens, Dion and the Belmonts, Freddy Cannon (Mr. turn up the volume until you can't hear yourself think). He pops up again in the 70's. the Dovells, the Crests, soul singer Ruth Brown. (Her husband was her musical director, a trumpet player who was shocked when we told him we didn't read music. It was a "Ruth hum a few bars and we will get it" moment.) Diana Ross and the Supremes three shy & very nervous girls, the amazing Jackie Wilson, John Lee Hooker and the list goes on. We also were, along with other bands from our agency, the opening act for The Beach Boys, Sonny and Cher, the Dave Clark Five, the Who, Ronnie Hawkins, Wilson Pickett, the Lovin Spoonful, the Rolling Stones and you get the point. Being backstage and mingling was another learning experience. I not only got to meet the artists but in most cases their managers or agents so my contact list was growing. Once we started bringing them in it made sense to book some of them other places in Canada besides Ontario so we started hooking up with agents, managers and promoters across the country and did a lot of exchanges of bands and artists. Our goal was to book everybody that was good and available anywhere. Somewhere around this time Caesar performed a date at Scarbourgh Arena. The opening act was newcomer Gordon Lightfoot.

CHAPTER 6

The Rock and Roll Dance Circuit

Toronto had and has some of the best musicians in the world so when the imports played here they spread the word talking up Toronto and that started a migration of musicians from everywhere. It's a thin line between rock and roll, rhythm and blues, blues, country, jazz and classical music. True artists have crossed it many times. Ask Canadians Randy Bachman, Dominic Troiano, Robby Robertson, Mike McKenna, Bernie LeBarge, Freddy Keeler, Lenny Breau, Tony Calicut, Doug Riley, David Clayton Thomas and on and on. Radio stations have tried to segregate the music but that's virtually impossible to do since the musicians won't co-operate and keep mixing it up with some great results. A lot of the music was rhythm and blues and a lot of fun to play and watch. Yeh Motown! Yeh, George Lorenz, The Hound, on WKBW Radio, in Buffalo, New York, my favourite r&b music show.

TID BITS

Years later, I tried to buy the tapes of all The George Lorenz Hound Shows on WKBW from his son. No deal. Big bummer. He has done nothing with them. What a waste. One of the greatest r&b music shows on radio EVER!

We integrated that music into our repertoire and did what we were best at: dance music. The sets were brutal. We played a one hour set and then two forty-five minute sets. We were exhausted by the end of the night. We caesarized the music with that old rule, KISS. "Keep It Simple Stupid", and that put us in a unique musical place that made the Consuls different from everyone else. Anyone could dance to Caesar no matter how clumsy they were. One of the best promotional things we did was to go to our tailor, Lou Myles, who was the go to tailor/designer for just about everybody in the business with clients from Frank Sinatra to the Beatles and Pierre Elliot Trudeau, Canada's controversial Prime Minister. Interesting guy. There were few prominent people that Lou Myles didn't know. We wanted split suits. Split down the middle, one half one color, the other half another. Lou never blinked an eye and put the suits together. Mine was black and yellow. Gave me a sort of bumble bee look. People remember those suits to this day. We started moving on stage and I became known as "Rubber Legs Wilson" as I danced my butt off. Even did front flips and splits for awhile. I'm no James Brown, George Olliver or Jon Lee all well known rhythm and blues singers that were famous for their dancing on stage. I paid the price for one split too many and ended up on crutches for a month with pretty blue, black, purple and yellow thighs. Fit right in with the suit. Anything for the show! We built all this into a short routine in the last number of the last set which was "Shout" originally recorded by The Isley Brothers; it was a crowd participation song that almost always got a standing ovation and encore, well except one night, in Belleville, at the Tiki Club run by Dave Charles the rock and roll dj at the local radio station CJBQ Radio. A very dedicated fan of Canadian rock artists long before it became fashionable. I was so into the dance, the music and doing my flips, I didn't notice that all the lights had come on and the crowd was leaving. The band, thinking this was funny, kept on playing to make sure my humiliation was complete. Felt pretty stupid but had to laugh at myself as was everybody else. Certainly put the ego in place. Charles was no help. He laughed louder than anyone. David was a very savvy promoter and made a lot of money from the dances. Two to three thousand or more a night which was pretty impressive in those days. A hell of lot more than he made being on the radio. As I said a huge supporter of Canadian talent, on air and off, he went on to a career as a consultant in communications all over the world. He booked most of his bands through our company, the rest through Harvey Glatt's Treble Clef Entertainment in Ottawa and Vern Craig's Agency, also in Ottawa. Vern was in the Esquires, the first band to get a Juno Award in Canada. There was also Don Tarleton's DKD Productions in Montreal. Charles worked closely with Brian Olney, who hosted CKWS-TV's Teen Dance Party; top show in the Kingston area that was patterned after Dick Clark's American Bandstand, the number one teen dance show in the U.S.A., and featured many Canadian artists and bands from all over the country. The other part of the trio was Gary Parr, also a dj, who had a hit underground show on CKLC radio, in Kingston, and had the same dedication to Canadian music as Olney and Charles. Gary and I hit it off and were great drinking buddies in Kingston and Toronto.

I am spending a lot of time on Caesar. A few reasons. The band was, along with the Mid-Knights, very instrumental in the initial growth and eventual success of our agency and me personally. A lot of musicians credit the Caesar with inspiring them to get started in the business. The band was exciting, fun and danceable. We were having as much fun on stage as the crowd was on the dance floor and it showed. Lest I forget we were also the most friendly bunch when it came to fans who were one of my keys to promoting the agency along with the buyers, all the media and with other musicians because I was in the band. I was meeting everybody face to face. The list is a long one. Nothing beats live and in person when you are dealing with people. Caesar opened a lot of doors for me and the agency. My payback to the band was that they worked more one nighters than anyone else on the circuit. At least two or three nights a week, sometimes more along with some occasional bar work. We made a lot of people that supported us over the years. Many are still friends today. Domenic Troiano (we will get to him) who first saw Caesar at Crang Plaza, a dance hall better known as the "Friday Night Fights", for obvious reasons. Everybody would be dancing then suddenly BANG! Fights would break out all over the dance floor. The bouncers earned their money. Then there was Masaryk Hall the home of rhythm & blues music. Both were Toronto venues. Gary Blackburn was the bouncer at Masaryk. One very large and muscular black dude who was my hero and also the reason why there were very few fights during the dance. One night a couple of guys were kinda hassling me something that was very unusual with the guys in Caesar. I was way out of my weight class on this one. Gary stepped in and simply asked, "Problem?" The problem disappeared. I Loved Gary!

TID BITS

Interesting sidelight, The Blackburn family can be traced back to some of the first slaves that escaped to Canada from the Southern United States via The Underground Railroad eventually settling in Toronto. I will get to that story later on.

Other future musicians like Jerry McCrohan (alias Jerry Edmonton,) eventually the drummer for Toronto band Jack London and the Sparrows which evolved into Steppenwolf and Jerry's older brother Dennis McCrohan later to be Mars Bonfire who wrote the iconic song "Born to be Wild". Both ended up huge artists in the U.S.A and worldwide. At the Jubilee Pavilion in Oshawa where we played a couple of Fridays a month Jerry and Dennis would stand at the front of the stage watching the band, specifically the drummer and the guitar player. What the hell happened to watching that exciting bass player!

The Jube was operated by their dad Owen McCrohan a most interesting character and one of the most knowledgeable promoters in the dance pavilion business. He was one of the first to make the change to rock and roll from the big band 40's music. First rock band in was the Lincolnaires from Oshawa who were the top band in that area at the time. Owen had an unbelievable collection of autographed photographs of every artist and band he booked including the dance orchestras and the rock bands. He had an uncanny insight on which bands to use which is why Caesar played there so often. We packed the place every time. Some nights Owen would have to turn people away but not before he had stuffed in every possible person he could. He sat downstairs in his office and never showed his face but he knew exactly what was going on in the dance hall at all times. He had the stage wired so he could hear everything. He would dock your pay if you showed up late or short a person. I spent a lot of time listening to Owen's stories and, of course, advice. He really loved having me available face to face as the agent. Nowhere to hide, nowhere to run. That came in useful later on when we booked The Jube exclusively. I never hid or ran. He loved putting me through the ringer but we did end up good friends. It was at The Jubilee that I met Marg a great looking lady from Oshawa who became my steady girlfriend for about two years which made juggling my life even more involved. Fortunately

Joanne had pretty well stopped coming to the dances and nobody in the band or their wives seemed to care about my sexual escapades.

Another location that became home for Caesar and a great place for all our bands to play was in the middle of nowhere. I was amazed that anyone even knew about the dance. The legendary Greenhurst Pavilion in Thurstonia Park in Dunsford near Lindsay, Ontario in the Kawartha Lakes Region where a lot of people made lifelong friends and met their future husbands, wives, significant others and many eventually created children. Again the first rock band in was the Lincolnaires from Oshawa headed up by Steve Macko, who later joined Caesar as keyboard, vocalist and sax player. The owner, Ma Lyons, had signed The Paul Minicola Orchestra, an old fashioned dance band, to a contract for Fridays and Saturdays through the summer. Didn't matter. She cancelled the dance band and put the Lincolnaires in first on Fridays and then every Saturday. Paul dropped around every week to pick up the pay check for his band. He had to do that for the whole season. Ma did have a sense of humour. Greenhurst was one of the best promotional vehicles we could have asked for. Once we started playing there on word of mouth people came from all over place. As far away as Windsor, Ottawa, Toronto, Vancouver, Montreal, the States and they spread the word. Ma Lyons was the female counterpart of Owen. She was a shrewd five foot two, 150 pound, demanding and no nonsense promoter. Visually she reminded me of my mom, the gentlest person on earth. Not Ma. As tough as nails, no crap, in your face mean, but underneath a heart of gold unless you messed with her. Her and her husband Joe, who was the exact opposite to Ma, a quiet unassuming guy who didn't talk a lot but who you had to like. During the dance season they lived in a 30 foot house trailer that was up on blocks and directly across the road from the dance hall. They wintered in Florida. As for the dance it was so successful even Owen from The Jubilee came out to see what was going on and was blown away. Couldn't believe this was happening in the middle of nowhere. He wasn't alone. Pavilion operators and promoters came from everywhere and went away astounded and jumping on the rock and roll train.

Within a short time Caesar would play the entire summer season at Greenhurst; almost every Saturday between the May 24 weekend and Thanksgiving as well as Sundays on the long weekends. It was in Greenhurst that the band's name was short formed by fans and then everybody from Little Caesar and the Consuls or the Consuls to **Caesar!**

I put other bands in when Caesar wasn't available. Around this time Wayne Connors our drummer was getting really busy with his metal parts business and left the band. He was replaced by Gary Wright. Ma loved the band. We practically became family. The dance was on the second floor of the building and held legally around 600 people. As Caesar's reputation grew a couple of times we even jammed in well over a thousand very sweaty bodies. The main floor was a restaurant with some tables and pinball machines. No booze. Ha! Make that no legal booze. Ma was at the door with two sets of tickets. One was for the government the other for her pocket. The heat was worse than a sauna and the testosterone levels were off the charts. Unbelievable! By the end of the night we could actually wring the sweat out of our uniforms and it would make a puddle on the floor. The wooden floor beams used to move about 2 or 3 inches up and down from the weight of the dancers. Never ever a security problem with anybody. Ma didn't need security. She would handle anybody that got out of line and nobody, not even the bikers, would mess with her. I have seen her go face to face with some pretty rough guys and stare them down or actually up because of her size. Of course facing the lifetime ban from Greenhurst rule for making trouble didn't hurt and she remembered every face. I do remember one incident. We were in the middle of the second set when this very big very drunk biker who was pissed off at something, cursing and yelling, comes barrelling down the middle of the dance floor like a freight train heading directly at the stage. To put this in perspective the stage was two feet high and our front line was three across. This was going to be a disaster. It was going to be like a strike in a bowling alley. I swear to God the guy tripped about four feet away and knocked himself silly when his head drove into the stage. His friends came over picked him up and walked him out of the building. Not a word from anybody, except one guy who did apologize for his friend.

This is where I first met Jim and Jerry McCarthy twin brothers and two of the funniest people I have ever known and who became lifelong friends. They should have been stand-up comics. They were from Buffalo, New York and had moved with their widowed mom to Willowdale, a suburb of Toronto. They both would later work with me in the business. Jerry would be master of ceremonies at some of the shows I was involved in and Jimmy worked as an agent. They and their eight friends had rented a one bedroom cottage behind the dance hall and the eight of them piled in to party all weekend.

At 8 pm the area would be deserted. At 8.30 BANG! The park would be jammed with cars and people that came out of nowhere. From the time we started to play until we finished they never sat down. The dance ended at 12 midnight. At 12.30 the park was deserted again as everybody disappeared into cottages to continue partying or into their cars for the ride home. Very science fiction. Another new word. A lot of drinking, recreational drugs and carrying on. Talk about a love in. Macko and Gary Wright were the chick magnets and lived up to their reputation. Bruce and Kenny were the straight men. No hanky panky. Norm and I, a lot of the time, worked as a team and were very happily busy. Good healthy activity. When we played the long weekends Saturdays and Sundays we partied in a cottage that Ma had. I leave that one to your imagination. I exclude Kenny and Bruce from all that activity. It's worth mentioning that we did from time to time bring our wives or girlfriends to the dances but that practice diminished over the years. The ladies got tired of sitting around all night while we performed. Moving right along I was noted for my cars and my driving habits. I loved speed. I had a 1949 Ford coupe that was missing first gear. It was a contest to see who got home the fastest from any dance. Once I got up to speed I always won because, most of the time, truth be known, I was the only one racing and never noticed that everybody else was driving normally. Being drunk may have had something to do with that. A couple of times the cops stopped me leaving the dance at Greenhurst and being Caesar fans told me to park it and sleep it off. Good advice. Better then jail. I hit the road as soon as they left. They knew it but they all loved the band. What's that old saying "God watches over fools and children."

One sour note here. My job was to keep Caesar working 3 nights a week which at times, required some creative booking and in some cases bumping other bands to accommodate our money makers. A common agency practice. I don't think the band realized what I had to do to keep them working. One really bad move was cancelling the Mid-Knights at Greenhurst when a job Caesar had fell through. When George Semkiw found out why they were cancelled he went ballistic on me and verbally ripped at least three strips off my ass. I point out here that was the last time I pulled that trick. On The Mid-Knights anyway.

Fortunately Caesar was always busy. In retrospect I should have told George that Scribner did it. HA!

One of the best and most visionary operators, in the summer dance pavilions business, was Ray Colbourne. His surname was actually Cockburn. The family had different choices on last names. Cockburn, Coburn, Colborne. Good fun. Ray operated The Pavalon Pavilion in Orillia known as "The Pav" which he had leased from the city in 1957. At first he used 40's dance bands. In 1960 he made a deal with the local Teen Town to run rock & roll dances as an extra treat for the kids. Within a year he started running the rock bands regularly every Friday and sometimes, Saturdays as well as on the long weekends. Caesar was the first name rock band in. With few exceptions the place was jammed for every dance and shortly, as usual, we were booking the dances exclusively. This is where I first met Ray Coburn Jr., knee high to a grasshopper, future keyboard player and Ray Sr.'s son. Ray Jr. went on to carve out a hell of a career performing with many top artists. Honeymoon Suite, Heart, Lisa Dalbello, Kim Mitchell, Peter Frampton, Alana Myles and others plus he was writing and producing music. He made the transition into management and has received Juno Awards and most recently a Socan writing award for "Feel It Again" a song he wrote for Honeymoon Suite. Socan is The Society of Composers, Authors and Music Publishers of Canada a not-for-profit organization that represents the Canadian performing rights of millions of Canadian and international music creators and publishers.

Another son, Paul Cockburn, played drums with the Hunt, a rock horn band, who had a impressive twelve year run. He also played drums for Derringer and the Blushing Brides. Yet another son, Brian Coburn, was more on the production side, writing great music and creating visuals with his wife Donna. All in all a very talented family in the music business.

In 1963 Ray decided to buy Dunn's Pavilion in Bala. Part of that decision was due to Scribner and Duff's success with The Purple Candle summer dances which Ray was very aware of. After he did the purchase he revised the entertainment at Dunn's from the big band orchestras to rock & roll. He changed the name to The Kee to Bala probably the most famous summer dance pavilion in Canada. Who could forget The Kee to Bala? It was a "Build it and they will come." Ray renovated the place and continued to upgrade over the years so it always kept its image as the place to be. You could literally eat off the floor it was so clean. Ray had great insight into what people wanted to see and hear. Bands from all over the world loved playing there. With a 900 person capicity it was often pushed way beyond that to as many as 1500 dancers or more.

Funny story told by Barry Hutt, a celebrity in his own right, performing with Domenic Triano and other bands and good friend over the years. In Barry's words.

"This was a night The Rouges were playing The Kee on a split bill with April Wine I happened on noticing several people, actually a lot of people in the crowd, that were soaked to the skin. Why? Later on I was told what happened as I recently reminded our great friend Tom Wilson for his account of info' for his incredible biography. A Canadian Music Book he's been working on. Turns out a slew of people tryin' to crash The Kee's great performance hall were docking their boats at the dock at back of The Kee where they were throwing their ropes way up to catch over the 2nd floor's balcony rail so that they could climb up and get' in for free. Well. I believe it was Ray Cockburn who was the then owner/operator that would either himself or his staff wait for the feisty Tarzan rope climbers to get up high enough climbing before Ray and his staff would throw the ropes back down and off of the Kee's second floor balcony which would of course cause the attempting free loaders take a total dip in the lake. Tom Wilson definitely recalls those gettin' dunked into the lake too when he was playing there with his Little Caesar and the Consuls. Which means this was a constant ongoing comedy of part of the Kee's behind the scenes action. Gotta' love The Kee of Bala with its huge beautiful hardwood floor and its outstanding acoustics".

Ray Sr. was a big fan of Bobby Curtola, a Canadian Teen Idol, who Caesar did some backup for along with other name artists that Ray Sr. was bringing in on Friday nights at The Pav and Saturdays at The Kee. Caesar became a regular at both The Pav and The Kee as did all our bands. The Kee was a magic place where the bands loved to perform. It was a great experience for Ray's kids and mine as they were exposed to the best in the business, and still got to hang out and have fun being kids. Even the agents and managers were hanging out. The house where the bands stayed overnight was legendary for the parties that went on. Oh yea. Ron and I booked The Kee exclusively too.

Another story as told by Ray Harrison formerly of Crowbar and Greaseball Boogie Band.

"In the early days of Greaseball we learned that if you dressed and looked like a lunatic people gave you a wide berth. So we would often travel on planes, in trains, etc., to the gigs, in costume and it would cause quite a stir with the public. On one particular occasion Ray Colborne, who owned The Kee to Bala, also had a profitable pool hall in Barrie that was being plagued by a couple of toughs who ruled the roost. Ray asked us to make an appearance at the pool hall in full Greaseball regalia to scare the stuff out of these guys. We made our entrance, all 6 of us, like the Bowery Boys on acid and scared the bejeesus out of these guys and they never came back. Ray was very grateful."

Scribner saw the writing on the wall and closed the dance in Bala and the other location in Skeleton Lake and Torrance to concentrate on Port Carling. Duff had already moved on and opened his own dance club on the second floor of an office building directly across the street from CKEY on Davenport Road in Toronto. Brave New World. Very successful and a place to perform for musicians. His house band was The Countdowns another one of the bands we did a lot of booking for. One night they couldn't make it and that opened up an opportunity for David Clayton Thomas, aspiring blues and rock vocalist, to bring his band in and, as we will see later on, the rest is history.

Another key location for our agency was Hidden Valley in Huntsville where, sometimes, there would be as many as 2,000 people in attendance on a Saturday night. Bill Waterhouse, the promoter, whose family also owned the famous Deerhurst Resort, brought in American artists such as Neil Diamond, The Association, the Left Bank, and many others. Three floors of bands every week, mostly Canadian.

Other operators that made the switch to rock and roll were Jack Robertson with The Sauble Beach Pavilion, Pop Ivey with The Summer Gardens in Port Dover that became home base for Ronnie Hawkins, The Dardanella in Wasaga and two Mid-Knights strongholds Peggy's Pavilion in Stroud and the Balmy Beach Canoe Club in Toronto. The list goes on. This trend was spreading to the dance pavilions across Canada. The point of mentioning these venues is that, once we put Caesar or The Mid-Knights in any of them, it would follow that all our bands got a shot. It gave our agency a heretofore unavailable market and helped us expand very quickly. You can read a great book "Let's Dance" written by Canadian writer Peter Young. It's a history on the Ontario dance pavilion business.

Our agency soon controlled the bookings in most of the pavilions the result was that the kids who attended the dances started calling our office to book the bands for their high schools, universities, CYO dances and private parties. This brought the commercial promoters on board. Our bands were in demand everywhere and our market and business was growing in leaps and bounds, creating new opportunities

Between Ray, Owen, and Ma, as well as the other summer pavilions, they opened the door for rock & roll bands to perform all over Southern Ontario, replacing the 40's-50's big bands. This created a demand for all our bands that spread through all the summer dance pavilions. Everybody jumped on the new music wagon. We were now booking all three locations exclusively and the rest of the pavilions in Ontario were getting on board.

CHAPTER 7

Bill Gilliland - Martin Onrot

n 1963 enter Bill Gilliland. Bill was the vp and a partner in Arc Records with president Phil
Anderson. Bill handled the record production side of the business and recorded a lot of first line recording artists that I will share as we go along. Bill was arguably one of the most knowledgeable people in the Canadian recording industry. He was also a lot of fun and played the game better than most. Edgy comes to mind. His parties were legendary. He was then and is now one of my favourite people. A lot of people liked him but a lot also wondered if they could trust him. He was the Neil Bogart of Canada. Anything for a hit. Over the years Arc recorded a lot of future stars like Anne Murray, Gordon Lightfoot, Billy O'Connor, the Ugly Ducklings, the Stitch in Tyme, Ocean, Ronnie Hawkins, David Clayton Thomas, Little Caesar and The Consuls, the Mid-Knights, Terry Black, etc. and was absolutely wired into a couple of the American record companies. MCA Record Label big time as well as Capitol Records and Neil Bogart's Kama Sutra Records.

I would love to read the book Gilliland wrote about payola and kickbacks and, I think mafia involvement in the music business in The U.S.A. and Canada. Unfortunately he was paid $150,000 not to publish the book plus a lifetime gag order apparently because of a concern about the content being embarrassing to some people in the business. Too bad. Would have been a hell of a read. Talking to Bill recently he told me he is rewriting the book leaving out the parts that had created the problems previously.

We had the similar mob problems in Canada but not a lot of activity in the one night rock music business mostly because there wasn't a lot of money in live music yet they were certainly active in the bar business, gambling, prostitution and whatever else they were doing. Later when the money started showing up big time they did get more involved especially when the drug market started to expand into the growing rock and roll business. I got to know Gilliland pretty well. We became good friends and were to share a few adventures in the future.

TID BITS

Bill was one of the investors in The Brickland Motor Company owned by millionaire Malcolm Brickland that built and sold the all Canadian Brickland, a sports car, manufactured entirely in New Brunswick between 1974 and 1976 by automotive entrepreneur Bricklin. It was touted as state of the art but that turned out to be a myth when it continued to have a myriad of problems and was actually banned in Canada. 780 cars were produced in 1974, 2,062 in 1975 and just 12 in 1976 when it was discontinued. A Bricklin car is worth a hell of a lot more today than it was then.

Same year I met Marty Onrot which was another important moment for me for a couple of reasons. He was the number one promoter in Canada at the time and he was later to become one of my best friends. I was aware of him because he was at first, in 1961, doing shows at The Fifth Peg, his folk club in downtown Toronto presenting artists like Peter Paul & Mary, Woody Guthrie and other well known folk artists. In 1964 Mary, of Peter, Paul and Mary, was really impressed with Marty and the way he ran their shows so when the group got back to New York she spoke to her manager Albert Grossman who, after hearing her story, called Marty to thank him for treating his artists so well and asked if he would he be interested in presenting more of Albert's artists in Canada. That opened the door. Over the years Albert also managed Bob Dylan, Janis Joplin, The Band, Gordon Lightfoot, Todd Rundgren, Odetta, , John Lee Hooker, Ian and Sylvia, Richie Havens, the Electric Flag, and Jesse Winchester. He was based in New York and, as well as being one of the top managers in the world, he was a most interesting guy and became a good friend of Marty's. Marty moved into larger venues. He picked up The Mariposa Festival in Orillia in 1964 and also started to use more rock and roll until he had moved himself into the position of being the top rock promoter in the country. I was connecting with everybody I could so I called and arranged to meet him at his second floor office on Front St. The first thing I noticed, other than the usual waiting room furniture, was a full sized barber's chair? I liked him already. A tad unusual, as is the man. (Yes Virginia I sat in the barber's chair and no I did not get a shave or a haircut until much later and then not by Marty). Let me count the times. Then there was his wife and right arm the beautiful Barbara who was very involved in everything that was going on with the company. Later on she became a member of the notorious "Strumpets". What was that you ask? We will get to them later.

Marty quickly became a very busy guy. I spent a lot of time with him. It was educational. We also had a lot of fun. He had a great sense of humour not unlike my own. He was meticulous on setting up his concerts. No detail was left out. He became a big influence in how I ran my business. All Marty's shows were top of the line organized which kept the artists very happy. We had some interesting times together. I got to meet many of the artists and their reps which sure didn't hurt. George Carlin, Elton John and the Lovin Spoonful. He was doing some 50 concerts a year in Massey Hall and Maple Leaf Gardens and co-producing in other major Canadian cities with promoters like Harvey Glatt in Ottawa as well as Sam Guesser and later Don Tarleton in Montreal. He went from Martin Onrot Productions to, in 1971, Encore Productions and a partnership with CBS Records who were looking to expand their activities in the market and they paid him a lot of money. That opened the door to worldwide contacts and access to the top acts in the world. Didn't last long. About a year and a half and that's when Marty turned his activity into management as well as continuing his concert production.

Speaking honestly, from the beginning, we never got a lot of our bands on Marty's shows except ones he was managing. Not a big deal. I got tickets to his shows and we had good times as friends and hung out a lot. Once he got into managing local artists we did do a lot more as we were booking the bands anyway. Over the years Marty managed Neil Young, early in his career, Crowbar, Barefoot, James Leroy and Scrubaloe Caine among others.

CHAPTER 8

The Support People

I first met John Rowlands in 1963 which makes it a good place to mention the photographers in the music business that has preserved the history of the industry. There were and are some great ones but Rowlands was and is still one of the best if not the best. John has travelled all over the world and has taking pictures of thousands of performers and his pictures have been in every entertainment trade magazine ever published. Even more important he is one of the nicest people I have ever met and worked with.

Bill King, as well as being an outstanding musician, songwriter, producer, arranger, journalist and broadcaster has taken some of the best artist's photos I have ever seen. His wife Kris King also has taken some amazing photos not just of people but some breathtaking landscapes and is well known on the concert circuit for great photography.

Another was Bruce Cole a newcomer who quickly became a dominate photographer in the business. I can remember him showing up in our office offering to photograph our artists or anything else he could, for free. In future he would also hit on Beetle Magazine, Walter Grealis at RPM , Stan Klees for The Gold Leaf awards, and eventually became one of the principal photographers for The Juno Awards, all of whom I have not talked about yet.

Pat Lacroix is an award winning photographer and he took some great promotion pictures of Caesar and He is also a very talented jazz vocalist, writer and producer. In his career he performed in the Four Winds with Gord Lightfoot, the Halifax III with Richard Byrne and Denny Doherty who later joined the

Journeymen with John Philips and his wife Michelle who later, along with Cass Elliot, created the Mamas & Papas and last but not least Zal Yanovsky who later, with John Sebastian, formed the Lovin Spoonful. Interesting eh! I would point out that there were a lot of amateurs that did some really interesting photos. One that comes to mind, Larry LeBlanc, who has taken some outstanding photographs on the road with the Guess Who and David Clayton Thomas as well as some great shots of my staff, or so Larry tells me. He can't find them. I'll have to take his word for it.

All of the photographers were essential to the artists we worked with and our business as an agency. A picture is worth a 1000 words and our industry has always been one of the most photographed in the world. On stage, backstage and some places we would rather not discuss.

Honourable mention here to Long & McQuade Music Store. A very integral part of the Canadian music scene. Jack Long, a trumpet player, opened his first store on Carlton St. in 1956 the same year as the Consuls started. No connection. He rented a room to Jack McQuade a local drummer who used it to give drum lessons. In 1957 the two of them got together and opened the first Long & McQuade Music Store at 333 Yonge St., just south of The Masonic Temple, in Toronto. The rest is history. A great staff of mostly musicians. Jack Long, Jack McQuade, Fred Theriault, Pat Coffey, Fred Deligo, Mike Holman, Pete Traynor, Tony Crivaro, Steve Macko, Bob Abbot ("The Super Salesman") and his amazing lady Yvette who did the books for the company. Many others passed through over the years. Spotlight on Bob Abbot who is the epitome of a great salesperson who cared about his customers. As I mentioned previously that was where I bought my first bass and all my music equipment for the rest of my career as did the other guys in Caesar and many, many other bands and artists. The best way to sum Bob up is to repeat a story he once told me and repeated here by Andy Cox who worked with and was trained by Bob way back when.

"It's about an old world Italian father buying his son a guitar. Bob did everything but pull the guy's wallet out and count his cash before he even started to talk to him. When he had the man set in his mind he approached him and explained to the father why it was so important to make sure his son had a finer quality instrument to start out with and guided him directly to the instrument he had already decided that the guy was going to buy. To be clear everything he told the man was absolutely true. The guitar was well worth what he paid for it. It was a great gift to the son because he did get a fine quality instrument. That was part of Bob's secret. He never pulled fast ones or tried to oversell anyone. Before I started working there he talked me out of a purchase and showed me a different option that made much more sense for me. Many would have just closed the deal and let me spend money I didn't need to but Bob knew I didn't have all that much to spend so he showed me the alternatives. You have to like a guy who works that way! That's Bob".

That was the attitude that prevailed throughout the company. They all took good care of the musicians making sure they had the latest equipment and personal attention. As anybody in the business will tell you they were then and still are the musician's music store run by musicians for musicians with over 60 stores across Canada now so no matter where you are they are just a phone call away. We often phoned from the agency to reserve equipment for some bands that were occasionally running short financially and we vouched for them. Our word was good with Long & McQuade. We knew where and when the bands were working. If you were broke, as a lot of musicians were and are, Long & McQuade would always work something out to keep you going. They knew what it was like out there. Caesar was a preferred customer. We paid cash for everything. I will never forget those state of the art Twin Fender Amps that we had.

At the rear of the store in the repair section another treasure, Peter Traynor. This is where Peter created the Traynor Amplifier that became the amp to have in the business. Just to test the amp's durability Peter would take one every so often and drop it off the roof of the two story building they were in. Passed the test every time. That was the beginning of Yorkville Sound that went on to become world famous and make a ton of money. Like a lot of the people that I connected with Peter was a good friend and another character. Also a bass player. A genius, a wonderful person, and a lot of fun. Also working there 1963 to 65, future Caesar guitar player Tony Crivaro. Another Caesar. Keyboard player Steve Macko who was in sales travelling around Canada and The USA for the company.

Later on when he needed more room as business grew. Peter moved his manufacturing and repair business to a River St. Warehouse in what was then a questionable neighbourhood in Toronto. The open door policy stayed the same. Help any musician that needed his expertise and work out a payment plan if needed. I went out to watch Peter play occasionally. I caught him one night at the Masonic Temple on Yonge St. I was a Mason at the time and this was where Corinthian my home lodge was. The Masons owned the property. The dance was called Club 888 A little vague here. I don't remember who the band was but Traynor was the bass player. His nickname was Thumper because he played sooooo loud. I played there a lot with Caesar. Norm Muir was the promoter and took good care of the bands in many ways to keep us all happy. Nick Jennings, a local music historian, reminded me that Norm Muir originally ran The Collegiate Club on Bloor St featuring artists like the Diamonds, Crew Cuts, Four lads and the Two-Tones Gord Lighfoot's duo with Terry Whelan. I remember one night I was standing backstage at Club 888 watching one of our bands when I felt somebody pressing up against my back and it was definitely female. I felt a hand slide around my waist and clutch my "business" and then a whisper in my ear. "Hi. I'm Pat. Would you like too?" I did and we did. Thanks Mr. Muir. My genitals could have been arrested for the places they were happily going.

At the Club there was a five foot high stage with a revolving stage built on top of it. The idea was that you would play your set then the stage would revolve and when it reached halfway you would stop playing and the next band would start. Whew. A couple of nights the stage stopped before the change over so the two bands were playing at the same time but two different songs! Had to have a sense of humour. One night one of the bands changed keys just so the two bands were synchronised playing 12 bar blues that became a mainstay whenever the stage got stuck. Now that's creative.

Muir also managed bands. One in particular Dunc & Judy and the Regents that became Dunc & the Deacons. Same problem. Why does everybody think they can be a manager? He would have been better as an agent. All he did was keep the band working and that was done by giving our agency an almost exclusive on the club. We made sure the band worked elsewhere regularly. While that was great for us it doesn't make a career for a band. Although they did record a couple of singles and an album at Hallmark Studios that were released by Quality Records who then made a deal with The Blue Cat label for a release in the States but nothing happened. The label folded and the band eventually split up. If there is a bright side all the musicians did move on to other bands.

Hats off to the unsung heroes. The Road Crews. They were considered members of the family and some even had their own fans. Some of the great ones that I dealt with in Canada were Jimmy Martin(Jumbo) with the Guess Who, Bruce Bell with Lighthouse, Pulombo with Domenic Troiano through most of his bands, Michael (Lurch) Hurst with Rush, Joe Owens with Triumph, and Roly Paquin with Crowbar. One that is outstanding in my mind is Mr. Bob Roper who I always thought of as a production manager and a good one. Bob has worn so many hats from artist manager and press agent to A&R working with artist like Burton Cummings, the Nylons, Rush, the Doobie Brothers and Supertramp.

In the beginning, hmm, sounds biblical, an easy go. Carry the amps; cram the guitars, drums, keyboards, and all the other equipment including yourself in the back seat and or trunk of your car. The musicians loaded and set up everything themselves. Sometimes with the help of friends. One positive it kept you in very good physical shape. The sound systems were whatever you found at the place you were playing. Usually a public address system that was used to make announcements and play records. Monitors systems you could use to hear yourself and everybody on stage were unheard of in the early years. Caesar had five singers that could do lead or background vocals. We had three microphones. Bruce had his own microphone because he was on the keyboards and Wayne on drums the same. The rest of us gathered around one microphone, centre stage, to sing our parts. You got to know who had what for dinner. Yuk! As things progressed we started carrying our own sound system and lights that Norm Sherratt built. We set everything up ourselves but, as we added more production, we had to hire a couple of guys to carry the equipment for us. I think it was more for show then need. Lenny Duncan and Ron Kerr, originally fans, were our roadies. Long story short it wasn't too long before the roadies became indispensible. These days as many as 30, 40, 100 or more people all ages are involved in organizing and running the shows for the known bands. For the most part each one is a specialist in setting up and operating the equipment and most of the time moved in and around the players like ghosts. With the roadies came contract riders. The requests started out simple. A stage where possible, a dressing room or at least something bigger then a closet, some refreshments then, as time went on, the production became more and more technically intricate. The now important riders went from a one or two pager to five to ten till it became a contest of who could ask the most outrageous things and get them. You are getting the picture.

Think as bizarre as young people with too much money and time on their hands can then double or triple the demands. Once it started the sky was the limit! As always the few got everybody painted with the same brush. The record holder at the time was Van Halen with 53 pages. There are lots of stories if you just browse rock and band riders online. The Canadian bands were, as with almost everything else except their music, far more conservative. The Guess Who rider was only 25 pages. The reason everybody used to justify this lunacy was that if they put a lot of irrelevant demands in the rider and they were granted it meant the important technical requirements would be taken care of for sure. If they were not then let the games begin. Now that was the rational anyway.

I would recommend you see the film "Who the F—k is Arthur Fogel" directed by Ron Chapman and produced by Wayne Thompson, both Canadians. A great documentary on the concert business. It does tell what goes on with the production crew behind the scenes really well. It also features a lot of the movers and shakers that did and do control a lot of the concert business in Canada and internationally. I am told it's on Netflix so you can download and watch it.

Lawrence Schurman is a person who has been very helpful with this book and is one of the agents that worked for me. One claim to fame for Lawrence was when he first met Arthur Fogel the future number one production manager in the world with such artists as the Rolling Stones, Mama Gaga, U2 and Madonna. Arthur was a waiter at The Edge Restaurant in Toronto looking for a job in music production. Lawrence referred him to Michael Cohl at CPI and Arthur got the job as producer for all CPI's rock and roll live concert shows. Productions costs can run into the millions. A long way from our "everything fits into one car days". I have been told it was the outrageous riders that killed the high school business. The school administrations rebelled and began to do their own riders for the bands to deal with which eventually caused a parting of the ways. By then the business had moved way beyond the high schools anyway.

CHAPTER 9

We go National - Larry LeBlanc

O nward and upward. Thanks to the bands we were working with and our own efforts the agency was on the map. Within a year I was a partner and the cash flow was getting considerably better. We started working with the bands, managers, promoters and agents across the country from Halifax to Vancouver as well as radio, newspapers, television and magazines coast to coast. Now we were finding other rock agents showing up in cities across Canada. We got in touch with them and explained what we wanted to do. We convinced them that they could be part of a national circuit in Canada with high schools, dance halls, universities, bars, promoters and anywhere else that would book talent including radio, television and even film work. We would all co-operate sharing each other's contacts and bands. We were already working with the major and secondary market radio and television stations. Something else we had started doing was booking the djs for the dances who played records during the intermissions on the dates our bands were playing. Just about every city and town had a local dj celebrity on the radio and/or the bonus of a television station. This was another way for us to connect and get airplay for our bands and get our name out there. We used djs a lot. They all got paid in cash and in some cases as much as the bands. All quite legal I might add. Win win. Got the records played and had fun. It was sort of a warped pre Cancon system that forced radio stations to play 30% Canadian content records. Every place our bands played, we called the local radio stations and newspapers and provided them with any material they needed to promote the shows especially records so that when the bands arrived it was an event. "A" rotation on the radio. This is a term referring to the amount of prime air time a record would get played which would be the highest rotation available. Where we could we got front page news stories or at least articles in the newspapers. My income soared from the $30 a week to a more comfortable level. Believe me I earned it! I was now doing the financial books for the agency. Good sign. We had books. Bad sign, I was doing them. Actually I was good with the company's finances but I did eventually turn them over to my wife Joanne who was a professional bookkeeper. Important to note here that we really were flying by the seat of our pants and learning as we went. We learned very quickly that recording and promotion were the most important things to be done. Oh yeah; and keeping the bands working regularly. Fortunately, and most important of all, we represented or were working with some of the best musicians in Canada and, as it turned out, the world. That combination created the international market we were after. Through this period I was travelling a lot more across Canada fitting everything in where I could around performing with Caesar.

Let me introduce 16 year old Larry LeBlanc later to be one of Canada's premier journalists who has interviewed and written about, well, everybody in the business. He still owes me a DVD from the Juno awards where he was honoured, in 2013. They asked me to comment on Larry in the presentation of the award as he was and is one of my best friends. I thought I was complementary for the most part. Nah. He is the most opinionated, determined, intelligent, creative, sometimes obstinate person, I know. Also one of the most honest which sometimes causes him grief or pisses people off but that was one of the things I always liked about him. Back to, I think, around 1964 he was booking the bands for Dunbarton High School in Pickering. You had to be involved in the extracurricular activities at the school to be the social convener, the person that hired the entertainment for the dances. Leave it to Larry. He started a chess club so he qualified to book the bands. I think the club met about three times. Even then Eh! He was almost a fanatic about wanting to know everything about the music business. I remember one time when he wanted to get to The Mimicombo Hall in Mimico, a roller rink/dance hall in the west end of Toronto, to attend a James Brown Concert. He hitchhiked from Pickering, got as far as College and Yonge Streets in downtown Toronto then, stranded, he called me to get a ride to the show. I was the agent and was going there anyway so I picked him up. Great show. An agent's dream. SOLD OUT! I have no idea how Larry got home. Neither does he. Even then he was obsessed with the music business and yes, even then, very opinionated. Did I mention that? If you asked Larry for his opinion you got it or, even if you didn't ask, you got it anyway. Those were his good points. Another one was that he could usually back up his stand. In late 1966 he was kicked out of school. He had a job at The Jubilee Pavilion in Oshawa as the disc jockey. Unfortunately he faced some pretty strict rules at home and because he arrived home so late all the time he was subjected to tough love by his mom. She locked him out. Undaunted our hero grabbed a ride to Toronto with the band that had played the Jubilee that night, Wes Dakus & the Rebels from Edmonton. They dropped him off in Yorkville. I don't know and he doesn't remember what he did after that. Larry and I have been friends pretty well since we met and have supported each other over the years. We socialized with each other's families. He has always credited me with being one of the catalysts that got him into the business. Flattering but it was his talent that got him there. I just opened some doors. I have heard other stories about his motivation. One was that on hearing David Clayton Thomas & The Shays Freddy Keeler's amazing guitar solo on their first record "Boom Boom" was another reason he was inspired to be in the business.

Fortunately, though both of us can be a pain in the ass, we never take any of our criticisms of each other personally. Be in big trouble if we did. Larry maintains to this day we have never had a fight. I guess that's as opposed to a strong disagreement. He went on to become a radio personality, a top entertainment writer in Canada and critic for many publications including Canadian Editor for Billboard Magazine, the music business bible, as well as publicist for The Guess Who, David Clayton Thomas and interviewing the movers and shakers in entertainment worldwide. An insightful, knowledgeable interviewer that does his homework. To expand his contacts and knowledge Larry had decided he was going across Western Canada to meet the influential people in the business and asked me for contacts that he could talk to in each city. Well. Revelation! Apparently we actually had established some very strong links. At every stop he used "The greeting Tom Wilson told me to contact you" intro and was more than well received in every city from Winnipeg to Vancouver. In Vancouver he called Bruce Allen, The Agent Man in BC, and got the same reception and ended up staying at Bruce's house for the night. Pretty cool for Larry. He and Bruce are still friends today. Great statement for our new network. For the first time bands could play coast to coast not just in the bars but one nighters. This was the real beginning of the Canadian rock music national touring circuit.

Toronto was alive with the sound of music and was firmly established as a major market luring musicians from all over the world. We were on the map and starting to get a reputation as the go to agency.

CHAPTER 10

We are booking Internationally

This is where our business began to change from strong regional to stronger national and international. Rock & Roll was becoming the mainstream music. The success of our agency and our national approach to the business as innovators helped to create another new market of promoters, publicity agents, managers, record producers, recording studios, A&R managers, magazine and music publishers and a host of other related companies that had previously not existed, were being ignored, or had ignored us. Now we were all more focused. Everybody helped create the market for our musicians who were the key people that weren't always getting the support or the recognition that we knew they were entitled too but it was improving. With few exceptions the radio stations weren't playing or promoting a lot of Canadian rock music. Wasn't profitable. There were some rebels that helped the cause. It was not just the bands. It was the people around and with them that worked their asses off. Many went on to become established internationally. Not all, unfortunately, but we did make our mark one way or another. We should recognise those that didn't and still made a contribution to the Canadian music growth. Old saying "It takes a lot of failures to get a win"

Special thanks to the import artists like Ronnie Hawkins, Bill King, Jessie Winchester, Jackie Shane, Rick James and other U.S.A. musicians that decided they liked Canada. Yuh Think? Refugees from what was going on outside our borders. The Vietnam War, hands down the dumbest war in history, that needlessly killed so many people was a big incentive to "Get the hell out of town", namely the U.S.A, where kids were getting drafted. No draft in Canada.

We had our problems in Canada. There was race discrimination for sure but not like U.S.A. and other countries. Ours was, for the most part, more subtle and generally not as violent. The Blacks and Jews were the most obvious targets as they were in other countries but our situation improved far quicker than then America and with the advent of rock music black, brown, yellow, white, or blue, we all ate in the same restaurants, used the same bathrooms, played the same bars and any other venues, eventually including the big hotels. We played to mixed crowds. Inter-racial relationships were getting pretty common and we all could enter through the front door with everybody else. These freedoms, as Canadians in the music business, we took for granted and surprised the hell out of the Americans and the rest of the world. Now let me qualify that. It applies to the music business, unfortunately, not always to the rest of Canadian life. Our black, Jewish and Asian friends were still subjected to the bullshit racism. Fortunately the music community was, for the most part, a safer place to be.

The talented imports have contributed amazingly to Canadian music specifically, in the early days. The Toronto Sound was born. Originally, it was mostly rhythm and blues thanks to the American artists passing through playing the bars and the dance halls. James Brown, Muddy Waters, Bo Diddley, Ike & Tina Turner, Wilson Picket, Jackie Wilson, Stevie Wonder, Ray Charles, Aretha Franklin and the list goes on. They were all very generous in sharing with us, the local musicians and us doing the same in return. It was a learning curve for both sides. It also gave our agency a boost as we provided more and more of their live play dates.

It was around this time that I first met Paul White the amazing A&R and promo person for Capital Records. Like me he started in the warehouse only at Capitol Records Canada. Prior to Paul's arrival in Canada in 1957 there were very few if any rock artists on the label. Paul, a transplanted Englishman, brought Capitol Canada to the front line by truly supporting and pushing Canadian artists and later, from 1972 on, independent record labels like Roman Records, Yorktown Records, Aquarius Records and Daffodil Records. A lot of our agency artists and bands were on all on one of those labels. On Capitol through the sixties into the seventies we had the Staccatos, later to be the Five Man Electrical Band, Edward Bear, the Esquires, the Ugly Ducklings, David Clayton Thomas,

Wes Dakus with Barry Allen as well as working with Ronnie Hawkins, Terry Black, Mother Tuckers Yellow Duck (loved the name), and Sugar Shoppe. Paul was an amazing guy. I am going to do something I probably shouldn't. Specifically highlighting "The Beatles Invasion of Canada" which has been beat to death but it was such an amazing accomplishment by Paul that I can't ignore the huge impact it had on the Canadian and world music scene. Most people in the industry know the story but not so many of the public. Paul was the person that introduced The Beatles records first in North America before the U.S.A. even knew about them. On the first two releases he couldn't get any airplay from CHUM or any Toronto stations at first. He did get the records played on an Oshawa station CKLB with disc jockey Jay Jackson and he gave them triple A rotation. That means they were played a lot. Previous to being in Oshawa Jay had been hired to do a short stint as the all night host on Chum filling in for dj Bob Laine, another one of my favourite people. When Bob briefly left CHUM to host a radio show at CKGM in Richmond Hill. There is little information about Jay, when I spoke to Doug Thompson, one of the creators of The Chum Archives along with Bob Laine, he tells me he has a photo but no bio on Jay. I do remember he was good to any of our artists that played in the area. The first station to chart the third release "She Loves You" was CFPL in London Ontario. Another disc jockey that jumped on it was Red Robinson on CFUN Radio in Vancouver. Not that this has anything to do with Canadian artists but it parallels how Canadian records were also being treated before we finally got on track.

TID BITS

Do you know who was the first on air person to play a Beatles record in Canada? Not many people do. This was in 1962 before Capitol released any of the band's product. A fellow named Ray Sonin was host on a show in Toronto with the name "Calling All Britons" that broadcast once a week on CFRB Radio in Toronto. A relative had sent him a copy of "Love Me Do" from London, England. Unfortunately he played it a couple of times then discarded it because of no reaction and no impact.

Back to Paul. He started The Sizzle Sheet which was a weekly hype mailing he put out to radio stations, record distributors, and agents and as many people as he could that were related to the business. Very successfully getting great reaction to providing the inside news on artist recordings, new record releases and other inside news all relating to Capitol's roster. I mention this because I used the same concept a couple of years later for my agency. Also very successfully.

Because of Paul and people like him all the Canadian companies had started to push Canadian artists more than they ever had before. Not to take anything away from the pioneers but the scene was changing and it started to become "Get on or get left behind" when it came to getting on board for Canadian artists.

CHAPTER 11

Ronnie Hawkins, Jackie Shane and The Bluenote

By 1963, thanks to the talent we were working with as well as our own abilities, we had established The Ron Scribner Agency as a national entity. At 23 years old I was the elder statesman in the company. I was doing three packs of cigarettes a day, 15 or 20 coffees and a fair amount of alcohol. No drugs as yet. For the most part I was surviving on 3 or 4 hours sleep. All day in Ron's basement and at night hitting the bars and anywhere else bands were performing. Of course I was still performing with Caesar two three or more nights a week. A gruelling schedule. Many years later I can still only sleep 4 or 5 hours a night.

The optimism was contagious. We could do anything. This is when Ronnie Hawkins approached Scribner and invited him to open an office on the second floor of The Le Coq d'Or Tavern on Yonge St. I think this was something that Scribner and Hawkins had been talking about for a while. They were good friends. Nobody had discussed it with me. When Scribner told me about it we both thought this would be a step up from the basement so we agreed and moved in. Being there was being in the heart of the music business in Toronto. Bill Bulucon, the Owner of the bar, liked Caesar so we got to play there a few times. I remember we got paid $450 for the first 4 day week. (That wasn't each) Another positive. We were booking some one night dates for Hawkins so Caesar got to play a date with Ronnie Hawkins and The Hawks. What a band they were! We played a split bill in London, Ontario and there was Robbie Robertson former

Little Caesar and The Consuls. At one point in their show Ronnie brought a noticeably overweight girl on stage and put her behind Levon the drummer and had her put her very ample breasts on either side of his head and squeeze them together. Levon never missed a beat. The crowd loved it but Levon was noticeably uncomfortable and the prude in me thought it was not funny.

Being at the Le Coq d'Or I had the opportunity to spend a lot of time in the local bars and got to meet a so many people who became lifelong friends. I swear every musician in Canada dropped by for a starter. The Hawks were playing almost every night in the bar.

Gord Josie who was the manager at The Friar's Tavern just down the street that eventually became the semi-home for Caesar as far as playing bars, and netted our agency a lot of bookings in another Kudlets stronghold where we ended up booking direct thanks to Gord. Hawkins played The Friars and also upstairs on the second floor in the Nickelodeon Club, as did we. It was the forerunner of The Hawk's Nest that was later to be on the second floor of The Le Coq d'Or. The Friars was owned by Jack Fisher who also owned The Concord Tavern where Hawkins later relocated his headquarters.

Another great club was The Colonial owned by Michael Lyons and family. Both Lyons and Josie became my good friends over the years. The historic Yonge St. Strip has its own stories that have been told a thousand times. As mentioned earlier Yonge St was the birthplace of the Toronto Sound. I first met the fabulous Jackie Shane at the Sapphire tavern on Richmond St. E. with the house band, Frank Motley and The Motley Crew. We had booked Jackie on some one-night dates around Toronto thanks to her 1962 Canadian hit single "Any Other Way" previously recorded by William Bell. On the original recording the word gay meant happy. Jackie was a gay man and a cross dresser and put a different sexual spin on the lyric that made the song her signature number and was a definite statement when it wasn't as yet accepted by the mainstream public. It was amazing that we didn't get heat from parents at the high schools we booked her into. I remember one night we backed her up at Crang Plaza. That was a night to remember. There is no question she was electric on stage and mesmerized an audience visually and vocally. She was originally from Nashville, Tennessee. An amazing performer and singer, an incurable tease, with a great sense of humour. One night I was sitting in the Sapphire with Jackie, Bill Gilliland and Bob MacAdorey, the newest dj at Chum, watching Frank Motley and his band perform and waiting for Jackie to go on stage. A lot of stories going around the table. Jackie's were always the funniest. Although she did continue to record everything in her career started to slow down so she never made it into the big time which is a shame. She was the forerunner of the glamour performers like Michael Jackson and Prince. At one point Ron and I had what we thought was a great idea. To combine the Funkadilics, a Detroit band, with Jackie. What a show that would be. Unfortunately never happened. In the seventies she faded from view and just disappeared. She was discovered years later living back in Nashville and refusing contact with anyone but she is still remembered. In 2010 I got a call from Elaine Banks a CBC producer who was doing a documentary on Jackie and asked for my help. I brought along Sonny Milne, Caesar's drummer, who has played with just about everybody and knows everybody including Jackie. Elaine had tracked Jackie down in Nashville but she refused to be interviewed. Elaine still managed to put together a great CBC documentary titled "I Got Mine" The Story of Jackie Shane" You can catch it on Youtube. More recently, in 2016, I talked to Rob Bowman, a local historian, who has somehow got through to Jackie and already has over twenty hours of conversations on tape and is hinting there may be a comeback brewing. I hope so.

Back at The Le Coq d'Or and Hawkins's World there is no question it was an exciting place to be. Although I was never a big mixer or that social, mostly because I was working all the time, I did meet a lot of interesting people from different backgrounds and all walks of life plus virtually every musician in Toronto and elsewhere. Hawkins had a boxing club and gym on the third floor where he held court. It drew a lot of people for various reasons. I won't even try to tell the Hawkins's Story. An amazing person with charisma coming out of his ass. Probably the best bio I have read on Hawkins was one in The Canadian Encyclopaedia. Worth your time to read it.

http://www.thecanadianencyclopedia.ca/en/article/ronnie-hawkins

One guy I met that I became friends with was Heavy Andrews, a very large man that was called Heavy for obvious reasons. Right out of a Damon Runyan movie he was part agent, part manager and there was a part I was never sure of. Maybe he was mobbed up, maybe he wasn't but he did have a lot of friends doing time in Joyceville and Millhaven prisons. His bands performed at both. I thought I met Heavy's wife in Toronto running a dry cleaners but apparently, according to Nick Panaseiko, a promoter from London, Ontario, Heavy, had one in London, Ontario. I don't know which one was before or after or were maybe one and the same. Walter Taylor from Fat Chance, one of the bands the Heavy managed, told me a lot of stories about the days with Heavy as have a lot of musicians that worked with him or were around at the time. Good one was when he got Fat Chance a new van to carry the equipment and the guys to their gigs. It had one small problem. You had to cross the ignition wires to start it. Never got stopped though. That would say either Walter was a good driver or Big Brother was watching.

It was at The Le Coq d'Or that I first met Robbie Lane, a true veteran of the music wars at a very early age and the perfect example of a survivor. Another Willowdale boy. He has often been compared to Dick Clark from American Bandstand with his perennial good looks. He had joined up with Hawkins as the backup band after The Hawks split to work with Bob Dylan. Always the business man, Robbie still managed to keep his band, The Disciples, as a separate entity and busy in the market performing live as well as on television and radio. Nice balancing act. I was always impressed. He had a great hit single with "Fannie Mae". Got some interest from American record companies. I thought he should have taken off. Luck of the draw. He has done well since still performing around Ontario and has a popular radio show on AM740 in Toronto. To my knowledge, he never had a manager. Hawkins was certainly involved in his career for a while but there was no formal agreement and I don't think Robbie wanted a manager anyway. He was doing fine on his own.

At the Le Coq d'Or Hawkins reigned as the King of Yonge St. and he literally held court. Same when he moved over to the Concord Tavern on Bloor St. It would be hard for me to top all the stories that relate to what went on there. The atmosphere around Hawkins was like a combination of the Playboy Mansion and The Best Little Whorehouse in Texas with an Arkansas twist and a smaller budget. A more down home good old boy feeling. One of his friends was Bill Clinton a decent musician who played sax and later, in his spare time, became Governor of Arkansas and then president of The United States. Would have been a great promotional package for Hawkins. He could have run for mayor of Toronto.

TID BITS

Bill Clinton's wife, Hillary, was almost the first female president in 2016 and, even though she won the popular vote, Donald Trump got the votes that counted and became the President.

There were a lot of people passing through or hanging out from politicians to lawyers, corporate types. Movie stars, celebrities, hookers, fans, groupies, the mob, street people and always the musicians. Some amazing musicians passed through those doors on their way to success and sometimes not. Hawkins was a taskmaster and made his bands want to be the best. Reminded me of Bruce with Caesar.

The Yonge St bars catered to what was, sometimes, a pretty rough crowd and it had an undercurrent of violence to it in the early days. Mostly blue collar workers out for a good time which included getting drunk and boisterous sometimes to the point of punch outs and sometimes weapons. Very seldom you would hear of any of the musicians having any problems. It was a kind of unwritten rule that you didn't mess with the musicians and most certainly not the ones connected to Hawkins. For the time I was there I wasn't hassled or threatened much. A couple of times but nothing I couldn't handle. There were things you didn't hear about. There were a lot of those. Murder wasn't common but it did happen.

I did run across something that was interesting. Hawkins was obviously athletic and intelligent. No surprise. I was told when he was a kid back home in Arkansas; he went to college on a swimming scholarship. He can, apparently, speak the Queen's English better than me. I have a lot of respect for him and what he has accomplished. Hands down one of the most amazing music careers in Canada ever. Never went to the superstar status as an artist but I think by choice. He always preferred to play the bars rather than the concerts and did create his own niche as a Canadian Celebrity. In his words "A legend in my own mind". True showmanship! If you would like to read an insightful article about Yonge St., and Hawkins era, check out one written by Juliette Jagger, a Toronto writer. (*https://juliettejagger.com/*)

Hard to believe she was only 16 when she wrote it. Another is by Toronto sax player Russ Strathdee who did an amazing blog talking about his years on the Yonge St. strip and sharing lots of pictures.

The legal drinking age in Toronto in the '60s was 21 years of age and bars closed at 11.30 pm on Saturdays and were not open on Sundays. For fun sometimes the bands would play Sundays and allow the underage teenagers in to dance and watch but no booze was allowed. Then there were the after hour clubs. One place where I loved hanging out was in a building right across the street from The Le Coq d' Or, on the second floor, over a store. The iconic Bluenote Club, owned by Jerry and Al Steiner, opened in 1958. It was basically a coffeehouse. No booze sold and stayed open till the early morning hours. Let's correct that. No legal booze and drugs. This is where you could see, hear and mingle with the cream of the Toronto musical community. Shawne and Jay Jackson, Diane Brooks and her daughter Little Joanne, Steve Kennedy, Dominic Troiano, Grant Smith, Doug Riley, Jay King, Wayne St. John, Shirley Mathews, Kay Taylor, Whitey Glan, Jack Hardin, Prakash John, Eric Mercury, George Oliver, Duncan White, John Finley, Terry Brown, Roy Kenner, David Clayton Thomas and the list keeps on going. Word was out that this was the place to be. People will be jumping on me for forgetting the names of a lot of the musicians who performed at The Bluenote. Think of all the singers, bass players, guitar players, drummers, keyboard and horn players that went through those doors. You would see artists like Stevie Wonder, the Righteous Brothers, Gene Chandler, Wilson Picket and other American r&b stars who dropped in after their own gigs elsewhere in Toronto. The agents, managers, radio people, and record company reps, were all there. That's where I made some great contacts and friends.

One of the first bands we booked was the first one to play The Bluenote. The fantastic Bobby Dean (Blackburn) & the Gems. Loved that band and Bobby! A great talent with an amazing family history. Here is where we test whether or not you have been paying attention. Remember Gary Blackburn the security guy at Masaryk Hall and the Tidbit on Page 42? Gary and Bobby are related. Bobby is the great grandson of Solomon Earls a slave that rode the famous Underground Railroad from the Southern U.S.A. into Canada. This escape route began operating in the 1780s and became known as the Underground Railroad in the 1830s and operated through to the 1860s. It wasn't really a railroad but a route that assisted escaping slaves to get safely out of the U.S.A. and secretly to Canada.

Soloman married Sahara Woods, a white woman from Owen Sound Ontario. Theirs was one of the first inter-racial marriages in Canada. Her family disowned them. The Klu Klux Klan tried to scare them out of town, to no avail. When the clan showed up at their house and Sarah came out with a shotgun. "I know all of you and if you don't get off my lawn you are going to have a problem". Very cool lady. I swear I did not know the Klu Klux Clan existed in Canada until I was doing the research for this book. Shocked the hell out of me. The other famous family story was about two more relatives and slaves. Thorton and Lucie Blackburn, that made the incredibly dangerous journey from Kentucky via the Underground Railroad and who started the first taxicab company in Toronto. What an amazing family history!

Next house band, Whitey & the Rollets, took over with Mike McKenna on guitar, future Luke & The Apostles star guitar player along with Whitey Glen on drums future Rouges, Mandala, Bush and so many others, with the fabulous lead singer Dianne Brooks and her daughter Little Joanne.

Then there was The Majestic's fronted by Shawne and Jay Jackson. There's a band that should have gone to the top of the music charts. They were always a presence in the Ontario scene and how you could not love Shawne Jackson. Great voice, knockdown gorgeous, a great performer, and a very talented actress. Jay Jackson could have been an ambassador for Canada in any country in the world. A born charmer and like sister Shawne, a good looking and also very talented performer. Over the years we have become good friends along with the guys in the band of which there were more than a few that passed through. A very strange story in regard to recording arrangements with The Majestics. The band never recorded together with Shawne and Jay because of record label politics. How stupid was that? The band did five albums with Arc Records and nothing. Minimal activity. Weird. Certainly wasn't a material problem. The tunes were good. Although they never had a manager to my knowledge they did make our agency a lot of money playing around Ontario.

TID BITS

Shawne and Jay's great-grandfather Albert Jackson was Toronto's first black postman. Another very cool eh! A quote from Shawne regarding the Blackburn family. "Thornton and Lucie Blackburn gave my great-great grandmother, Anne Maria Jackson and her seven children, a place to stay after they'd come to Canada through the Underground Railroad!"

Grant Smith & the Power was another band that knocked them dead at The Bluenote. I'll get back to them later. Not to be left out the fabulous Jack Hardin and Silhouettes great band, and performer that never got the recognition he and they deserved. Who can forget Jay King and the Spices who almost made it on Motown. What a voice. Note that all the bands I have named, to my knowledge, did not have a manager. Usually the leader of the band talked to us direct and confirmed the dates. What a great showcase club to invite Buyers down to see the talent!

Back at the Le Coq d'Or the plot thickens. I'm not sure what happened, or why, but Hawkins and Scribner, as far as I know, made a deal to work together without me being involved. Just like that I was out. Never did get a reason. Still can't think of one. I was very good at what I was doing and Scribner was my friend. Maybe I should have been more social. We did not have a written partner agreement so I had no comeback. At the time I thought this was pretty cold but that's business. Live and learn. It was in retrospect one of the best things that could happen for and to me. "Thanks Ron and Ronnie." For the record Wanda, Ronnie's wife, was and still is, my favourite Hawkins. Up the proverbial creek without a paddle I was forced into doing something right away. I did and commenced on what turned out to be the beginning of an amazing journey!

CHAPTER 12

Bigland, Domenic Troiano and Irving the alternate life style Dog.

I am a firm believer in that everything happens for a reason. I immediately called Fred White, a newcomer in the business, who was working as a salesman at CHUM; very ambitious, very young, working with a couple of local acts The Big Town Boys and Shirley Mathews both of whom were recording with Stan Klees at Tamarac Records. Fred was starting to get a name for himself especially in the media and record business areas. I had met him a few years earlier when he was the entertainment/ buyer social convener for Leaside High School in Toronto. Fred was Mr Personality a publicist who would go where people feared to tread. His contacts were the top of the pile in the media business. Always a suit, shirt and tie and all about make money and have fun. His attitude was a contagious. Every company needs attitude and he had plenty. Fred was one of the boys. I will never understand why he doesn't have the image that Scribner and I ended up getting. In our case "The Bash Brothers" a rude reference to our golfing abilities or rather lack of.

Fred was awesome! Madison Avenue! He was one of the movers and shakers in the Toronto music business in the media, and the record labels for around three years. I tried researching him and found very little. I did know his family. When I called him he had just finished working with Duff Roman at Roman Records but left because Duff didn't have the budget to carry him full time so he had moved to CHUM in sales and was a very popular guy in the station but looking for other opportunities. My timing was perfect. We made the deal to combine our talents and contacts to open a new agency of a type never seen before in Toronto or, for that matter, anywhere in Canada. Plans were well underway and we were close to opening the doors when Scribner called me. He had changed his mind about working with Hawkins and wanted to join us. The news was out on the street about our new agency. Fred and I discussed it. We agreed it would make sense to have Scribner on board with all his contacts, booking abilities and organizational skills so it was a yes. I made it a no questions asked. What could I say? Everybody has stupid moments in their lives. Who knows better than me? As far as I was concerned Scribner had a brain fart now let's move on. We agreed to have him come on board and never discussed what had happened. We were on our way and it was really exciting. 1963 was the pivotal year for our future in the agency business. We opened the office in a two story office building we named "The Music Canada Building", at 1940 Yonge St., a couple of doors north of Davisville Ave and a five minute drive from CHUM which was to become a huge part of our growth in the industry. We named the agency The Bigland Agency. Our logo was a map of Canada. That sort of said it all. We expanded our staff to 4 agents adding Jack Manning and Bob Wilton. I have no Idea who Bob was, why Bob was involved or what Bob did. I never saw him book a band or anything else and even still he made the centre of the cover of the Bigland Catalogue which was a first for agencies, the catalogue, not Bob. It listed all our artists and bands plus hype for RPM Music Weekly and Fred on the back cover. Interestingly enough many of the advertising agencies began using our catalogue as a guide regarding information on rock music artists that they could use in their commercials. Back to Bob, one of life's many mysteries. I would love to ask Fred or Scribner but they both have gone to the big agency in the sky. I know he never invested any money. Maybe Bob will read this book and enlighten me. Only thing I did know was that he was a friend of Fred's so I assumed he was working with Fred. Scribner and I plus our amazing secretary Cheryl McDonald ran the agency. My wife Joanne did the books as well as anything else that needed looking after. Fred opened Fred White Promotions with the "Young Man on the Move" theme. He would handle all the agencys publicity and promotion as for most of our bands. We bought an AB Dick 350 printer and put it in the basement so I could do all the printing for the company including band pictures, bios, and other propaganda. I was a printer for the Ontario Government in a former life. That was BM (before music).

Tom Wilson, general manager/agent/musician/printer and "the go to guy" for, well, everything. No room for egos here. A little later we hired Chris Vickery printer/bass player and friend to take over my printer job. It helped to pay his bills. Chris played bass for The Majestics on his way to being one of the most respected players in the business working with jazz and blues greats Moe Koffman, John Lee Hooker, Lenny Breau, Bob Seger, James Cotton, David Clayton Thomas, Jackie Wilson, Peter Allen, Rick James and many more major artists in the world. He was a jobber player. Happy being a sideman as are many other musicians that are the backbone of the business. Guys like Sonny Milne, drummer and Bernie LeBarge guitar player and Dennis Pinhorn, bass player all of whom have played with a numerous top performers in Canada and the USA and had no interest in being the star. They just wanted to play.

The key to our eventual success as an agency was very simple. We respected the people we worked with and for. The most important people which was something a lot of the people in the business forgot and still forget to do. We respected our clients, the artists, the musicians and, after all, I was one. We let the musicians that needed it use our address as a mail drop because they didn't have one of their own. Anybody could stop by at any time, and would be welcome. There were no set hours. Our lobby was a meeting place for musicians, managers, agents and media people as well as radio and record people from all over Canada and The U.S.A. The place was like a magnet for everybody and we encouraged them to drop in. We put up a bulletin board where people could post jobs wanted, jobs available, looking for players for a band, instruments for sale and wanted. Anything anybody wanted to post. It was a busy board. We broke everything down into departments. One for concerts and one nighters, one for bars, one for conventions and corporate business, one for high schools and one for cross-Canada and international tours. Another first. We never opened one for management but we probably should have since almost everybody in the company was managing an artist or band. Our network was spreading coast to coast and we were getting a name as the agency to deal with for dates, information or anything anybody needed or wanted. One thing the guys were doing is what I mentioned earlier. This agents being managers thing. Scribner was managing Bobby Kris & the Imperials for a short time and, while the guys loved him, it really didn't work because he was agent first manager second so nothing was accomplished except the band got booked a lot more. He actually had a list of band rules and band fines. I can't imagine! Only Scribner. Later Fred took over and according to Bobby Kris it got worse. Bad move. Fred tried to turn them into a rock band. Wrong!!! He actually told them they were playing The Lovin Spoonful tunes too heavy! My question would have been why in hell are they playing Lovin Spoonful at all? Bobby was always an r&b big band sound. From there out of the pan into the fire when they signed with Mitch Martin, Randy Markowitz's little brother. I always had the urge to count my fingers after I shook hands with him. He wasn't Randy.

Through our contacts Scribner had picked up the Funkadilics and the Parliaments from Detroit for management and booking which gave us some strong Detroit ties and another open door. In addition he was working with Duke Edwards, a drummer from Detroit, on Jon & Lee & the Checkmates one of the hottest local bands we had but, according to Jon, not as managers just advisors. I didn't pursue the manager thing. I was too busy with the agency and Caesar. In 1964, we sub-let the second floor of our building to Walt Grealis, a former Mountie, and a Toronto Cop. A gay Mountie. I thought that was very cool. Walt got into the music business with Apex Records and London records as a promo rep. He had just put RPM, a new Canadian music business trade magazine, on the market that very quickly would become the Canadian Record Business go to trade mag. The other tenant was Stan Klees his partner who had formerly worked at CHUM and London Records. Now he had his own independent record label, Tamarac Records that he had just started. Walt and Stan came as a package. Stan had just made a deal to go into partnership with Art Snider, ACT Records and Duff Roman, Roman Records to collaborate on a brand new label, Red Leaf Records, with the intention of recording and promoting Canadian Talent. We moved Fred, who had a good relationship with them, into his own office on the second floor with his Fred White Promotions. He was to be our liaison with RPM and Red Leaf Records making sure our artists and bands got all the publicity Fred could get them plus setting up some recording deals. Credit due. Walt Grealis worked his ass off to make RPM become a big part of the "Canadian Revolution". It was a great promotional tool for us. He was incredibly kind to us and our artists and bands although some people say to a fault. Just jealous! The RPM record chart became a major influence in the market. Artists and bands that had barely been heard of before became news. Not to say that the chart wasn't accurate but it was biased. Someone told me it took a lot of donuts to get a mention or a chart position in RPM. Just sayin. I have heard so many stories about the motivation behind Walt and Stan's dedication to supporting Canadian music. It's hard to criticize what they accomplished for the Canadian Music Industry whatever the motivation and whether the stories were true or not was probably not important as the results.

They had this beautiful German Sheppard dog. First gay dog I ever met. I had never considered the thought that animals could have different sexual preferences same as people. His name was Irving. He would go through the office nosing men in the crotch. Never the girls. Only the guys. Nice doggy, but really? We were sure Irving was in love with Fred and were all so happy when we moved Fred to the second floor which got us out of the direct line of fire from Irving's questing nose.

Another band that had a problem with mismanagement was the Big Town Boys. Not with Scribner. With Fred. He was great at promotion but management? Tommy Graham, the leader and guitar player did say that Walt Grealis was a big help in the early days helping to build their profile and hooking them up as house band with CTV's After Four Show. To his credit, Walt never tried to manage an artist. I thought that Stan was managing the band but Tommy tells me no.

A very special meeting for Scribner and me. We were approached by Randy Markowitz aka Dandy Randy aka Riff and Mr. Personality. A very talented flamboyant character as well as a great manager. He wanted us to represent the band he was working with, the Mandala, for bookings. Randy had a cane that had a fold out banana seat that he would, when he was meeting, sit on instead of a chair. I always wondered, "What if it folded up by accident? Would it become a serious anal problem?" With Randy was Dominic Troiano leader of the Mandala. One of the most talented musicians in the business and respected by everybody. Domenic had previously played with Robbie Lane and the Disciples as well as replacing Robbie Robertson in the Hawks for a short time until joining The Rouges and changing the name to the Mandala when Markowitz took over their management. Dominic was one hell of a guitar player, writer, producer, performer, and person. In later years he played with the James Gang, and the Guess Who. Every once and awhile you meet greatness. That was Donny. I was and still am a huge fan of the musician and the man. I have seen the best and he was one of them. He became a good friend and confessed that he was a fan of Caesar. He was impressed on how we made simple music work. "Don't want to say that too loudly around other musicians Donny"! He also told me later that at the meeting with Scribner and me he was very nervous. Excuse me? Ditto pal! We stayed friends through all the years and I booked most of the bands he was in. He also married one of my favourite ladies on earth. Ms. Shawne Jackson. We made the deal with Markowitz and I can say without reservation he made us do our job and earn our commissions. When he took over as the Mandala's manager he gave the group a step up over all other Canadian bands using aggressive, inventive promotional tactics and developed a state of the art lighting system for their live shows that blew everybody away. All the ideas came from Randy's experiences in television and theatre. Troiano said it all. "He came in like a hurricane and the locals were just flabbergasted! They were shell-shocked because they were used to dealing with 15 year-old kids and suddenly they're dealing with this professional entrepreneur."

Wearing matching pinstripe suits onstage the Mandala became known for their live shows and stage presence. I can speak from personal experience having, with Caesar, played a lot of split shows with the Mandala plus attending quite a few more shows as the agent. They were exciting!

Markowitz's background included a run of some very successful children's shows on CHCH-TV in Hamilton. In the early 1960's *The Randy Dandy Show*, produced, of course, by Randy Markowitz. A great show that grabbed the kid's attention starring clown Silly Willy and the beautiful Magic Lady. Very creative in its day but the one that became a television classic was The Hilarious House of Frightenstein. Both were way ahead of their time. With all of Markowitz's expertise at the helm the Mandala were signed to Chess Records and recorded their first hit record "Opportunity" in Chess Records studio in Chicago. The song was number one on the record/radio charts in Canada and made some inroads into the U.S. A The band played some amazing dates performing with a lot of major American artists but never broke the invisible barrier between Canada and America into the upper level of the music business. In 1967 the lead singer George Olliver left the band and was replaced by Dominic's best friend Roy Kenner from the Toronto band R.K. and the Associates The Mandala folded in 1970, Troiano put together Bush, another great band but it just lasted a year. He went on to an amazing run with the James Gang in 1972 that also, later, included his friend Roy Kenner as the lead vocalist. Troiano joined the Guess Who in 1974 which only existed until they did their last show in Montreal in 1975. Troiano started writing, successfully, themes for television shows, and toured as a jobbing musician with artists like Joe Cocker, Diana Ross, David Clayton Thomas as well as producing some other artists and himself in the studios. Many years later, in 2005, I visited him, along with Vic Wilson, at his home in Toronto (Thornhill), during the last days of his life. He had cancer. He had been fighting it off and on for years. He was now sleeping a lot. There was nothing to be done. He was dying. Vic and I were standing beside his bed arguing about the past and stuff to do with music and just hanging out. He woke up and smiled just happy to listen and enjoying being with friends. His favourite place to be. He died May 25 shortly after our visit. What a huge loss to the music world, his family and his friends. The memorial service was a standing room only event. Domenic would have loved that. He was, and still, is one of the most influential musicians in the history of Canadian rock music. He was a good man! Always had time for the people around him and always gave one hundred percent to whatever he was doing. Still miss him as do many others. The good die young and he was definitely one of the best! Never to be forgotten.

TID BIT

Markowitz moved to Palm Springs, California and, with partner Mary Jardin, created the fabulous Palm Springs Follies, a dance and musical revue show that played at the historic Plaza Theatre and ran till it folded in 2014.

Back to Bigland. We were now officially the go to guys. We controlled most of the high schools, universities, one night dances and shows in our area and expanded the territory very quickly. We had re-started our fledging business in cross country tours and it was working. We had great relations with the other agencies around Ontario as well as The Maritimes, Quebec and Western Canada. Then came bonus time. Radio host Al Boliska left CHUM and went to CKEY. He and Johnny Lombardi from CHIN Radio began running concerts in Maple Leaf Gardens featuring name acts like the Beach Boys and English band the Dave Clark Five. We were providing all of the support acts for the shows. Next perk! CHUM set up a trailer in The CNE just inside the Princess Gates and featured our bands performing on top of the trailer for the three weeks of the fair exposing them to thousands of people and the bands all got paid. This all sounds like it was easy but it took a lot of work and hours of schmoozing to get those contracts.

TID BITS

Larry LeBlanc, the up and coming journalist, used what he called a writer's dream. He got to use my state of the art Selectric Typewriter to write the first band Bio for the Ugly Ducklings. Thought he had died and gone to heaven. Whoops. Didn't get paid for writing it. I didn't charge him to use my typewriter. Note here. Typewriter not computer.

There were two unusual people hanging around the Toronto bands during this time. One was semi-retarded Freddie McNulty, who always wore a suit, white shirt, tie and a fedora. Freddie would get on stage, usually invited, and sing mostly Ronnie Hawkins hit record "Forty Days". All the bands knew Freddie and liked him. The other was a lady named Moiré (Myra) who was a whole different kettle of fish. She loved the guys in the bands and knew all of them. She was very aggressive in showing her affection. She was dwarf short, plump, with stubby fingers and not good looking, but not ugly. She showed up everywhere sometimes with a briefcase stating she was the band's manager. As I said Myra was aggressive and would wrap her arms around a musician in a bone crushing hug as well as trying to kiss them and, in couple of instances, actually bit guys. She was not a fan of the women that were around the band and would sometimes push them out of the way. She had a special fondness for Kenny Pernokis, Caesar's guitar player, and would literally chase him around the room looking for a hug and a kiss. One day when we were playing on the CHUM trailer at The C.N.E. she showed up. When we finished our set and got down from the top of the trailer she went after Kenny for "THE HUG!" Kenny was having none of it and fled the scene. Myra went ballistic and starting hammering her head on the iron trailer hitch. We stopped her and held her while somebody called The St. John Ambulance people who showed up and took her away with her head bleeding. Welcome to Rock & Roll!

CHAPTER 13

The Toronto Musicians Association.
Big brother is watching

It was Billy O'Conner that set me up to run for the Executive Board of The Toronto Musicians Association. The most powerful musician's union local in Canada. I had joined with the guys in Caesar in order to be able to perform in the major venues and do television. I was also licensed with them as an agent. Billy was connected and respected. The association (union) controlled the performing market in the Ontario and where they didn't they had very close ties with the other locals across Canada that assured control. I was, to my knowledge, the first rock & roll member elected to the Board in the history of the Toronto Musician's Association or any other local in Canada.

You had to be in the union to perform anywhere in Canada, the U.S.A and, for that matter, the world, including radio, TV, film, recording, bars, concert halls and any major music or entertainment venue like The CNE, Maple Gardens, Massey Hall and virtually any other venue that provided music of any kind. That excludes the non-union and garage bands that had their own circuit. Even when we didn't have the support acts on a show at Maple Gardens or Massey Hall we now contracted most of the standby musicians which was a deal made with the major venues to provide an equal number of Toronto musicians to the number of foreign musicians performing. These musicians got paid for hanging around backstage. Helped a lot of broke musicians pick up a pay cheque. The leader's fee was double what a sideman made. We had to file union contracts on every gig for at least scale which was the musician's minimum wage. Most of the bands were not even close to making that so we had to do two contracts. One for the actual fee, the other for the union. The union contract had to have a leader and a steward who checked everybody's union cards. Right! Not! Sometimes half the members of the band were union, the other half not so they would lie when the union rep would show up. Forgot their union card, used somebody else's, anything to avoid getting caught. Few of them knew what the hell a steward was. Fortunately the rep was hip to the game and was open minded enough to sometimes look the other way. In the end we did talk a lot of the musicians into joining the union when they started recording and doing television and other media but, honestly, most of them didn't know anything about the union or give a shit. They just wanted to play. This was where I met most of the top jazz musicians and big band jobbing musicians in Toronto. Peter Appleyard, Dalt Russell, Moe Koffman, Rob McConnell, Doug Riley, Oscar Peterson, Quido Basso, Paul Grosney, Terry Brown, Russ Little, and Sam Levine to name a few. I already knew O'Conner was very influential with the union. As it turned out a lot more than I thought. He was one of The Old Boys. I knew pretty well everybody that was anybody because, sooner or later, most ended up in front of the board for whatever reasons good and bad. It was a great source for contacts. That helped us to do combined dates with the rock bands and the dance orchestras with the convention and corporate clients. We also advertised a lot in their quarterly newsletter, The Crescendo, which helped keep our name in front of everybody. We and our company got into trouble with the union from time to time but thanks to my guardian angels we were okay. Gurney Titmarsh was the union secretary and a legend in the business. Behind the gruff exterior a walking heart. The stern father, grandfather and "Mr. Fair." Loved to have him grumble and yell at me for whatever I had done wrong that week. Throw in Alan Wood, favourite uncle, the president, of the Toronto Musicians Association and VP from Canada of the powerful American Federation of Musicians in New York. He became my mentor in the union business. I think he had ideas of grooming me for bigger and better things. Then there was Sam Levine vice-president and father of Mike Levine future star with the rock band Triumph. Sam was the union's conscience and a devout member and board member. He lectured me a lot and apparently everybody else too. Between the three of them they managed to keep my ass out of the fire. Another one was Vic Bridgewater, the union agent, who would drop in at the bars to check everybody's card to make sure they were union. It helped if they said they worked with Bigland Agency. Other agents and operators were not so lucky. Not that I was doing anything totally illegal. I take the fifth on that. Just taking care of business. I am sure part of the reason for bringing me into the union inner circle was to try and find out what was going on out there in the rock and roll world. A mole. What were the chances? I warned them that they had better address the new electronic music and put some rules in place now. They listened but did not hear. Eventually that music changed the whole landscape of the entertainment business. My thanks to Gurney, Al, Sam and Vic for keeping me almost honest. You were my fire extinguishers. Truth be I never got into any real serious trouble anyway. Just pain in the ass stuff. One time Alan Wood and I flew to New York on the union's dime to meet with the president and board of the AF of M. THE AMERICAN FEDERATION OF MUSICIANS. THE BIG GUYS! What a trip. It was like a combination of the tv series West Wing and the film Good Fellows. These guys controlled all the business related to music in North America and pretty well everywhere else in the world. Mob connected? Hard not to be but? Here I was one of the first rocker board members of one of the most powerful locals in the Federation. Toronto. Yeh us! It was cool to be so respected and treated so well. Meanwhile, they too seemed to be oblivious to the revolution in music. On the other hand they were so well connected I guess they didn't really care.

CHAPTER 14

The Birth of The Guess Who and David Clayton Thomas

Going through my stuff preparing for this book I came across a contract we did for a five piece band from Western Canada that we brought in on tour in 1964. It was for a one nighter. Their total fee for the night was $125. Expenses and commissions came off that. Imagine! We had brought them in from Winnipeg to tour across Ontario and the Maritimes. All in all they would probably do 15 or 20 dates. Their name? Chad Allan and the Expressions with lead singer Barry Allen. They were managed by Bob Burns a dj in Winnipeg that I had connected with through Caesar's record "IF". I got to know the guys in the band fairly well and we had some good times. My favourite was Jimmy Kale the bass player. We became good friends and have stayed so even today. Got along with Gary Peterson the drummer and Randy Bachman the guitar player too. The guys really liked Toronto and the feeling was mutual. We toured them again in 1965 and Quality Records had released a single originally written and performed by Johnny Kidd & the Pirates. The song was "Shakin All Over" this time recorded by a band called the Guess Who, sshhh big secret, alias Chad Allan & the Expressions. It was a hit. They had done the impossible. A Canadian band with a number one rock and roll hit in Canada, charted in other places in the world and nobody knew who the hell they were. In 1966 they showed up with a new lead singer, 18 year old keyboard player Burton Cummings, an amazing talent and performer. Wherever we booked them they brought the house down.

Now at $300 sometimes $400 a night. Wow eh? We started getting offers to tour them country wide. George Streuth, v.p. and general manager from Quality records made a deal to release the record for the band with Sceptre Records in America. The single was successful selling a quarter of a million copies and reaching number 22 on Billboard's chart. Hard to believe but I was told the total royalties paid to the band were only $400. How can that be you ask? I don't know I say. The royalty rate must have been horrible or the record company's money advances to the band were off the chart. Based on the band's financial situation, is highly unlikely. We toured them in Ontario at much better money and with Bob Burns out we met their new manager Don Hunter who was, to say the least, a character. Don was hmm, interesting, with no connection to the music business previously other than a desire to be a blues singer. That never happened. I think he was in the wholesale grocery business. The story goes he met Burton Cummings when Burton was his paper boy as a kid in Winnipeg. When Burton got into the band he remembered the businessman that he had met that he was so impressed with. He got the guys to bring Hunter on board. Hunter's management fee was five percent of the net income of the band. That's the lowest fee I have ever heard of next to zero. He was obese and missing a lot of teeth. Had a bad attitude about women. Pissed off all of the ladies with a tongue roll thing he did. Even I was disgusted. He hit on anything that moved. Hell he thought they were free game if they were breathing. He believed he was desirable because he managed The Guess Who. I heard stories of how the guys fixed him up. What can I say? We spent a lot of time together. Hunter and I were sort of friends despite his issues. At this point the band was on a roll so we kept them busy. The band was hot and was starting to make some decent money and it was going to get a hell of a lot better. Once the band hooked up with Jack Richardson there was no looking back.

A word here about the Go Go dancers, true soldiers in the business. On stage with the bands either on a raised platform on either side of the band or sometimes in a cage or on a swing above the crowd. WHAT!! Pretty skimpy outfits and eye-candy for the patrons. The ladies were terrific although it was a whole different way of dealing with entertainment. Performers with cramps or that time of the month or asshole husbands and alcoholic boyfriends and lest we forget, being women, much more honest than guys. They could swear like stevedores.

Nothing more startling then these beautiful and, for the most part, intelligent women, letting their hair down. They made the guys look prissy. I separated them into two categories "Go Go Girls & No Go Girls" They thought that was funny. I was driving two of the ladies to a Saturday night dance at Oshawa's Central Collegiate known as "The Get together club". We were late so I was doing the pedal to the metal thing on the 401 Highway. Some idiot cut in front of me. I had to swerve to miss him lost it and away we go across two lanes of traffic across two more lanes of traffic going the other way. All the time the ladies were screaming and mouthing words that turned the air blue. We finally came to a shuddering stop. At that point total silence. I looked around at the ladies. I heard a "well, fuck"! I said, "Everybody okay?" "Yeh" the reply. I gunned the engine, had an interesting moment getting back on the highway. With the tires spinning at top speed we managed to lurch back on the highway. We still made the gig on time. Another day in the life of an agent. That night it was Caesar playing (my two hats). With my usual mingling in the crowd I ran into Bobby Orr. He was with the Oshawa Generals then and was a big fan of the band. Later he joined the amazing NHL Boston Bruins and became one of the most famous hockey players in the world. I was a huge fan of his so it made my night as did the sell out crowd and my adventure with the ladies.

This is off topic but since I was making much better money Bob MacAdorey, Fred White and I bought investment properties. We each bought ten acre adjoining parcels just north of The Stouffville Road and east of Hwy.48. I think we paid $7500 each. Bob was the only one to build on his property. A great looking cottage with a deck that overlooked the pond he built by diverting the water from the creek running through all three properties and stocked it with trout so we could fish off the balcony. Later I turned my property over to my wife as part of the divorce settlement. Fred sold his.

Another feather in Bigland's cap. This was the first year that we booked all the talent for a live show called Teenage Fair, at the CNE in Toronto. It ran for 3 weeks, promoted by Al Slaight, CHUM Radio, and Harry Ornest, a promoter. Harry later bought the Toronto Argonauts with Wayne Gresky and John Candy. The show featured a contest for amateur bands competing to win a record deal. It also showcased a lot of our agency bands, plus there was a Miss Teenage Beauty

Contest. I hired Jerry McCarthy, my Greenhurst buddy, to MC everything. He was great. He had been in the U.S.A. Air force and had worked his way up to sergeant. He was also a sharpshooter and was recruited by the CIA but he turned them down. He was semi- babysitting Al Slaight's son Gary who was about 12 years old at the time. Jerry drove him home and to school just about every day.

Back to the Mid-Knights hit record. The song was "Charlene." Huge Canadian hit so it begs the question. Despite having the number one hit, an appearance on The Dick Clark Caravan of Stars at Maple Leaf Gardens and a sell out show with The Rolling Stones why no album? The answer is there are several reasons. The record company, Arc Records, said they didn't think that the band had any material strong enough for a follow up single or to support an album. I have never heard of a band not getting an album to follow up a number one hit single. Judgement call? Arc did try to promote the single on radio in the Northeast U.S.A without any success and without any interest from the U.S.A. labels so the company gave up. Another reason. The Sevilles, an American group, had released the song in 1961. It hit the Billboard Top 100 and peaked at number 84 not high enough to be a factor. Last and not least the Mid-knights were managed by Neil Martin who came and went very quickly. I only mention him because none of the guys in the band remember much about him and he may have been part of the problem of dealing with the record company and breaking into the U.S.A. Neil was the person, along with Doug Chappell the bass player that snagged the Dick Clark Caravan show at Maple Leaf Gardens. I couldn't find anything else about him other then he was from Detroit. It was a "what have you done for me lately?" moment for the band. Another manager gone astray. I don't remember him or dealing with him. Everything I did with the band was with George Semkiw.

I was given one explanation that sort of made sense. Arc was not experienced at working with hit records so when it came time to move ahead, they didn't know how to. The reason I mention this stuff is whatever the band did to make a name directly affected on how well we could book them and for how much. The Mid-Knights were hot and were a door opener for the agency. We could keep them busy making money for all of us but they never moved up the star ladder and that's a shame. Not all their fault. Our first 'One hit wonder." Certainly not the last. They had another problem that was not uncommon and will come up again with Caesar. Some of the guys did not want to quit their day jobs. Certainly dispelled any ideas of going international.

Another band that bears mention. The Mynah Birds. One of the best known bands in Toronto, especially in Yorkville. The band only lasted a short time. 1964 to 1967. One of the most unusual groups that I ever worked with. They had numerous talented people involved and pass through the band but they couldn't get the Mynah Birds to fly. Many went on to amazing careers. I got to know some of the guys. Jimmy Livingston, the lead vocalist, an amazing performer was a regular in my office just to talk. He later moved on to The Just Us, The Tripp, and Livingston's Journey all of whom we were booking. Jimmy later relocated to Los Angeles where I met him couple of times when I was passing through but he was into drugs and eventually became another casualty. Goldy McJohn keyboards and Nick St. Nicholas bass player both future Steppenwolf members, the other lead vocalist Rick Mathews was an American AWOL from The U.S.A. Navy who changed his name to Rick James and he went onto become a Superstar with Motown Records as a writer, producer and performer. He was busted by The F.B.I on the AWOL charge when the band was recording in Detroit at Motown's Hitsville Studio. After he was released from military prison he managed to go on his own to make millions of dollars that he blew on drugs. Ricky and I talked a lot about what he was doing with his life and to himself. What a waste of a great talent. At one point I suggested he re-locate to Montreal just to get away which he did for a short time. Unfortunately drugs were just as available. Another bass player Bruce Palmer had been in the Mynah Birds and also the Sparrows. Neil Young was with the Mynah Birds for a short stint in 1966. I met him a couple of times in Yorkville at The Riverboat and The El Patio but that was just a "Hey. How ya doing?" He later he tied in with Bruce Palmer to put together Buffalo Springfield then Neil moved on to Crazy Horse then Crosby Still & Nash & Young until, eventually, he went out on his own. Not a lot of people remember but Domenic Troiano was also in the Mynah Birds for a short time. The Mynah Birds did have a manager, one Colin Kerr, who owned The Mynah Bird night club in Yorkville. Colin got them a one record deal with Colombia called "Mynah Bird Hop". It was a total bomb and Colin was shortly history. They got lucky and got support from the very wealthy local entrepreneur, John Eaton of The Eaton's department store chain. He bought their equipment and set up an expense account for them. They got a new manager Morley Shelman who was another count your fingers after shaking hands guy. Rumour was most of the money Eaton was giving to the band was going into Morley's pocket. They did go back in to the Motown studio with a new line up that included another new member Neil Lillie aka Neil Merryweather another bass player formerly with the Tripp. and the Last Words in Toronto. The producer was R Dean Taylor, also from Toronto, who we had booked a few times but was better known for his abilities in the studio, his song-writing and his huge hit song "Indiana Wants Me" that hit number #1 in Canada and The U.S.A. as well as England. He was best known for his work as a producer with the Rare Earth band. What an amazingly talented group of musicians! Too bad about the drugs and the lack of direction We booked dates on all the different bands up to Buffalo Springfield and that was that.

It was around this same time that we picked up The Spasticks for booking and I first met Jim (Soupy) Campbell. First single record for them; "Love's Got a Hold on Me" b/w "If That's What She Wants" on Apex Records. Soupy reminded me of the story about a contest CHUM Radio ran to choose the most popular band in Toronto. The Spasticks got their friends together who sent in over 3000 votes for them. Damned if they didn't win! That's what got them on The Toronto Sound show at Maple Leaf Gardens. Bigland was booking all the bands for the show and helping out with the production. We kept the band working around the high schools up until they changed their name to The Cat in 1968 and Gary O'Conner, Billy's son, who had been working with the Cynics band, joined up. Billy set up the introduction to Jack Richardson, owner and record producer at Nimbus 9, who was also the bass player in Billy O'Conner's band and Bob Ezrin as engineer who later producer for Alice Cooper and Pink Floyd. Ezrin also sat in on keyboards with Gary on guitar. When I first met Gary at his Dad's house he was playing drums? No manager but lots of support from Jack and dad.

Another band that was making noise in the market, The Checkmates, a really strong band for us who I thought was managed by Duke Edwards, a very aggressive musician producer from Detroit that was pushing all the right buttons for the band. Turned out not so. He was just advising the band which means working without pay. Hard to believe. When they added Jon Findley to split the lead vocals with Lee Finley (Mike Fonfara) in March, 1964 they changed the name to Jon and Lee and the Checkmates, the whole image moved up a couple of notches. They became one of our top bands. Jon and I became friends and still are today. He had James Brown down cold. An exciting performer and vocalist. A most interesting career as he grew as a talent. Great song writing. He and Lee together were magic. After Jon and Lee & the Checkmates folded in 1967 Finley, Danny Weis on guitar and Mike Fonfara on keyboards auditioned for Electra Records in Los Angeles for a new band the label was putting together with the name Rhinoceros. The band was managed by Sid Berstein out of New York. Despite some great marketing and performing as the opening act for many top rock artists like John Mayall, the Grateful Dead and Blood Sweat and Tears the band never really happened and the guys were having more success writing songs that were picked up by such artists as Three Dog Night and Rod Stewart. The band finally split in 1971 and the guys returned to Toronto.

Then there was David Henry Thomsett (birth name), aka Sonny Thomas, the legendary David Clayton Thomas. I won't get into the details of his story other then how it relates to mine and the agency business. There have been thousands of articles about him and he has written his own autobiography that documents him thoroughly. Absolutely iconic in the world of music. He is Canada's "bad boy" success story. He left Millhaven Prison at the age of 21 with a guitar. An aspiring blues singer he ended up in Toronto hanging out at The Le Coq d'Or bar with Hawkins and doing guest shots at The Bluenote as well as in Yorkville and other bars and clubs around Toronto sitting in with anybody he could. That's where I first met him. He started first with his own band Boom Boom then along came Scott Richards on bass, Freddie Keeler guitar, John Wetherall drums and Gord Fleming on organ; a garage band called the Shays. They hooked up with David when they met him at The Le Coq'dor tavern where he was performing occasionally with Hawkins. David joined the Shays and they quickly became one of the hottest bands in the area. The first one to book them was Sylvia Train, an agent in Toronto that was booking mostly actors and models. She was another Billy O'Conner find. She also owned Acta the record label that the band first recorded for. That's when I met her. Later on she became the celebrity columnist with The Toronto Sun and was a celebrity in her own right as well as a great source of information and contacts. She had two partners Bill Kearns and John Hardin who were not as memorable as Sylvia.

The band recorded "Boom Boom" a John Lee Hooker tune. The guitar solo by Freddie Keeler was amazing, inspired by Robbie Robertson's guitar style. Keeler was 16 years old and did it in one take. We did manage to get some airplay, not a lot, but enough to put the band on the local map that helped us increase the amount of work they did and increase the price.

So far so good. We took over all the bookings for the band. As an agency we were obviously very interested in David and the Shays. It didn't take a genius to know the talent here so we got very involved. It was that Willowdale connection. David's name was all over Yonge St., Yorkville, and the rest of the city and gaining recognition in Ontario and across the country. Freddie Keeler was already getting a reputation as an amazing guitar player. We got to know the guys pretty well. We assigned Scribner as the principal agent to work with them. I got to be friends with Scott Richards. It was a bass player thing and he was free with his advice on how to play better. DCT (David Clayton Thomas) signed up with Duff Roman for management and recording which was what moved Sylvia on as she and Duff didn't see eye to eye although Duff says it was more her partners than her that caused the split.

David and the Shays recorded on Duff's Roman Record label. The first record released was a remake of "Boom Boom". Interesting. Freddy's solo on this version was not as good as the Acta version nor was the recording itself, engineered by Bob Vollum, but it got enough airplay and recognition that it served the purpose. The follow up "Walk That Walk" was a hit and took off. Duff contacted his friend Norm Perry, a local promoter in Ottawa, who knew the Anka family. Paul Anka was a huge star in The States with a string of hits from "Diana" to "My Way" plus writing hits for other artists. He was living in Los Angeles. Perry spoke to Andy Anka, Paul's father, who agreed to call Paul who was one of the MC's on a new hit television show, Hullabaloo, out of New York. It was a Dick Clark American Bandstand clone show and prime time on NBC and Paul agreed to book David and the band for a performance of "Walk That Walk" which was getting some airplay in the U.S.A. on Acto Records. NOTE! They were first Canadian band to be on the show. The record was released on Acto Records in the States and the publishing was by Spanka Music, Paul Anka's company. The price of admission?

The show was cancelled after a year but it served the purpose for the band and allowed us to once again book the band more often and for more money. This was the first time I talked to Sid Bernstein at GMC Agency in New York who was the exclusive agent for Hullabaloo TV show. Sid was the agent that booked the first North American date for The Beatles at Carnegie Hall in New York in 1964 and August 23, 1966 at Shea's Stadium. He also did the first American concert with the Rolling Stones. Great contact and we stayed in touch. I would check in with him whenever I was in New York.

Back home everybody was starting to hang out in Yorkville as well as the Yonge St. Strip. A lot of music going on. We continued to book dates for David and the Shays until he moved on and formed a new band. The Bossmen.

A memory of Tony Collacott, the keyboard player for the Bossmen. An amazing musician/writer who, though he had a drug problem, wrote and played brilliantly. He wrote one song, "Brainwash", which was a blend of rock and jazz. An amazing tune that still holds up today. Rumour has it he may have been involved in writing "Spinning Wheel" also. Just a rumour but it makes sense.

I forget where we were. Some club in Toronto. Could have been the Friar's. The band was getting onstage to play and I remember Tony had to be helped up and set down at the piano. He just sat there with his hands over the keys until the song started and he played. When it came to the ending he played it over and over at least four different ways until someone touched his shoulder and he stopped. I so remember he said."Let the mother-f--kers copy that!", and he was right. Brilliant!

One time when we had the Bossmen out on tour up north and then west heading for Winnipeg. They had mechanical problems with the van all the way finally arriving very late at Lakehead University in Thunder Bay. Bad mood all the way around. Drugs and booze didn't help or solve the problem. I got a call around one in the morning from the organizer that Thomas was on stage waving a gun at the crowd and apparently shot a hole or holes in the ceiling. My first question was "And what is it you want me to do at 1 o'clock in the morning a thousand miles away?" After about a thirty seconds silence I said."Has the show finished?" The answer, "Yes"."Then relax, do nothing. The band will pack up and leave. Okay?""Yes." Then, with a "Have a good night", I hung up. When the band arrived back in Toronto nothing was said about the incident however for some reason Thomas was unhappy with the promotional material Fred White had provided. You didn't want to make Thomas unhappy. Not a good idea. A few days later he and some of the band arrived at our office very angry and carrying a large wooden box and looking for Fred? The word coffin crossed my mind. Up the stairs to Fred's office they opened the box and turned it over to dump all the promotional material in a heap in the middle of the floor. The plan here seemed to be to burn all of it then and there. Another not a good idea. We'd miss the building. I managed to calm Thomas down and get the guys out of the office. Fred was hiding. Good idea Fred. I think the truth be known the promotion material was fine. Reality says Thomas was unhappy with the problems that had happened on the road with the van and the "incident" during the show in Thunder Bay. He was tired of the grind. A gun. Really?

Thomas finally got tired of the same bars and dances week after week and left Toronto to live in New York City in 1967. In 1968, he joined Blood Sweat & Tears. Their first album with him as lead vocal was released in December with the huge hit song "Spinning Wheel" and the rest is history. Oh yeah. Bill Gilliland owned the publishing rights to "Spinning Wheel" along with CBS Records and David Clayton Thomas.

Meanwhile back to 1965, with the success the agency and Caesar were having, Joanne and I decided to move up a notch and rented a two storey 4 bedroom real penthouse in an apartment building at 45 Baliol Ave. which was around the corner from the agency. It was great for parties and became our entertainment centre for clients and friends. Joanne's younger sisters, Judith and Jane moved in with us. Their mother had just died and their dad was having trouble coping and into the bottle so Joanne and I became the girl's guardians.

CHAPTER 15

My Girl Sloopy.

As previously mentioned Caesar had backed the Vibrations, a great 5 piece vocal group, a few times at Masaryk Hall and a couple of other places. Through my association with RPM we had hooked up with Stan Klees who wanted to produce our records for his Red Leaf Record Label. Stan was not the easiest person to get along with. An over active ego and a tendency to pout if he didn't get his way. I was surprised to learn that the record "Big Town Boy" by Shirley Mathews had been produced by Bob Crewe, a heavyweight producer in the U.S.A., not Stan. The Canadian engineer was Bob Vollum. It was a great record and on the brink of breaking out in the USA market. It could have become a major hit but on November 22, 1963, American President John F. Kennedy was assassinated by Lee Harvey Oswald in Dallas Texas. everything froze for many days. All music on radio in North America was suspended in order to constantly report new information regarding the assassination as it became available. That delay killed a lot of potential hit records including Shirley's and most never recovered from the delay. Unfortunately neither did Shirley's career. We booked her on a few dates and Caesar performed with her a couple of times. She was a talented lady. Another what If?

Caesar went into the Hallmark Studios. I had hoped we could get the RCA studio where George Semkiw was the engineer. Didn't happen. We recorded "My Girl Sloopy" a song we picked up from backing The Vibrations. They had released it in 1964 and it went to #26 on the top 100 chart in Billboard Magazine. We recorded "My Girl Sloopy" and put "Poison Ivy" on the flip side.

Bob Vollum the engineer and the band did the arrangements for the songs. It took a couple of hours to finish recording the music tracks and then we went to mix everything together. Not once did Stan offer an opinion. The band didn't think the recording was that good but we agreed we wanted to release it and take our chances. "One man's junk is another man's treasure?" Sometimes you just have to believe. George Semkiw told me that when he heard it at RCA it was so slow he thought that something was wrong with his turntable. Nobody can tell me why we recorded it so slow. Other people loved it some saying it was a great blues song. Go figure!

When the first pressing went out in 1965 the producer credit on the label went to Bob Vollum not Stan, justifiably so. Reality was Stan didn't think the record was good enough to put his name on. Despite that we got a big push from Walter's RPM Music Weekly.

With the help of the band and a lot of my own contacts we hit all the media across the country. I did television music shows including CTV's teen shows, After Four hosted by Susan Taylor and It's Happening, hosted by Robbie Lane with his band the Disciples. Jay Nelson top dj from CHUM was the announcer. I did these gigs a few times along with radio and other media interviews without the band because all the guys were working full time jobs and couldn't get the time off. It's not easy to promote a record. It's a lot of time and work. You can't just throw it out there and hope somebody listens. Hope is not a strategy. Thanks to so many people like Sam Sniderman, Sam The Record Man, Mac Kenner at A&A Records, and all the wholesalers and the other retail outlets in Toronto and across the country. The Telegram newspaper and The Star in Toronto and all the other print media across Canada were on it. and CHUM picked it up as did all the rock radio stations in Canada and the record caught on. Sloopy took off. YEH! It became a national hit. One dj that went to bat for us was Dave Marsden aka Dave Mickie. I had first met him when we were promoting "IF" and he was on CFCO in Chatham. I hooked up with him again when he was with CKEY with one of the hottest shows on radio in Toronto. When he took over as host of Music Hop, a top variety show on CBC in 1965, I did an appearance promoting "My Girl Sloopy."

As an aside with the success of "My Girl Sloopy" Klees was now basking in the glory with his new moniker "The Genius in Blue Jeans". He was also now touting the fact that he was the producer of "My Sloopy" and "Poison Ivy". Bob Vollum had once more been relegated to engineer.

TID BITS

Larry LeBlanc shared this story. *"I was hired by Stan to write the liner notes for the Caesar album. I was really excited. I did a good job on it. Small glitch. I never got paid nor did I get a credit on the album. I didn't know until it came out with my liner notes on it. Bummer."*

Right about here Stan got a call from Wes Farrell from New York. Wes wanted to make a deal to release the record in the States on his Bang Records label. He offered Stan a 5% royalty which was pretty good at the time. Wes co-wrote "My Girl Sloopy" (same song different title) with Burt Burns a New York writer that started in the business at 32 years old and who had an impressive track record of 51 hits in 7 years. He was only 38 when he died. He was connected up his ying yang with The Mafia as was Wes. Should have been a no brainer. Another note of interest. Caesar's live song list included some of Bert Berns other hits like "Shout", "Twist and Shout" and others that would have set the stage for recording some great follow up singles and albums. The Genius in Blue Jeans turned him down and instead signed with Larry Utal's Bell Records Malta label. Utal was a very tight friend of Stan's. Caesar, unfortunately, knew nothing about all this. "My Girl Sloopy" was released and went Top 50 in the States on Billboard's Top 100. Also on the Cashbox Chart. WOW! I started getting calls from the U.S.A. Dick Clark's American Bandstand in L.A. was one of the first. I was working with The William Morris agency in New York on an offer to tour 15 days in The U.S.A. with The Beach Boys. We had just finished opening for them in Ottawa, Kingston and Toronto. It was a very successful tour so the American dates made sense. I was chasing offers and setting up tentative dates all over the place. All of this subject to meeting with the band for a final decision on touring. With everything ready to go I met with them and after a lot of discussion, including begging and pleading, the guys turned all the offers down not wanting to jeopardize their day jobs. Out voted 4 to 1. I was pretty well destroyed at the time, incredibly angry and disappointed, as it turned out it was a sensible decision under the circumstances that were about to unfold because of Klees.

Wes Farrell was upset; nah really pissed off at the turn down on the record by Klees. He went into the studio and recorded "Hang On Sloopy". Same song new name and a lot more upbeat version. The band that went on the road was an unknown group of musicians with lead singer Rick Zehringer and called Rick & The Raiders. Wes took them into the studio to add Rick's vocal as the lead singer and some background vocals plus Rick's guitar solo to a music track that had been recorded by The Strangeloves, an American rock band, on a previous album. He renamed the band the McCoy's derived from The Hatfield & McCoy's famous family feuds. Their record was released in the summer of 1965 and, as the saying goes the rest is history. Within 6 weeks they had blown past us on the way to number #1 in Billboard and we disappeared off the charts so the deal with Larry Utal turned out to be nothing while the five percent from Bang records would have probably got us a number one in the U.S.A., a gold record, and a lot of money. Boo hoo. Hindsight is a wonderful thing. I never did find out what was behind Klees problem with Bang and Wes Farrell. I suspect it may have been the heavy ties that Burns and Farrell had with the Mafia even though that was a pretty common situation in America. Another obvious reason in that Stan was so tight with Larry Utal.

We went back into the studio and recorded our first album. Not much you can say about it. I know my Mom loved it and it is worth more today than it was then. It didn't sell that well. I guess one positive would be that in the 1965 RPM Awards we got the award for "Best produced single". The producer was listed as Red Leaf Records Stan Klees which because of Stan's connection to RPM is probably the reason we got the award. I have read articles where Klees took credit for the success of Bang records and Burt Burns because of "My Girl Sloopy". Nowhere in these articles did I read "at the expense of Little Caesar & The Consuls."

In 1965 we played Maple Leaf Gardens with the Beach Boys, Ritchie Knight and The Mid-Knights, The Checkmates and yes Virginia, the Vibrations. In the dressing room, as the agent, I was told by the Vibrations leader that Caesar could not play "My Girl Sloopy" as it was the Vibrations hit. Really? We weren't backing them this time. I think The Mid-knights were. We played the song. We released a second single "You Really Got a Hold on Me" flip side "It's So Easy" which was a much better recording and actually did better than Sloopy and went to #1 on RPM in Canada but got lost in the shuffle in the States. I'm still waiting for the Canadian Gold Record for that one or for that matter a royalty cheque for anything we did. "You Really Got A Hold On Me" saved us from being a one hit wonder. The one dubious claim to fame we had when it came to recording. Other then Chad Allen & The Expressions we were the only Canadian group to attain a # 1 slot twice on the RPM charts in that era. I read that in a trivia book. Caesar did three more singles with Red Leaf. They got some airplay but not enough to have any impact.

Back to the drawing board. The band had a final meeting with Klees in the basement of his house. What started out as a discussion turned into a screaming match between Klees and Pernokis our guitar player who had an amazing selection of curse words and pretty well used every one dressing Stan down. We ended our relationship with Red Leaf and I can tell you Klees know how to hold a grudge. With all fairness to "My Girl Sloopy", despite all the Bullshit going on, it did establish Caesar as a national band and we got some mileage in the U.S.A. for what that was worth. I did at least pick up a pile of new contacts in Canada and the U.S.A.

A little payback. I knew that it was childish I but I couldn't help it. We did play a date at The Eglinton Ave. Arena in Toronto on a triple bill with The McCoy's as the headliner. Larry LeBlanc and Jack Manning were the promoters fronting for Don Little from The Gouge Inn another popular dance spot in the east end of Toronto. I was supposed to be helping since I was the agent but I was preoccupied with playing in the band. The third act was the Mandala. Caesar wisely asked to open the show. The room was packed. We did great. On come the Mandala and as always they blew the people away. By the time The McCoy's went on stage well over half the crowd had left the building. It was hard to be sympathetic. I didn't stay to watch.

In 1966 we switched back to CBS Records and did two more singles, "Mercy Mr Percy" and on the flip side "I'll do the same thing for you". The last single we recorded for CBS was a song that I wrote "My Love For You".

One night, at twenty-seven years old, I got myself involved with another nineteen year old lady and this time it got crazy. Shawn. She looked like Goldie Hawn and I knew my marriage was in trouble the first night I met her. At Club 888

Caesar had just finished playing and she came up to me and introduced herself. She had just moved to Toronto from Vancouver and didn't know very many people. I tried to set her up with a couple of guys in the band but no takers. She asked for a ride home and I agreed. It didn't take long before I was spending more time at her apartment that she shared with Gloria Sinclair, a friend, than I did at home. This was all sex and I was wallowing in it. This also where, thanks to Shawn and Gloria, I first tried drugs starting with hash and grass and moving up to coke. That was bad enough but here is the oh! oh! Shawn got pregnant. To complicate things on April 10, 1967. Joanne gave birth to my daughter Lisa and was making a last ditch effort stop my promiscuous antics and save our marriage. I loved my daughter but I was thinking more with my crotch then my brain in those days. A year later I left Joanne and, stupid me, moved in with Shawn and Gloria. I continued to pay for the penthouse and I still had access to Lisa on a regular basis. Joanne had no idea what I was doing. Finally accepting that we were over she moved out of the apartment out and rented a house. She got a job as a bookkeeper working for Julie Fine at his restaurant, Julies Mansion, on Jarvis St. Julie was a good friend of ours and was also Lisa's Godfather. Shawn and I moved into the penthouse along with Gloria. My son Tommy was born on Sept 16, 1968 and the plot thickens. Both Joanne and Shawn were using the Wilson name and had lots of credit cards to play with. The shit hit the fan one day when I went to pick up Lisa. Joanne opened the door and threw some paper at me, called me an asshole, and slammed the door in my face. I was stunned! I picked up the paper. It was a credit card statement and one of the items listed was a baby's crib. Somehow the department store had mixed the Wilson accounts up and sent a Shawn bill to Joanne. That was how Joanne found out I had a son. Needless to say our relationship changed from reasonably amicable to sub zero frosty. I was denied access to my daughter and was shortly summoned to court where Joanne was suing me for child support, a divorce and alimony. She also asked the court to have me examined by a psychiatrist because of what she called my sex addiction and my sociopathic personality disorder. The wrath of a woman scorned! Whew! I was ordered to attend a session with a shrink. I did but nothing came of it. I agreed to the child support and the divorce, not the alimony and got my visiting privileges back. One big positive in this soap opera. My mom got to be a grandmother and she was in her glory. She loved both Tommy and Lisa and they felt the same about her. After the rough life she had lived with my father she was now enjoying the life she had earned. She spent more time with the kids than I did taking them to places like the zoo and the C.N.E. on all the rides and buying them stuff. I was so happy for her. She must have been exhausted but so loved her grandchildren. Sadly she died of cancer on my birthday February 8, 1969 in Women's College hospital. Jimmy handled the arrangements for her funeral. I'm sure she would have been happy with her send off. I wish she had had more time to hang with the kids. Strange thing. I went through all the motions of sorrow but it wasn't until a year later, on my birthday, that my mom's death hit me. I completely broke down, fell apart, and finally felt the full weight of our loss.

CHAPTER 16

Yorkville Village and Bigland makes a difference

By this time The Yorkville Village had brought a complete change to the Toronto Music scene. That was when the hippie generation kicked in. Yorkville was our Haight Ashbury in San Francisco or New York's Greenwich Village. It was made up of mostly small cafes and coffee houses open till three in the morning. Drugs were sold and used openly and it was a very different lifestyle. All kinds of music r&b, rock, jazz, blues, folk, classical, poetry, even comedy and artists not just from Toronto but from across the country and the world the experience in the new gathering place and Toronto was the place to be. For the bands the money sucked but the exposure, the atmosphere and the experience was great so it paid off in other ways. More gigs for money outside Yorkville. All the markets were heating up from The Maritimes to B.C. Most important for us Bigland was on the map as the go to booking agency.

In 1966 we sent Scribner on a Western Canada trip to solidify our network and find new contacts to help tour our bands, scouting new talent and established acts for touring rights. Late one night I got a call from Mel Shaw, manager of The Stampeders, a 6 piece rock band from Calgary that was starting to get noticed. He wanted to let me know they were coming to Toronto. WHAT?!!! The story goes like this. Scribner had booked them July 11 to16 at the Blue Spruce Motel in North Bay for a week. On to July 18 to 23 at The Lock City Motel in Sault Ste. Marie and then the long drive straight through to Toronto. Scribner had told

Mel to call me when they got to town. Here's the rub. Scribner forgot to tell me they were coming! Up to this point we in Toronto had no idea what was going on. They arrived around 10.30 p.m., families and all in a very large 1962 Cadillac limo with a packed, trailer and with no place to stay. I hate surprises! My first call was to Harry Finegold owner of The Nite Owl Cafe in Yorkville to explain the situation and that I would needing his help. I called Fred White and told him to meet the band at the Bigland office then gave Mel directions to get there to meet him. I told Fred to bring them down to The Nite Owl. They all drove down to meet me and Bob MacAdorey from CHUM. Yes. Mel had called MacAdorey who had called me. Hard not to lose our sense of humour here. There was one very pissed off dj and SIX STAMPEDERS WEARING THEIR COWBOY HATS AND DRESSED IN YELLOW COWBOY SUITS in The Nite Owl Cafe! Where the hell was my camera? After sorting everything out, we put Mel, his wife, 2 year old daughter, 4 year old son, and a couple of the band guys up at Nancy's home, a CHUM Chick friend of Fred's and the rest of the band crashed at my place. We had a lot of bedrooms although it was still a tight fit. The next day we moved them all to The Ford Hotel at Dundas and Bay St. in downtown Toronto. I spent the next few very stressful days explaining to MacAdorey and others at CHUM as well as Basset at The Telegram and a lot of other people in the media why we didn't have any dates for the band. Talk about crash booking. We had to bump dates on other bands and create others out of nowhere. July 25 to 30 at the El Patio, a one-nighter at The Broom & Stone in Scarborough with the Rogues and then Sunday with Ronnie Hawkins in Kitchener. Everybody hit the phones and we did get everything straightened out very quickly so the band worked steadily from that point on and went on to become an established act in Canada and good recognition in The USA. Whew! Dodged a bullet!

We had Wes Dakus & The Rebels from Edmonton in town at the same time but them I was expecting. Wes, the leader owned Alberta as far as being a booking agent and his own studio for recording. He was a busy guy. He eventually became part of our network. His agency, Spane International Booking Agency booked our bands as they passed through Alberta on cross county tours. With lead singer Barry Allan they did have an RPM Top Ten hit called "Love Drops", in 1965, with Capitol Records, and were voted Canadian Instrumental Group of the year in 1966. Barry Allan was voted the most promising and then top vocalist in 1965-66. However they never broke in the U.S.A.

It was the connection with Wes that hooked me up with Keith Hampshire who was working As a dj on Radio Caroline the pirate station off the coast of England that had an audience of up to 20 million listeners. His theme song on his radio show was The Rebel's song "Sidewinder" and he also played the hell out of the rest of the band's records. Relocating to Canada, Keith became a major recording artist as well as a radio and television host. I hooked up with him at CKFH when he arrived in Toronto. He didn't stay there long. He turned up working with Bill Misener, former Pauper, at the RCA studio with old friend George Semkiw. That didn't happen either but he did click with A&M Records in 1973 and did alright but it to be short lived which turned out to be a good thing. He went to TV with CBC doing the rock variety show Music Machine and did great with 25 weekly productions. I was certainly happy for him as well as us as he was using a lot of the artists & bands we were working with. The Bells, Copper Penny, Lighthouse, Shawn & Jay Jackson, Roy Kenner, Eric Mecury, The Stampeders and away we go again.

TID BITS

Allan Slaight Canadian media giant headed a sales agency for Radio Caroline out of the UK in 1966, but the acceptance of commercial radio was still years off in England so he returned to Canada.

Bigland was now the number one rock and roll Agency in Canada. We were working with the new breed of agents and promoters right across the country some born out of the rock and roll explosion.

On the west coast, in B.C., Bruce Allan of Bruce Allan Talent Agency in Vancouver. One of the first to work with us. Bruce had complete control of the B.C. market and was also pretty strong in Washington State. He was a control person and seemed to be tense a lot with a low boiling point. Almost kidding, but he always seemed so uptight with, well, everybody. He had one of the best office managers in the business. Ingrid McDougal kept his agency running smoothly. He did later turn out to be one of the best managers in the business.

I was also talking a lot with Drew Burns who owned The Commodore Ballroom in Vancouver the best concert venue in BC that rivalled many of the concert halls in Canada and the U.S.A. I got bands in once in a while, sometimes through Bruce, sometimes direct. Burns was another visionary and had an amazing run with The Commodore. His contacts were mind boggling. He knew everybody. Definitely one of the nicest and most helpful people I have met in the business. Reminded me a lot of Ray Colbourne from The Kee to Bala. I remember spending a lot of time in the clubs in Vancouver, the Cave, the Body Shop, and Oil Can Harrys in Gastown which was Vancouver's Yorkville. My favourite place was The Granville Market where a lot of the folk artists played.

Alberta was Wes Dakus's Spane International in Edmonton. He owned a studio and had a hit band with The Rebels. We were touring them a lot through Ontario and The Maritimes. He always took good care of our bands in his market. He was tied in with Norman Petty who owned a studio in Clovis, New Mexico. That's where Buddy Holly and The Crickets did most of their recording. That's also where Buddy Holly produced Waylon Jennings first recording. Waylon was the bass player in Buddy's band.

The other heavyweight in Alberta was Ron Sakamoto a Japanese Canadian, with Gold & Gold Productions in Lethbridge, Alberta. Sakamoto was and is one of the best promoters in the business. Like many of us, he started as an agent and then branched out into promoting and, of course, management. An amazing career! A great guy.

He originally did mostly country artists but jumped into the rock business and went ballistic bringing in the top artists including, the Bee Gees, Santana, Van Halen, our own Stampeders and the Guess Who. He finally hooked up with Michael Cole's CPI and Tarlton's DKD in Montreal which gave him access to the best in the world including the Rolling Stones. An amazing promoter! He summed up his philosophy on being an agent in an interview with Larry LeBlanc. "What's the sense of having 100 acts on your roster when only 10% of them work and make a living and the rest are mad at you because you are not getting them work?"

Grey Thomas, Studio City Agency in Calgary and Edmonton had a good hold on his market as an agent and manager. Also a former musician. Nothing terribly exciting to mention but he could deliver when it was needed. Didn't do a lot with him because of our relationship with Wes.

David Tkachuk, Actron Agency Saskatoon, Saskatewan, the only agency in town and the province. Dave was booking a lot of the local talent and could provide dates for our bands, as they were passing through. Regina, Saskatoon, Estavan, Lloydminister, Moose Jaw, North Battleford and many other places we had never heard of before. David later went on to become a Senator in The Canadian Government, a dubious step up.

Frank Wippert Winnipeg, Manitoba, an independent promoter, semi-hippie, intelligent, knowledgeable and certainly one of the nicest people I have met albeit a bit loopy. He did tour bands from Winnipeg to Vancouver. He used a lot of our bands. A good thing about Wippert was that he would take chances on borderline artists as opening acts on his shows that we would have otherwise had to put in the bars to get exposure across the country because other promoters were leery of losing money on one-nighters. Wippert did not lose often. He, Larry LeBlanc and I, became good friends and did a lot of dates together.

Frank Weiner, The Hungry I Agency in Winnipeg, Manitoba. The home of the Guess Who. Weiner and his partner Dick Goldman opened The Hungry I Club on Portage Ave in 1967. The first rock and blues club in town. Weiner was the number one agent in Manitoba so everybody wanted to be around him and he wanted to be around Bigland. Next came the well known watering hole for musicians, The Pink Panther, owned by Fred Munster. That was his name believe it or not. Maureen Murphy, vocalist from Sugar & Spice, remembers the club as the place to be seen in Winnipeg. There were a lot of teen clubs operating in the city and Weiner booked most of them.

He was one of the busiest hustlers I ever met and did control the business in the province. Locally bands like the Eternals could draw 500 at a teen dance even in rural Manitoba. Who knew? One band we did work with was Harlequin, another hometown band, with 3 gold records on Epic and travelling the world. The bass player, Ralph James, joined Hungry I as an agent and did well until he relocated to Toronto years later and landed a job with The Agency.

Weiner also dipped into Grand Forks and Minneapolis in the U.S.A. for artists like Overland Stage, Backstreet Journal, and The Triad. At the Pink Panther club you would meet regulars Neil Young, Maureen Murphy, Harlequin, Lenny Breau, Jim Martin/ Jumbo, road manager for The Guess Who, as well as the guys from the Guess Who and just about any artist passing through town. Great connection in our network.

Another great link for us was Franklin Records, an independent label, in Winnipeg that basically catered to local talent and supporting "The Winnipeg Sound". Sugar & Spice, Exhibition Earth, The Fifth, The Mongrels, Blakewood Castle, The Electric Jug, all great bands that helped put Winnipeg on the map along with the Guess Who. One small item. Franklin Records was owned; you guessed it, by Frank Weiner. Talk about controlling your market!

Caesar only played live outside Ontario a couple of times in the entire lifetime of the band. Once, in 1958 when the band recorded in New York. Another was a gig we played in Winnipeg for Frank Weiner in 1965 when Sloopy was at the top of the charts in Canada. The Winnipeg gig was in a converted courthouse and most of the equipment was provided by Weiner. The place was small but packed. I hung out with Donnie Burns, local dj on CKY radio and Jimmy Kale bass player from the Guess Who. That meant a lot of booze and drugs! We ended up at two in the morning at Randy Bachman's apartment trying to rouse him out of bed to come party. Didn't happen. Randy Bachman, party? An oxymoron.

Donnie Burns was a well known person in the media, and eventually ended up on CHUM in Toronto. A lot of booze and drugs. Too much party time, 24/7, until the drugs and the booze took over and he started getting delusional. I hear he did clean up his act later. Caesar had no idea what was going on. We did the gig and headed back to Toronto. For me a very quiet flight.

Toronto now had more booking agencies than all the other provinces combined. Same with promoters as well as the Canadian head offices of the record companies. Toronto was the centre for the music business in Canada and gaining a reputation internationally.

There were no courses you could take to learn to be a manager or an agent. It was a "learn as you go" school which could be and sometimes was disastrous for the artists and bands. Thanks to Scribner I learned a lot about booking bands the right way Much later I actually ended up teaching a course about the business called appropriately "This Business of Music" for The Colombia Academy in Vancouver. It was once a week for 3 months. Sold Out! Very gratifying.

The promoters and agents have something else in common. They all, with few exceptions, managed artists at one time or another. Very few were successful.

Management is a personal commitment like marriage. A lot of divorces going on along with shattered dreams and a huge dose of frustration.

On top of all this there were a whole slew of agents in towns around Ontario who grew up with rock & roll. They became part of our network which increased our control of the market. We were also making contact with artist's reps in the U.S.A and overseas.

As I mentioned Billy O'Conner handled most of the entertainment going into the C.N.E. and other fairs around the country thanks to his affiliation with a guy called John Barry. He set me up to meet John who had a lot of influence in the fair business including booking the talent for the CNE in Toronto and a lot of other fairs and exhibitions in cities and towns across Canada. Billy thought it would be beneficial for me to meet him. Ah Yes! As I was about find out that was an understatement.

John owned The John Duck Tavern on the Lakeshore Road motel strip in the west end of Toronto next door to The Palace Pier, a beautiful dance venue right on the water with a huge deck hanging out over Lake Ontario. A popular spot from the 1940's to 1973 before an arsonist burned it to the ground. It was right out of the 1969 movie "They shoot Horses Don't They." Just standing on the dance floor you could picture the dancers swirling around the floor 0and the big bands doing the Glen Miller thing. Then the agony of "The Marathon Dance"! Gruelling hours of virtually non-stop dancing turned into days and with minimum breaks the dancers who, exhausted, would literally pass out on the dance floor and the last couple standing was the winner. It was brutal and very surreal. I remember playing there once backing Paul & Paula, an American vocal duo with a couple of hits, notably "Hey Paula". They were alright on stage but backstage Paula turned out to be a total bitch who ripped a strip and a half off the latest Paul for missing some lines. There were many Pauls apparently. I thought she was going to beat on him. I could have booked their backstage show as a comedy. This is also where, much earlier in my career, I had a job putting up posters for Saul Holiff a promoter from London, Ontario for a Conway Twitty Concert. Saul was also the manager of Johnny Cash! He was very helpful with contacts and introductions later when I was working on Nashville and the Southern USA market agents and artists. Small world.

Back to the John Duck Tavern. I had to meet Barry there. Interesting man, interesting mix of people in his bar. It was a trip back in time almost like the prohibition days. A lot of off duty cops, bikers and a few guys in very expensive suits that Barry later said were from Detroit. The way they were dressed I had a flash back to Harold Kudlets and his connections so I'm thinking this is my first direct encounter with a "mob connected" person". I introduced myself, shook hands, listened to a couple of tunes by the band, a mix of jazz and blues, and then we headed upstairs to Barry's private apartment. First issue I had to face was two very large fucking dogs. Dobermans. They just looked at me then laid down their eyes locked on me. A little unnerving. The apartment was like a penthouse suite in a luxury hotel. Definitely a bachelor's pad. Right off the bat he pulls out a revolver from behind his back and sets it on the coffee table. Didn't say anything. I did a "What the hell?" Other than that I was kind of at a loss for words at this unexpected situation and not sure what was supposed to happen now! However, since I was still standing, the dogs still half asleep on the floor and the gun wasn't pointing at me, I figured I wasn't in trouble, at least not for the moment, but it was uh, un-settling. I was sure I was dealing with The Mafia. After a couple of minutes John laughed and explained that he loved playing the role as a connected guy and loved the music business and that the dogs were pussycats. We sat down and he offered me a scotch which I readily accepted, actually needed. He had a lot of questions and did seem to know a lot about me. I guess O'Conner had filled him in. Rumour had it he was everything from Mafia to he was under investigation by the RCMP and he was very wealthy. Only the money thing was true. He had bought the tavern in 1963 and set it up to be "The place for special people". It was like a Humphrey Bogart gangster movie only more like the real thing. Found out later that among his acquaintances were celebrities like Bill McCormick, a homicide investigator then and later, Chief of Police in Toronto. Wally Croutier on air host from CFRB, the Argos football team and their coach Leo Cahill. Musicians like O'Conner, Gordie Tapp, Peter Appleyard, and many of the artists appearing in or passing through Toronto. Everybody that was anybody were friends of Barry's. Film stars, politicians, the mayor, the police chief, developers in real estate, construction and other "business people" from Detroit, New York, Chicago, Los Angeles and Montreal. All of these people could be seen in The tavern from time to time. He gave me some of his background. I mentioned that I thought the gun was a nice touch for his image. He laughed. Another purpose of the interview was, apparently, to test my capacity for drinking. By this time I was pretty experienced, not necessarily an admirable attribute. I held my own until the wee hours of the morning. Well, truth be told, I thought I was holding my own. We were relaxed enjoying discussing people and everything under the sun. He was an intelligent, informed man and a huge fan of the music business. Both of us were still reasonably coherent as far as we knew. Barry, as it turned out, was, besides being one of the most interesting people I've ever met, a very sociable guy. He appeared to know everybody that was anybody and a lot more in between. As I left in the wee hours of the morning he shook my hand and patted my shoulder. "I like you" For Barry that was a contract. If you Google John Barry The Bar owner you will get his story. A fun read. An amazing guy who, over the years, became a good friend until, in the late 70's, I lost touch. He also owned The Lakeshore Film Studio, a limousine company and the company that co-ordinated a lot of the big acts that performed at the Canadian National Exhibition's Grandstand shows and other fairs across the country. Coincidently O'Conner told me that now I could start putting acts into the CNE and he would give me contacts for the other fairs. Passed the test I guess?

From there Barry introduced me to Jack Thomson who was his front man for a number of enterprises including something to do with the CNE. Thomson worked out of The Lakeshore Film Studio. O'Conner had introduced me to Colonel (Cliff) Hunt, musical director of the CNE, and a very influential person in Canadian music. He was an interesting guy, very old school army but we hit it off okay. We discussed my getting involved in booking some of the artists into the C.N.E. He didn't really know the bands and artists I was working with but I threw in the names of some of the guys from the musicians union and the fact that I was on the board. That broke the ice. Later I met his son, also named Cliff, who was a trumpet player in the Brass Union, a Hamilton horn band that we had been doing some dates for and who, eventually, came to work with me, as an agent. O'Conner also introduced me to Dave Garrick, who was general manager of the CNE at the time and later on manager of the CN Tower. We were about the same age. He was another fun guy to be around. We went to a couple of The fair association conventions together and the connection with him led to a lot of fair bookings across Canada. I remember being in Vancouver for The Canadian National Fair Industry Convention. Garrick was very helpful in introducing me to the people that booked the entertainment. On the last day of the convention it snowed and, within a couple of hours, the city was paralyzed. Vancouver is not used to snow. All flights out of town were cancelled. There was a lot of juggling so we could keep our rooms. One lady asked me if I would share my room with her. Of course I agreed and we had a fun night. Moving on we went to The International Fairs Convention in Vegas. This was the big one with reps from all over the world. Fair people do know how to drink, party, gamble and have a good time. Garrick was at the slot machines in the airport before we even got our luggage and he was winning. We booked into The Stardust which was the favourite hangout for a lot of the fair people as well as politicians, Hollywood celebrities and the Mafia. It was owned by John Factor half-brother of cosmetic's Max Factor who leased it out to Moe Dalitza well known American gangster. We spent lot of our time in the casinos meeting the performers, other influential people in the business, and enjoying the first class treatment. The CNE was one of the big players in the world of fairs so the association with Garrick sure didn't hurt and besides he knew how to party. A very successful trip. Something new happened. Because of the connections I was making, I was now invited on occasional junkets to Vegas. All expenses paid, first class flights, luxury suites, meals, shows, everything. All I had to do was gamble a minimum of $500 a day win or lose. It was a strain. I am not a gambler. I camped at the blackjack tables and sheer luck ended up ahead most of the time but it was nerve-racking. Other players spent their money like they hated it and never blinked an eye.

CHAPTER 17

Bigland closes. Now What do I do?

B ack in Toronto, I was approached by Stan Freeman, acting for The American Music Corporation that managed The Sparrows forerunner of Steppenwolf. AMC wanted to get into the agency business. Les Kahan and Stan Heller were the principals. They wanted me to head up the new company and they assured me that they would provide any connections I needed plus the money to back it up. I agreed to accept the offer but only if my partners were involved. They agreed and so did Ron and Fred. Before making the deal they asked to place a bookkeeper in our office to monitor the activities and verify income and expenses. That was an Oops! Things appeared to be progressing fine for about a month until I found out the bookkeeper was trying to talk our artists into leaving Bigland and join an agency she was setting up on her own. I mean really! I couldn't prove that Kahan and Heller were involved but we agreed not to agree. So much for that deal. Bye bye money. What a bummer! I did stay in touch with Kahan. He was a classy guy and fun to be around. More importantly, I continued to work with The Sparrows and later when they became Steppenwolf did do some dates in Canada.

It was about this time that Bernie Finklestein picked up the management of The Paupers after the group had parted company with Duff Roman. They had been rehearsing a lot and we booked them as much as we could when they were available. We were very good at short notice booking. Great mention in Bernie Finkelstein's Book "True North". He was one of the managers hanging out in the Bigland lobby hoping to get those last minute bookings for The Paupers. He didn't say so but he did get the bookings. Bernie got things happening for the band very quickly and gave them an open door to go all the way. We knew this band was one that had a for sure shot at top spot. You can read Bernie's book for the whole story. Another what if? I was really disappointed when they didn't make it. So close. Loved the band most when they had the two drummers. Again drugs and booze were a big part of the problem for them.

Thanks to Billy O'Conner I met Jack Richardson who was, among other things, Billy's bass player. Jack later on became a major force in the business with his Nimbus 9 Recording Studios and award winning productions for Coca Cola and along with Bob Ezrin was involved in producing Bobby Curtola, The Guess Who, Five Man Electrical, Alice Cooper and Pink Floyd among many others. He had just left McCann-Erikson Advertising Agency and I got to know him very well. He was one of the sharpest and nicest people I've met in the business. What you see is what you get. He shared his knowledge and experience without reservation. He was a gift to me. I was working the ad agencies for commercials business and he knew that field better than anyone I'd ever met and was very helpful with contacts, suggestions and introductions.

TID BITS

In 1966 my friend Mike Burton and I bought new Sunbeam Alpines sports cars. What a great car at least until I had my mechanic Eppie Wietzes, the well known formula one driver, redo the engine, the suspension and some other stuff so it would be much faster. I had so much fun with that car. One night I was racing myself, as usual, on the 401 Hwy and I blew the engine. For no car people that means "I killed it". I was so sad.

1966 was the highs & lows year for Bigland. One high was May 8 thanks to John Basset Jr., owner of The Toronto Telegram newspaper, Bob MacAdorey from CHUM and Martin Onrot. They promoted a date with the Lovin Spoonful at Massey Hall. On the support bill were Little Caesar and the Consuls, Bobby Kris and the Imperials, Tom Graham and the Big Town Boys and Susan Taylor, John Basset's protégée. I had certainly heard about Zal Yanovsky the guitar player from Ottawa and Denny Doherty vocalist but had never run into either one. Backstage I introduced myself to Zal as the agent for the other artists on the show and congratulated him on the amazing success the band had achieved. I added that I was also the bass player with Caesar and he acknowledged our success with "My Girl Sloopy" which surprised the hell out of me. A memorable few minutes. The night was an outstanding success for all the bands. As part of our show Caesar had been playing "Do You Believe in Magic" the Spoonful's first giant hit in 1965 and the one that put them on the map. It was one of our strongest numbers. No Virginia. We didn't play it that night.

The ultimate high. On September 24, once again thanks to John Basset Jr. From The Toronto Telegram newspaper and Bob MacAdorey from CHUM Radio, Bigland was hired as the agent and co-ordinator of "THE TORONTO SOUND SHOW" at Maple Leaf Gardens. Over 16,000 fans jammed the place. We invited record companies, producers, managers, a&r people, agents and media people from all over North America and overseas. Just about everybody showed up. It spoke well of the power centre Toronto was becoming. CHUM broadcast live and every band on the show was represented by Bigland. It was like a family night. Everybody knew everybody and the stories flew. A lot of the people had played together in other bands. The line-up was Little Caesar and the Consuls, Luke and the Apostles, the Secrets, the Five Rising Sons, the Ugly Ducklings, Stitch n' Tyme, the Last Words, the Paupers, Bobby Kris and the Imperials, Susan Taylor and the Peyton's, the Big Town Boys, R.K. and the Associates, the Tripp and the Spastics. 14 bands in 14 hours, two shows each, and we ended up only nine minutes late! Almost all the bands had a positive response from the show and opportunities were being presented right, left and centre. It was a first! A great showcase that started some things happening with the bands in the U.S.A. It should have become an annual event.

In October this same year we had the Counts, Big Town Boys, the Del Tones and the Apostles on a show with Headliner Neil Diamond at the new hot venue in Toronto, The Club Kingsway, in The Seaway Hotel on Lakeshore Road. This was a new approach. We had started booking multiple bands on shows as often as we could. This was the forerunner of the bigger festivals. I remember booking Little Stevie Wonder there when he was just sixteen and already a major artist. I met him in his hotel room before the show along with his managers. He spent a lot of the time going around the room sometimes on his hands and knees touching and feeling everything. A couple of hours later he was on stage blowing people away.

TID BITS

In 1966 the Iconic Hawk's Nest dance club opened on the second floor of The Le Coq d'Or Tavern and became the "Go To" place for the music people.

What a year eh! Bigland booked a show in Peterbourgh at the Civic Auditorium. The event featured Wilson Picket and his band as well as Little Caesar and the Consuls and the Ugly Ducklings. Wilson Picket's band was amazing and all three bands did the encore together. To die for! 3 bass players, 3 guitars, 3 drummers, many horns and three keyboards. Wilson Picket's drummer was the world famous drummer, Buddy Myles. The guitar player was the legendary Jimi Hendrix. What a night to remember!

Then came the lows. Trouble in paradise. Despite our success we, the principals, were all getting individual offers right and left. The guys were getting antsy looking for greener fields. Young people bore easily. This turned into an "every man for himself". Within three weeks I closed Bigland. Fred White was the first to bail. He called Ahead Corporation's (Arc Records) Bill Gilliland and asked for a job with Bill's new setup. Gilliland agreed and also hired Jack Manning to run the new booking agency division World Canadiana. In addition they had Yorktown records distributed by Capitol. Later, when the deal with Capitol expired, the label changed to Yorkville Records and began to manufacture and distribute their own product through Arc. So now everything was in house. The Yorkville management and promotion division, which was Fred White and Bob Wilton (Still don't know what Bob did). They were overseeing the Stitch in Tyme and Sugar Shoppe. The artists had access to Arc's recording studio as well as other studios in town and apparently liberal financing all geared to a one call does it all approach to handling artists. The accountant was Ross Atchison another Fred White friend. Arc had already recorded some of the top artists in the country including Anne Murray, David Clayton Thomas, Ritchie Knight and the Mid-Nights, Little Caesar and the Consuls, Ronnie Hawkins and now the list was growing quickly but Arc was not usually involved in promoting the record releases.

Gilliland had one artist he was working with. Bill Amesbury who I had first met in 1968 when he was lead singer with the Five Shy band managed by George Elms. George kept the band working but it basically never got beyond the local market although not from lack of trying. Having left the band Amesbury, a very talented singer, had signed up with Yorkville and was recorded and managed by Gilliland. His biggest hit was "Virginia Touch Me Like You Do" that made a lot of the charts and created a fair buzz in The U.S.A. Gilliland made a record deal with the Kama Sutra label in New York and owned by his friend Neil Bogart. It went well at first but ran into problems. Amesbury's career stalled and in the early 1980s Amesbury changed course, had a gender change, and became Barbara. She left the music business and, with her partner Joan Chalmers, the Maclean-Hunter publisher's heiress, became an arts patron and dealer in New York City.

One of the first projects with the new company was the Ugly Ducklings and they recorded some great tunes. Huge potential. I thought they could be the next Rolling Stones. Their first single "Nothin" established the band as a contender. After a few more singles on the Yorkville label their single "Gaslight", in 1967, went #1 on the charts in Toronto and a few other cities in Canada. It was recorded in New York by some of Doc Severinsen's Band from the Tonight Show without any of the Ugly Ducklings in the studio except Dave Bingham the lead singer. We had booked them through Bigland since they started in 1965. The band performed on all the big shows including with the Rolling Stones. They never went beyond touring the Ontario circuit and some northern USA dates. Yorkville's agency, World, did the best they could but couldn't keep the band working regularly. Not sure what the problem was. For one I guess drugs as usual but there was something else. Bill Huard, the band's manager, was a great guy and was certainly competent in handling the Canadian business. They never went international despite some great recordings. Started in 1965 done by 1968. For sure they were hot out of the box but never really got off the ground in the long run.

With Bigland out of the picture the market was in chaos with everybody fighting for their own niche in the business. It should have been a no-brainer for World Canadian to control the agency business however, as it turned out, the agency wasn't making any money and Jack was out. He could have stayed but when they cut the salaries and went to straight commission there was no point. He did a short stint working with Bud Matton Agency then left to start his own booking agency called Alvin Munch Talent. Initially he was working out of his apartment then went into partnership with Susan Morgan and added a third partner Terry Fillion of Canadian General Artists.

TID BITS

1967 was one of the most notable years in the decade in Canada.
It was the centenary of Canadian Confederation year-long celebration.
The Toronto Maple Leafs wins the Stanley Cup for the last time!
The first McDonald's restaurant in Canada opened its doors in Richmond, B.C.

Definitely a low point in my life and career. Thinking positively I like to call it my re-grouping. Fortunately I was still performing with Caesar. Finally I gave the agency to Jimmy McCarthy and, in late 1967, joined Yorkville as The Wilson Agency booking their artists. McCarthy closed up his agency and joined Bert Mitford who was doing a lot of the middle of the road acts and bands working out of The King Edward Hotel on King St. McCarthy helped Mitford to expand into the rock market by bringing in American artists. We worked together on a lot of dates. I took over booking all the Yorkville artists that were still with Gilliland and Fred White plus the ones I had on my own. I had difficulty getting motivated and after about 3 months I quit. It just wasn't exciting. They were doing a lot of recording and getting lots of action in Canada but not in the American market or internationally. I could keep the bands working locally but none of my contacts were interested in taking them into The States. Earlier Bill had brought in Rich Hubbard aka Ritchie Knight to meet me with the plan of expanding the agency but when I left Gilliland set him up to take over the booking which, unfortunately, by the time he got there, was almost nonexistent. Gilliland closed the office and moved everything to Arc's head office. Rich did some work with Edward Bear and Terry Black but ran into the same wall I did. No heart and no excitement. He got out of the music business completely and opened his own magazine publishing company. Fred White went back to CHUM as a salesman. That was that and the last of mystery man Bob Wilton.

Gilliland kept Yorkville the label going and it was one of the busiest in Canada. The Stitch in Tyme were now house band at The Flick Coffee House. The rumour was they owned the building. Gilliland told me they started the rumour themselves to make it sound as if they had lots of money which they didn't but the story worked. Meanwhile I had called Jack Manning and asked him for a job as an agent. He said yes. Whew! So I joined Alvin Munch Talent working for Manning, Susan Morgan, the dragon lady, and Terry Fillion who I had known earlier when he had his own booking agency and later along with Jack when we both had done a short stint with Bud Matton. I loved Susan. She was one tough, smart, good looking lady. They paid me five percent of everything I did. The other agents were Mike Watson and Leonard Alexander from Ottawa who had been booking some of the local Ottawa and Kingston bands The agency office was in an old three story house at 48 Hayden St. in downtown Toronto south of Bloor St. just off Yonge St. Great location. For a while it was "The Alvin Munch Hotel." The agency had the first and second floors in the building. Jack had an apartment in the attic. Murray McLaughlin, budding folk singer and writer, along with his girlfriend Pattie, were renting the main floor rear of the house. Bruce Colbourne another aspiring folk singer and writer lived in the rear on the second floor with his wife and their dog Arue. Brian Massey from the Big Town Boys also lived there off and on.

This is where Jack as "CHESTER FIDGE" created a new and easier way for the high schools with limited budgets to afford the better bands and of course to make money. ALVIN would book the band CHESTER would pay the band, help the dance committee co- ordinate the dance, and pay the school a percentage of the sales. It was a good deal all the way around. Win win and gave us that much more control over the high school market. Somehow I had managed to keep my relationship with most of the agents, managers, promoters, record companies, the media and fortunately, with the musicians. After all I was one of them. I think that is what saved my ass and I was always straight with everybody. We picked up all the bands that were working with Gilliland's Yorkville. I was back booking everybody and having a good time. It was exciting times again!

CHAPTER 18

Lawyers and Promoters.
What do they do?

The definition of a lawyer
Someone who solves a problem you didn't know
you had in a way you don't understand
See also wizard, magician.

One area that I have not addressed so far. The lawyers. They were on one hand a very necessary service that you couldn't exist without. We sometimes nicknamed them liars sort of tarring all with the same brush as in any business where the good guys get lumped with the bad. There were some great lawyers that did a lot of good in the business. So many lawyers. Lawyers for artists, promoters, agents, managers, record companies, corporate, publishing, divorce, immigration and on, and on, and on. Even some of the road crew guys had lawyers. Worse! Lawyers had lawyers! What the hell was that all about? The excuse was "Any lawyer that represents him/herself represents a fool". Now that does not garner a lot of confidence. What kind of lawyer needs a lawyer? Acting on behalf of their clients instead of working on behalf of their clients. Acting conjures up all kind of images. Why are lawyers always practicing? Can't they ever get it right? Favourite lawyer phrases of the day; Talk to my lawyer -I don't know call my lawyer- my lawyer says-according to my lawyer. - Lawyer's favourite word NO- favourite phrases I will take that under advisement- No problem I'll get back to you –I'll talk to my client- and my all time favourite "Fuck you"!

Good example is the story about Burton Cummings buying all the songs that he and Randy Bachman had written for the Guess Who. All were originally owned by Jack Richardson's Nimbus 9 Corporation who just happened to be going bankrupt. Jim Martin (Jumbo), the Guess Who's road manager who was now working just for Burton, was strolling through Yorkville where the Nimbus Studio was located. He ran into one of the employees from Nimbus 9 who asked him if he'd like to buy Nimbus 9's publishing catalogue which included all the Guess Who songs that Burton and Randy had written. Jumbo called Cummings and told him about the offer. Cummings called Abe Summers, his lawyer, and Summers told Burton to make the deal which he did. Read Bachman's book "Vynal Tap Stories" for Abe's response when Randy called him to get his songs back.

Mention lawyers and you have to talk about contracts. Like every business there were some incredibly bad contracts signed by the musicians that tied them up, robbed them blind and, in some cases, destroyed their careers. Same with publishing contracts where the writers gave away everything to the record companies, managers, agents, lawyers and others. This was because they didn't know any better, didn't care, or because they didn't have a clue about how much money was involved and, of course, their reps didn't tell them. Some very sad stories. It took years but as the artists got more business experience that practice started to slowly change when we finally realized how much money could be involved. In a lot of cases deals were done without any lawyers. That could have been a disaster or not depending on whom you were dealing with. I was not surprised to find out how many artists had no written agreements and were just working on a handshake. I did it myself with most of the bands we worked with. There were only a couple we did sign exclusive contracts with. One thing I did learn while writing this book was that a sizeable percentage of the deals made were verbal.

At the time there were a few lawyers that were the "go to guys' in the music business in Toronto. Bernie Solomon (Bernie the attorney) was one. He could have been the inspiration for the song "My Attorney Bernie." You can catch it on

Youtube. Solomon was flamboyant. Always immaculately dressed. Early in life he had lost part of his left leg in an accident with a streetcar. It was replaced with a wooden artificial extension which, when he got mad he would take it off and hurl it at clients. Bernie Soloman was one of The Three Bernies. Bernie Finklestein who was managing the Paupers and Bernie Fiedler who owned The Riverboat coffee house . I didn't know at the time but Marty Onrot was also involved which explained the concert side of their business. They put together what appeared to be a "one call does it all" company to manage, record and promote music artists.

I knew Solomon but had never done business with him. I ran into him on a few occasions at industry events or when he was involved with some of the people I was working with such as David Clayton Thomas, Marty Onrot, Bernie Finklestein and Domenic Troiano. He was the king of Canadian music lawyers representing artists, record and publishing companies, managers as well has having his own record label. His biggest client was ATV music publishing, the largest publishing company in the world. His Amex credit card bills were running around ten thousand dollars a month as he wined and dined and travelled all over the world. Solomon was a character and over time we became good friends despite his unorthodox practices in business. You couldn't help but like him although his occasional lack of ethics and often representing both sides as clients and that was what almost got him disbarred for conflict of interest. He was told by The Law Society to take some time off and re-evaluate what he was doing.

Eddie Glinert was the new kid on the block who opened the Fredrick Lewis booking agency with partner Jeff Gold. The agency income paid Glinert's way through Law school. Glinert was brilliant and wore many hats. Agent, lawyer, manager, promoter, publisher, and went on to be a major influence in the music publishing industry in Canada. As well he was promoting concerts at The Rockpile in the Masonic Temple on Yonge St. and making a name for himself very quickly. He was a marketing maniac, a hustler, and the master of the deal. Glinert was fun to work with. I don't think he trusted a lot of people in the business but he did take care of his clients. We got along and were arm length friends.

Another busy music lawyer was Peter Stiemetz. Mr corporate who, while keeping a low profile, managed to carve an impressive and long career in the Canadian entertainment world as a top negotiation lawyer. I didn't do a lot with Peter except call him for legal opinions from time to time. He was always very helpful and it was always pro bono. He was a partner with Ritchie Yorke in a couple of trade papers. First one was called "POP" and later "Rainbow" with Ritchie and Marty Melhuish. I dealt with him briefly when he was acting for Daffodil Records when Alvin Munch Talent was the booking agent for many of their artists. Peter was counsel for the Canadian Recording Industry Association and the executive producer of the Juno Awards annual television shows and many other organizations. A backstage star in the entertainment business.

Then there was Sheldon Vanek. Shelly, my lawyer, who was only 25 years old when we first met and I retained him. He was six foot four and 275 pounds. He could be very intimidating. He covered my butt and my family's for over forty years. Shelly had some interesting clients. His uncle was provincial court judge David Vanek who wrote a great book "Memoirs of a Criminal Court Judge". Interesting read if you are into criminal court stories. Besides his other talents Shelly was a criminal defence lawyer who faced his uncle in court many times defending, among others, some members of the Hell's Angels and Vagabond motorcycle clubs. Must have made for some interesting conversations at the family get-togethers. As far as I know Shelly never had clients that were in the music business other than me which was probably a good thing. I had no reservations about trusting him with my life.

There were other lawyers that were well known in the business but above mentioned are the ones I dealt with.

I insert the following on behalf of my friend, Michael Lyons because I can't convince him to write a book of his own about his days in the entertainment business which would be a sensational read maybe even a movie. Michael was the operating partner in The Colonial Tavern which his family had owned for years. Besides booking bands for The Colonial, he was a big time player in the entertainment market from 1967 on with his company, National Variety Productions. He and partner Steve Propas were promoting shows in The O'Keefe Centre, The Mirvish theatres and later, The Sky dome and Roy Thompson Hall in Toronto. Originally he was doing Vegas type shows, Broadway Musicals and big name artists like Ella Fitzgerald, Frank Sinatra, Liza Minnelli, Don Rickles, and Cher. He also produced the musical "Pirates of Penzance" starring Barry

Bostwick and Andy Gibb, the youngest brother from the Bee Gees family. He arrived in Toronto for rehearsals and Michael parked him in a country place he had north of Toronto. Gibb was depressed about a recent break up with his girlfriend, Vicki Principal, when she gave him the ultimatum, "Choose me or choose drugs". Andy had taken the journey into depression and drugs. Three days later with little change in Gibb condition Michael finally had to sit down with him and read the Mike Lyon's riot act which is gentle but firm persuasion. "Walk softly and carry a big stick". No punches pulled and whatever Michael told him worked. Mini rehab. A recovered Andy made the show and it had a successful run but he was still a train wreck waiting to happen. Gibb was only 30 when he died. Another "what a waste"

National Variety also co-produced shows with Roy Cooper in Montreal booking shows into The Forum and Place De Sar. They did The Queen Elizabeth Theatre in Vancouver with Hugh Picket who was the local promoter and partners with Red Robinson. Red was the top dj at CJOR radio, the number one station in Vancouver and consequently, very influential in the business in Canada and in the western U.S.A. Red, a huge Canadian music supporter, was directly responsible for Bobby Curtola's records breaking out in Canada and the U.S.A.

Branching out Michael also put a co-op together involving some dance and bar owners outside Toronto that bought their bands through Michael as an unlicensed agent. Michael was managing some half dozen rock bands including some we were booking and the co-op was how he kept them working. He was busy booking the bands in The Colonial as well as promoting shows and wearing a lot of different hats. He eventually attracted the attention of the powerful Toronto Musicians Association which was concerned about all his activities that criss-crossed all over the union requirements including conflict of interest rules which was primarily due to his activities with the co-op. They were threatening to charge him and shut him down. As a board member I voiced my concern as he was booking some of our artists and was doing a lot to put our city on the map. I think that may have helped the problem with the union going after Michael. He didn't stop his activities but he did become less visible. Yeh for us! Glinnert was Lyon's corporate lawyer and as well Michael put all the booking contracts through The Fredrick Lewis Agency except for the ones he did with me. Glinnert was running the rock shows at The Rock Pile Concert Hall on Yonge St. booking artists such as Frank Zappa, Led Zeppelin, John Mayall,

Chuck Berry, Savoy Brown, Jethro Tull, John Lee Hooker, Paul Butterfield, the Who and the Grateful Dead.

A big moment for Michael and his wife Vicki. In 1979 they flew to New York as guests at the opening night of Liza Minnelli's record setting sold out 17 consecutive concerts at Carnegie Hall where she was also recording her fourth album Live At Carnegie Hall. More goodies. Michael and Vicki were invited to the after show party at Studio 54 the hot spot nightclub in New York City at the time. The guest list was the who's who of the entertainment business. During the evening one of the people they were introduced to was Milton "Mickey" Ruden, the most influential entertainment lawyer in America, with a star-studded client roster that included Frank Sinatra, Marilyn Monroe, George Burns, Lucille Ball, Elizabeth Taylor, Cher, and Liza Minnelli. Mickey had strong suspected ties with The Mafia. Major heady company. Mickey shook Mike's hand. "You're the kid from Canada?" Michael nods yes. "Thanks, you're doing a good job" referring to Michael's work with Frank Sinatra and other Mickey clients promoting their shows in Canada. "You and your wife enjoy yourselves" One of those moments. This is one of many stories that Michael shared which I hope we will all read about in his book when it is written. Michael sold the Colonial in 1978 and parted company with Glinnert and Propas around 1979 and moved on to other pursuits continuing doing a number of variety acts that were non-rock. Later he and his real estate partners started buying and operating golf courses in and around Toronto.

Steve Propas and partner Neil Dixon, along with Eddie Glinnert, were booking a lot of rock acts and now working with other promoters across the country. Neil and Steve opened Dixon Propas Management consulting for nightclubs. The El Mocambo and The Colonial Tavern were two of their clients. They were the exclusive entertainment consultants for the Ontario Place Forum and produced concerts featuring major artists ranging from rock to classical. They used a lot of our bands. As a management company they guided the early careers of Triumph, Toronto, and the Good Brothers. All bands we were doing some bookings for.

They opened Solid Gold Records where their artists earned a dozen plus Gold and Platinum records and Juno Awards. Unfortunately in 1985 Solid Gold Records filed for bankruptcy protection. They ended up getting an advance from

Kama Sutra records and paid off the debt they owed to A&M Records and then declared bankruptcy.

TID BITS

Steve Propas & Eddie Glinnert were cousins.

CHAPTER 19

The Times They Are A-Changin

966 Don Tarlton opened DKD Productions in Montreal initially as a promoter and later added a booking agency and record label. Up to this point anything we were doing in Montreal had been with Sam Guesser who asked Donald to take over the rock and roll part of his business By 1968 Donald owned the market as well as connecting with every decent promoter in the country and connections all over the world. In Toronto he was originally working with Martin Onrot and using Canadian artists often. I liked him as soon as we connected and I started spending more time in Montreal with him and his partner Terry Flood. They were great guys, not only easy to work with, they were fun. We spent a lot of time in the bars on Crescent Street the hot part of Montreal. They are legendary and respected in the music business. You can Google both of them and see the amazing impact they had on the rock and roll business in Canada.

We had been booking J.B. & The Playboys, a Montreal band, for a couple of years. They were big in the area. The plan was to tour them all over the country with the hope of getting enough exposure to take a shot at the U.S.A. They were signed to RCA Records and Ed Preston was great to work with providing us with lots of support. I worked closely with their manager Lionel Pazon. He was good. In 1966 they relocated to Toronto to work closer with us and changed the name of the band to the Jaybees to get away from the confusion with the red hot American band Gary Lewis and the Playboys. They had two more name changes Peter & The Pipers and the Carnival Connection. Didn't help. Although they had a lot of Canadian hits and despite a great push from RCA they had no impact on The American market so in 1969 lead singer Alan Nichols split to New York City to join the cast of the new hot musical "Hair" on Broadway as one of the leads. After "Hair" Nichols returned to Montreal, briefly, to play with Mashmakan, one of our top bands, managed by Donald and Terry, then split to Los Angeles and the film business. Another crossover. He did some great films acting in "Slapshot" with Paul Newman and "Nashville" working with Robert Altman. He also worked with Lorne Michaels on "Saturday Night Live" and then moved into video production. I've often wondered what happened to Lionel. I asked Nichols and he doesn't know.

In 1967 Caesar headed back into the studio to record the last single for CBS. An exercise in futility (great title for a song). This time we hired Duff Roman as producer with a song I had written "My Love For You". Would not have been my first choice to record. We had a lot better, stronger material, and it was not a Caesar type song. I think, by this time, the band had lost focus and needed a change to get back on track. Once again into Hallmark Studio. I don't know whose idea it was but Duff hired some studio musicians to augment the sound. I don't know why. Some of the top jazz musicians in Toronto. Quido Basso and Moe Koffman who were taking turns on the phone a lot. Peter Appleyard who kept leaving the session and coming back in. Old school. I think he was in a phone booth outside the studio. This was before cell phones. It is difficult to imagine a world without cell phones. Dalt Russell's son was on bass to fix my parts. I should have been insulted. What's to fix? I knew the parts. His dad was an amazing bass player. Dalt had an old Gibson bass I would love to have got my hands on. We were on the musician's union executive board together. This time the record cost the band $10,000. Released on CBS Canada Records it went nowhere, very quickly I might add. I couldn't think of a good reason to promote it. The flip side was an instrumental cut of the same song. The whole exercise was a huge waste of time and money. Nobody's fault. It was wrong from the get go and anyone of us should have spoken up and nipped it in the bud. I had written the song as a slow love ballad. The end result was an up tempo something almost Latin but not quite rock and roll so, in other words I have no idea what it was. Maybe we had created a whole new sound. NOT! So what went wrong? Well remember back in the beginning. The Secret of Caesar? The

Caesar Shuffle. The Kiss Principal. "Keep it simple stupid" We didn't and paid the price. Fortunately the band was working more than ever so we ate the $10K and kept on trucking.

Bigland had been booking dates for Mike McKenna's Luke and the Apostles around Ontario at all the regular venues plus the bars up north since 1965. I don't remember ever dealing with a manager. I do remember they did do bookings with Wayne Thompson and William Tenn. We put them on The Toronto Sound Show at Maple Gardens in September, 1966. On July 23 1967 they were the opening act for Jefferson Airplane and the Grateful Dead at Toronto's City Hall's Nathan Philips Square. The show drew more than 50,000 people. Following that, with the same line-up, they played July 31 to August 5 at The O'Keefe Centre and sold out! It was promoted by legendary rock and roll promoter Bill Graham from San Francisco. Larry LeBlanc and I did a tour of bars in Toronto that week, particularly downtown, to see what impact the shows were having on the bar business. You could have shot cannon through the downtown streets and not hit anyone. Very few people, if any, in the bars and the whole area was as quiet as a church mouse. Unheard of other than on a Sunday. The repercussions were bigger than anyone realized. Electronic rock was taking over and absorbing blues, rhythm & blues rock and roll and pop rock in its wake. The original "Toronto Sound" was evolving. Bill Graham and Albert Grossman had previously approached McKenna to discuss managing the band when they were performing in New York's Cafe Ago Go for a couple of weeks opening for the Grateful Dead, the Yardbirds and other bands. The Apostils did have a manager of sorts. Bernie Klugman, the owner of Boris's, a coffee cafe in Yorkville, where they were the house band. He had signed the band to a personnel management contract. I can testify, as the agent, I had never talked to him or dealt with him all the time we were booking the band. It bears the question. What the hell was he doing other than having the band play at his club? Obvious answer. Nothing. When Albert Grossman, one of the top managers in the world, and Bill Graham, one of the top promoters in the world, wanted to manage the band Bernie, taking care of the band's business, tried to hold Albert & Bill up asking a for a huge buy out of his contract. Not exactly working for the artist. Surprise! Albert & Bill passed and the band ended up getting nothing. Perfect example of a greedy man who played manager and screwing up a band that could have gone all the way. What a waste. Another one of the gifted bands that never got the shot. To add insult to injury their go to guy at Electra Records in New York, Paul Rothschild, a talent scout for the label, who had arranged to get them signed and was overseeing the band because nobody at Electra had, up to this point, worked with rock bands before. Rothschild got busted for marijuana possession. He ended up serving a year in prison. That put all the plans on hold. With all this going on in August the band split up. McKenna moved on to the Ugly Ducklings another great band that had success in Canada and played in The U.S.A. but didn't break the American barrier either. Finally Mike got together with Joe Mendelson and they formed a blues band that, after a few changes of personal, would become McKenna Mendelson Mainline. They relocated to England and got a deal with Liberty Records. On the release of an album called Stink they played live dates in England, Europe and Australia with bands like Led Zeppelin, Rod Stewart, Jeff Beck, Jimi Hendrix and the Guess Who. Everybody was expecting the band to take off and rise to the top but Joe Mendelson quit in 1969 citing artistic differences. Mike reformed Luke and The Apostles which shut Mainline down. So close but no cigar again.

Shep Gordon is worth more than a mention. I first met him when he was working with DMA agency in Detroit and managing Alice Cooper. In addition he managed Anne Murry in the U.S.A as well as Teddy Pendergrass, Luther Vandross, Blondie, Raquel Welch and Groucho Marx. He was also a Hollywood film agent and producer. Shep is an industry legend who knows just about everybody. Many claims to fame and all true. One of his stories relates as follows. In 1965, in a Los Angeles motel room, he got punched in the eye by Janis Joplin. He had heard strange noises coming from her room and thought she was being raped so he gallantly rushed in to intervene. Turned out it was consensual. Janis was pissed and punched Shep. Her secret partner was Jimi Hendrix who, after getting over the surprise, started a conversation with Shep asking if he was Jewish. Shep replied "yes" and Hendrix's next question was did Shep want to be a manager? Gordon once again said "yes" which led him into managing Alice Cooper who Jimi introduced him to. Later in his career he was featured in Canadian Mike Myers film documentary production "Supermensch. The legend of Shep Gordon". Shep was one of the nicest and kindest people it was my pleasure to know and do business with, keeping mind, as long as you agreed with him. The man is a genius. He was around Toronto a lot so we spent quite a bit of time together. He made a deal with Bob Ezrin at Nimbus 9 to produce an album for Alice Cooper for Straight Records in the States This was the last album of a three record deal. The first two were disasters that died quickly. The Ezrin production got a hit out of the box with "I'm Eighteen" that went to hit 21 on the on The American charts in 1971. Immediately after that Warner Bros. Records bought the contract from Straight Records.

One thing that Shep shared with me was his three rules on what a manager and an agent must do and they are rules that I never forgot. "(1) get the money (2) always remember to get the money and (3) never forget to always remember to get the money." Sage advice!

As told to me by Wayne Thompson prior to the Alice Cooper famous chicken episode at the Toronto Rock Festival September 13, 1969, at Varsity Stadium. Great show. Prior to that show I had booked Alice for Wayne who was promoting a show at a Catholic high school, in Scarbourgh. Until Wayne reminded me I did not remember that Alice Cooper did his whole "Scaffold Hanging Show" including throwing a chicken, rubber of course, into the crowd from the stage. The priests were not impressed with the whole, in their words, disgusting performance and banned Wayne and Alice Cooper from the school for life. Quite a scandal. Alice went on to perform at the Toronto Rock Festival where the real chicken episode happened. A chicken was reportedly thrown on stage and thrown back into the audience by lead singer Alice Cooper; Various reports ranged from Alice biting the chicken's head off before returning it to the crowd. Alice's claims that audience members in the front of the crowd tore the poor bird to pieces in a frenzy of rock and roll pandemonium. a photo of which was sent by wire around the world. Welcome to Rock & Roll! The incident went viral and was the beginning of the turnaround in Alice's career.

As the market grew so did the number of participant's involved in the national scene. One of the best agent/musicians was Gil Moore, a drummer, who I tried my damndest to hire. Drove me crazy but he liked his independence. We did a number of dates together and I ended up running him for The Toronto Musicians Association Executive Board and he was elected. We continued to work on different dates and bands together. Later on with Mike Levin and Rik Emmet he formed Triumph one of Canada's most internationally successful bands. They did have management for a short time, Dixon/Propas, but were better at marketing themselves so parted company and did their own management.

It was around this time that Larry Envoy and Edward Bear appeared on the scene, showing up in Yorkville booking with Eddy Glinnert at first, then some dates with us and Scribner at Music Shoppe. No particular affiliation with anybody else until, in 1968, Larry hooked up with Jack Manning from our office. Manning managed the band until 1969. Not exactly a lifetime commitment. They parted company with Manning then Larry immediately signed a record deal with Capitol Records working with Paul White handling the A&R and promotion. In my few discussions with Larry I was impressed with his knowledge of the business but it was obvious he was gun shy when it came to tying up with anybody for anything other than short term. That said he then signed a deal with Ross White, Fred White's brother, also from our office, as manager/agent. Somewhere in there, according to Danny Marks. the guitar player from the band, they also worked with Bruce Bell from Lighthouse for a short time. Larry's history is well documented, both personally and with the band, but as far as the agents and managers he worked with a long list without any positive results to talk about. He was and is a talent, a great pop writer and performer so one has to wonder why he had so many problems with managers, record companies and agents. Could be he thought he was better at the job than they were? He may have been right. I know he did respect Paul White at Capitol. The band did some opening act gigs with Paul Butterfield and Led Zeppelin at The Rockpile. Their first Hit "You, Me & Mexico" did well in Canada plus top 3 internationally and #68 on Billboard. On the strength of that record they toured Canada but not through Concept. That tour was a disaster with poor attendance on all the dates and they finished up stranded in Vancouver. Their next hit "Last Song" soared up the charts hitting #1 in Canada and top 30 on Billboard, but the end was in sight and finally Larry shut the band down. Since then he has had a pretty good solo career plus owning a horse ranch just north of Toronto. Danny Marks, the guitar player, has established himself in Toronto playing local clubs regularly and doing a great blues show on Jazz FM 91 on Saturday nights. The managers that Larry had really didn't have the juice to break into the international scene consistently. Should have been huge success. I think he would have been a great fit with Albert Grossman. It seems that the odds were astronomical for a band to find a good knowledgeable manager in Canada. A very rare bird for sure!

The Collectors from Vancouver was another band starting to get national recognition. Bill Henderson was the guitar player/vocalist along with Howie Vickers the lead singer. The manager was Keith Lawrence, the brother of Claire Lawrence, who was in the band. We brought them east a few times and all in all it was looking good. The manager seemed to know what he was doing but I suspect Bill was running things behind the scenes. I point out that they were one of the bands we were booking direct from Vancouver as opposed to through Bruce Allen. In 1969 the band, which we had booked since 1965, decided to change their name to Chilliwack and Bill Henderson took over as lead singer. With some personnel changes and signing a record deal with Mushroom Records in Vancouver they began to hit the mark and had some solid hits, gold records, albums and singles and high profile film scores. They were soon on their way to being one of Canada's top bands, a big money maker for us, and the best was yet to come. Michael Cohl and Bill Graham loved the band. Michael booked them for his Winter Pop New Year's show at Maple Leaf Gardens in 1970 which also featured the James Gang, Johnny Winter, Sha Na Na, Rare Earth and, Steel River another one of our bands. Chilliwack peaked in 1973 when the single "Lonesome Mary" hit big in Canada and got into the top 100 in The States. I thought we had another Guess Who on our hands. They did almost do it but, when Mushroom Records went bankrupt, it left them hanging. They lucked out and signed with Solid Gold Records. The hard luck streak continued. Solid Gold records went bankrupt. The band had done several changes in personnel over the years and that kind of inconsistency was a part of problem that kept the band from breaking out live internationally. As far as I am concerned Keith Lawrence was a good manager but again the band missed the mark. Bill Henderson has gone on to establish a stellar solo career as a writer, producer, and performer.

A big supporter of Chilliwack and Canadian artists in general was dj Terry David Mulligan. The first time I met him was when he was working with Red Robinson at CKLG in Vancouver. Later, in 1969, he showed up at Chum as the all night guy. August 8, 1969, a new dj started at CHUM. Roger Ashby who had just come over from CKOC in Hamilton. He was sitting in on the all-night show with Terry learning the ropes when Terry got a phone call and informed

Roger that he had to leave immediately to deal with a family emergency. Are you ready? In Vancouver! So Roger had to take over the show and went on the air cold, at about 3 a.m., playing "And I Love Her" by the Beatles as his first song. Talk about baptism under fire. Terry never came back. I hooked up with him again later in Vancouver where he was busy doing television shows, radio and had worked himself into a successful career in film.

In 1968 Caesar leader Bruce Morshead was totally frustrated with everything that was going on with the band as he was not as much in control as he used to be and was very unhappy with many of the decisions that were being made. He decided to leave and was replaced by Steve Macko, formerly of the Lincolnaires from Oshawa, on keyboards. Vic Wilson, formerly with Little Diane and the Starlights and the Majestics, joined shortly after on baritone and tenor saxes. I left the band soon after Bruce, in the same year, to concentrate on the agency which was now off the wall busy. Caesar wasn't fun anymore. The music was still good but the image went down the tubes. They became a grunge band as far as costumes and they ceased being a headliner. Around the same time Norm Sherratt had moved into the penthouse with me and my family. I did continue to book the band but they had lost the momentum that we had built up since 1960. They started auditioning for new members one of which was guitar player Tommy Graham who told me this story.

"This had to be early 70's. I remember going to an audition for the band at some bar". (Blues on Belair.) This gets interesting because I know Steve Macko was smoking pot pretty regularly and I thought, he & Gary were both into it but, I guess not for Gary, until much later". I asked, "Did you finish the set?" , "Finished the set fine only the rest of the band during the show kept looking at Gary Wright, the drummer, because he kept giggling and was being silly and kinda out of it. He did keep the beat. I swear I thought he smoked…oh no…. sorry guys."

TG.

Tommy really felt tongue in cheek bad about the incident. That may be why he wasn't with the band for long. Just as well. Wasn't his thing. He moved on and has done some fabulous record productions in South America and Ecuador. Now I should be his agent.

By this time Shawn was working full time in the music business and had picked up a lot of contacts. I didn't keep track of what she was doing. I know she worked for Duff Roman for a short time and that ended badly. Call it creative differences. She was also in partnership with Larry LeBlanc in a promotion agency they called Media Machine. She was sort of friends with the guys in Caesar as well as their wives but arms length. I had introduced her to Ray & Shirley from The Pav in Orillia and The Kee to Bala in Bala. She became great friends with Shirley. We were all social alcoholics and, eventually, in 1969, Shawn and I introduced them to marijuana and we became doobie smoking buddies. The first night at their house in Barrie we bought an ounce of marijuana from a local dealer. Ray was the designated roller. He was rolling Jamaican and didn't even know what that meant. Huge cigar sized joints. We did the whole ounce which, normally, would have been a couple of weeks supply. Needless to say we got really stupid and spent the evening laughing our fool heads off. I tried to go to the bathroom on the second floor. I couldn't handle it. The stairs were too huge. Ray Sr. was a most favourite person in my life and Shirley ran a photo finish second.

CHAPTER 20

Alvin Munch. Let the games begin

T hanks to being able to concentrate on the agency business full time it wasn't long before I became a partner in Alvin Munch. It was cheaper than having me on commission. Here we go again. The roller coaster ride continues. We changed the name to Canadian General Artists which was Terry Fillion's original company. By mutual agreement I bought out Jack & Susan for $10,000 which gave me controlling interest in the company and, in 1969, I changed the name to Concept 376 Agency. I didn't like Canadian General Artists. It was, well, to general. We brought Mike Watson along with us. He had formerly been an agent first with garage bands and then with Bert Metford who did everything at the King Edward Hotel plus a lot of the convention and dance band type bookings. Mike worked with me putting together the Guess Who dates and handling Don Hunter the manager and that was becoming a full time job.

Within a year I fired Mike telling him he wasn't cut out to be an agent. He agreed. It was an amicable parting. He had talents better served elsewhere. Mike went on to manage Buckstone Hardware for a short time, moved on to a successful career as a promo rep at CBS Records and then Capitol. Next time we met was in 1972 at a Gold Record presentation to John Kay of Steppenwolf. All this and Mike was just 21 years old. We hired a couple of new agents, George Elms and Chris Summerton. Elms was originally from Angus, Ontario, and grew up in Thornhill which is where he met Chris. I first heard of George in 1966 when he was a butcher working at Loblaws and managing/booking a local rock band The 5 Shy, later Manchild, on the side. He went into partnership with Larry Cuthbertson who was managing Carnival a decent pop band. Elms and Cuthbertson started a company called Metropole Management that handled both bands. They promoted dates themselves around Southern Ontario using many of our bands as well as their own. Elms had called me to join the agency and I agreed. Cuthbertson and Summerton came along with him. They worked together through to 1974 and continued to use our bands on their shows. Cuthbertson left to form his own company, Crossroads Entertainment, about a year later. In 1969 Elms recruited Lawrence Schurman from Newmarket High School where he was the entertainment rep. Lawrence was a great addition to the agency. Larry meanwhile had arranged an audition for Carnival to take over "After 4", the television show that Robbie Lane had hosted for a couple of years. The producer was Gerry Rochon. We did a lot of shows with Gerry. He was producing most of the variety shows on CFTO Television including the Ian Tyson Show, It's Happening, After 4 and many others that featured musical artists. A great promotional vehicle for all of us as well as international performers. Carnival was one of those bands that worked regularly made decent money and got some great promotion created by Larry but they never really took off other than in Ontario. Cuthbertson on the other hand did well as an agent and show producer and has become a major player in the convention business all over the world. I think he was a decent manager at the level the band achieved.

At Concept we had hired the most unbelievable secretary; Shawn's friend Gloria Sinclair. She was one of the best promotional vehicles we ever had. The apt description I can think of is "a presence." She was built like a well, just built, and very, very Gloria. Didn't matter that she was a great office manager. I didn't care. Everyone that came in contact was mesmerized and, while we all loved her, we were all in awe. She probably bought as much business to the agency as the agents. She was the only woman I knew that could go to an afternoon party, whip home, change and attend a dinner party, split, change and hit the early evening in crowd then gone, change, and onto the all nighters just about every night and always looked sensational the next morning. Never ceased to amaze me. To our dismay she died a few years later. Choked on a chicken bone. Not the ending I would have envisioned for her. Loved Gloria.

Lest I forget Erika our little blonde German secret weapon. Mini skirted five foot two and yes Virginia, eyes of blue. To watch her bend over to file something was a religious moment. She always had boyfriend problems which, at one point or another, we all offered to be available to console her. She just left one day never to be seen again. Two other ladies we added to the staff. Rosemary Perruzza who was referred to us by her friend Loretta who worked in my lawyer's office. One of truly nicest people I had ever met who was handling all our promotional activities. Her husband Enzo had a decent rock band called Titeass that was making a small buzz in the market but he was really better at selling real estate. A truly great example of "keep the day job".

Yorkville Records had folded their World Canadiana agency and were concentrating on recording and publishing so we picked up their bands for representation. No question our roster was the strongest in the country. This was a great location for us close to everything. We had the token greasy spoon next door called Lucy's Open Kitchen. The food wasn't bad for what it was and as long as you didn't look at it too closely. For meetings we had the historic Spadina Hotel known for its rooms for the night or by the hour policy. It was on the corner of King and Spadina. The Spadina was famous for amazing fish & chips. It became the hangout place with an eclectic mix of people from the resident alcoholics, the hookers, the suits, blue collar working people and our people thrown into the mix. Our people being musicians, radio, television, record promo reps, record producers, artist managers, promoters, bar and restaurant owners, feature and promo writers, and other agents. A lot of people still have a fond place in their heart for The Spadina Hotel and we did do a lot of business out of there. Also close by on Spadina Avenue were two amazing delicatessens. Shopseys and Switzers. We rented out the second floor of our office to Jim McConnell and Dave Blakney They owned Special Records and Target Promotions. Special was the label for Downchild Blues Band first album Bootleg, which was recorded in 1970 in the famous, infamous, Rochdale College on Bloor St. W. What a trip that place was. Could have started a pharmacy with the drugs going on there. Target was the band management company. Downchild was and is one of my favourite bands and Donny Walsh, the leader, a favourite person.

In1969 some radio stations threw us a bonus; at least that's how it looked when it started. The Maple Leaf Radio System. This was a group of 12 or 13 Canadian radio stations plus a couple of associate stations that all got together to create an opportunity for Canadian artists to get more airplay. The idea was that the radio stations from across Canada would review Canadian content singles every week and then select one to get "A" rotation airplay and promotion for a minimum two weeks. Up to this time the normal, unspoken practice for Canadian records, was dubbed "The Beaver hours" a nickname by listeners and critics for a programming philosophy used by some Canadian radio stations as the government was making rumblings noises about regulating the mandatory playing of Canadian records to be played in prime time hours. The CRTC had already kicked in a minimum 25% rule for Canadian Content but didn't specify prime time. Some Canadian radio stations, rightly or wrongly, felt that their audiences did not want to hear Canadian music. They would designate certain program blocks in off-peak listening hours such as late evenings or overnight, on weekdays, or early on Sunday mornings, to play almost exclusively Canadian music reducing the number of Canadian selections that would have to be played during peak listening hours. The practice was controversial hence The Maple Music System. There is some confusion about who started it. Depending on who you talk to the author was J. Robert Wood at CHUM, Stan Klees from Red Leaf Records, and Walter Grealis from RPM trade magazine who was appointed as co-ordinator and resigned in the first year or possibly Nevin Grant at CKOC in Hamilton. My money would be on Nevin. He had been with CKOC since 1966 as a dj and eventually as program director. He was an amazing supporter of Canadian Talent and was situated strategically close to Toronto and was popular in the Kitchener area which was perfect for us and our associates Dram in Kitchener. We could drop by the station and provide all the records that our artists had recorded and count on Nevin to play them. On top of all this he was a great guy and fun to know. This Maple System was a great idea that appeared to be a win win when it started but, unfortunately, fell apart when some of the stations didn't follow through and actually play the records. Questions came up why some great records didn't get voted on and others did only because they were Canadian content, and not that good. Other times no records were voted on because none were submitted or were ignored. It was a very loose organization and that plus the politics made it a given that members would start resigning! Within a very short time that was exactly what happened. What a mess! It didn't affect what we were doing as an agency. It just pissed me off that they blew a great opportunity to really do something positive for Canadian Artists.

One thing I have noticed while writing this book. There were a small number of radio stations programmers and dj's that were actively supporting Canadian Artists long before it was fashionable to do. As far back as the 1950's. We were working directly with all the stations program directors and dj's pushing our own artists better then the system was. We made sure when our bands were playing live in a markets we used local promoters, local radio dj's as mc's and always, where possible, the shows were radio sponsored or at least supported. In Canada that was what agents had to do. I have to say we were very fortunate to be working closely with stations like CHUM and others doing shows and other live promotions. It paid off for us and our bands. Eventually the government brought in Cancon, the minimum 30% Canadian content programming law, but in my opinion, it was a mute point because the business was already moving forward a lot quicker after 1968 and more artists were breaking in the states anyway and that was what we were all looking for. I think Cancon gave it that extra push. The boomerang effect. Win in the U.S.A. win anywhere was still the watchword but now it was working towards win in Canada and everybody was starting to pay attention. Our Canadian artists were always world class but without a star system to support them it was a grind to get on the bandwagon enjoyed by The Americans and The British.

CHAPTER 21

*Concept 376 Walk softly
and carry a big stick.*

A word regarding my remaining partner Terry Fillion. We had known each other since the early years in the business and had been partners in Alvin Munch through to Concept. Terry was a great agent. A good local manager, from what I was told, and a good partner. He was managing a couple of decent local bands, Taxi aka Tote Family aka Sea Dog, who we hooked up with CHUM on their Much Records label. The other band was a new one, Homestead, that I had seen unknown to the band. It was "the sneak a peek" way to see bands and get in and out quickly. Avoids having to voice what may be a negative opinion. Bill King was the leader/ keyboard player. He was a transplanted American with an impressive track record including playing keyboards for Janis Joplin, Linda Ronstadt, and Martha Reeves. Bill had already lived a lot of life and only 24 years old. He truly hated The Vietnam War and everything about it so avoided the draft. Then he had a visit from an FBI agent who told him they had been trailing him for around two years Long story short he had to serve ten months in the army which is a story of its own which Bill will probably write a book about some day.

More long story short. I can't imagine how they felt when he and his lady Kris were smuggled out of the USA, undercover, and across the border to Canada. As for being a draft dodger, in the same position, I would have left a lot sooner and faster to get away from that pointless war in Vietnam that America was involved in and losing.

Back in Toronto and 1969. Bill and Kris are both top photographers as well as having many other talents. Together they are a formidable couple. They have experienced more good and bad then most people will in a lifetime. They are also two of the most beautiful people I know. Bill recently reminded me of my first words to him after hello when I went openly to see the band at The Elmacombo Tavern in Toronto. "I like your music but you should quieten down on the politics." The Vietnam War was obviously a big item for a lot of the Americans who showed up in Canada and rightly so. It was a stupid no win war. I am surprised he didn't tell me to fuck off. I have told him and Kris since then that Canada is very lucky that they made Canada and, in particular Toronto their home.

Fillion got involved with the Homestead through The Tote Family guitar player Fred Cacciotti who he had previously managed. Immediately they were playing a lot and doing the opening act thing which is the usual sign of personal interest by somebody in the agency. Fillion asked me to connect him up with Jack Richardson which I did. He got a deal with Richardson to do an album with the band for Nimbus 9 Records. They recorded in the RCA studios on Mutual St with old friend George Semkiw, formerly Ritchie Knight & The Mid-Knights and one of the hot engineers in town at the time. Jack and George both told me the session was a challenge. Not my problem until the same problems started happening on the live touring side involving drugs out of control which was my problem. I mentioned to Fillion that he needed to get things straightened out in the band. One complaint had come from Don Tarleton, our most important pro-moter, regarding a date in Kingston with Mashmakan one of our hottest bands and managed by Donald and his partner Terry Flood. Not a good thing. Fillion assured me he would take care of the problem. Bill King has written an excellent article about the band and the drug problems. Fillion was not someone who could take the band where they could have gone internationally, Jack Richardson could but it was a mute point since drugs were destroying them anyway. Being the agent is not always the easiest gig. Drugs and booze were major problems with a lot of the bands as well as other people in the business.

I first met Marty Melhuish during this time. It would be easier to list what he hasn't done rather then what he has. Before I met him he was a guitar player. In 1966 he owned Britannia Enterprises an agency booking non-union garage bands. That's where I first heard about him. Later another agency. Talent in Canada Promotions (Tin Can) with Ray Danniels, Don Peltch, Wayne Thompson and Les Webber. Three of the five, Marty, Ray and Wayne, would go on *to* great success. Marty moved over to journalism working with the underground newspaper The Tribal Village in Yorkville and finally landed at Beetle magazine, the new music industry magazine, as an editor. I'll pick him up from there again but this is a good place to talk about the non-union bands or, more aptly named, garage bands. New, all fairly young, and just wanting to play. Most of the time they played for very little or nothing. A lot were doing it for the fun and eventually went on to other careers. The few that stayed at it would move up into our world, a more professional level. There were some agents booking them. Mike Watson and Pete Rumble with their Camel Trek Productions. Others like Ed Glinnert, Fredrick Lewis, Bobby Roman and Julie Brown, along with Mike Watson and Pete Rumble, put their own circuit together. We didn't consider them competition to us at the time but they were watching what we were doing. It was similar to the situation Ron and I had when we first started out and learned what we could from Harold Kudlets, Bud Matton and Billy O'Conner.

I decided to talk to two of the new players in the booking scene about joining Concept. William (Skinny) Tenn and Wayne Thompson both agents/managers. Skinny, who managed Fludd, one of our busiest bands, was originally from Saskatoon and came to Toronto with a band called Witness Inc. looking for a job as an agent. He wasn't sure but I think it may have been Bud Matton that he talked to first because his roster would match Skinny's description of the agency's line up of middle of the road lounge bands with the exception r&b band Grant Smith and the Power. Matton had tied in with Jimmy McCarthy at Bert Metcalfe's office for a couple of the rock tours. McCarthy was touring Roy Orbison and put Witness on as opening act for 9 day tour, doing 10 shows from Victoria to Winnipeg and another few dates with The Bee Gees in Western Canada. Skinny eventually bailed and returned to Toronto. At first he worked as a partner with Ray Danniels booking and managing Rush before that meant anything and then split just before things really started to happen. When he left Danniels the band was making a big $150 a night. Who knew! Skinny chased

Ed Glinnert at Fredrick Lewis Agency for a job, got it, and that's where he first hooked up with Wayne Thompson who was also working there as an agent. Wayne had dropped out of law school because he made more money with the bands then he ever would as a lawyer. He had first worked with Marty Melhuish at Britannia Enterprises. Wayne was the one that worked out the same plan as Jack Manning had for us with "CHESTER FIDGE" our in house promoter. We booked the high schools and promoted the some of the dates ourselves and paid the schools a percentage of the door and concessions. But Wayne took the idea a step further to include the schools with limited funds and going for dances during the week instead of weekends when the bands would work for a reduced fee happy to get the extra money. Bonus for the bands and the schools. He made a lot of money. He did often use our bands because that's who the schools wanted. He was managing McKenna Mendelson Mainline and later the Nylons which he did break big time in the U.S.A. He was very impressive in his ability to meet and work with some of the top movers and shakers in the business. He later moved on to an impressive career in the film business as a producer, manager and promoter. He also worked with some of the biggest artists in the world. Frank Sinatra, Liza Minnelli, George Burns, Whitney Houston, Steven Segal and many more promoting their concerts worldwide. Wayne has won 4 Juno Awards and has more than a dozen gold and platinum records. More recently he produced the CBC movie "Keep Your Head Up Kid, The Don Cherry Story". Another award winner.

Eddy Glinnert and his partner Jeff Gold ran a tight ship. Wayne and Skinny both told me that they had tried to work with Eddy but it was such a pressure cooker atmosphere it took the fun out of everything. Glinnert was in law school so hardly ever in the office and when he was they say he made it very difficult with a gruff, unfriendly attitude, towards them. He had made commitments to the bands and the boys had to produce maximum dates or be fired. A totally different image than I had of Glinnert. We did some stuff together and I enjoyed working with him. We also did some dates for each other's bands and got along very well. As their own bookings increased Wayne & Skinny decided they had enough, left Glinnert and opened up an agency across the street in Yorkville at 80 Schollard St. where a lot of the high school kids were hanging out. They created a small but busy agency called Music Factory that caught my attention. Skinny was still managing and booking Fludd. Wayne still had McKenna Mendelson Mainline plus they booked some of my bands, fairly regularly.

Quick story here shared with me by Wayne Thompson.

Ray Danniels, manager of Rush, was working with Pete Rumble and Mark Franklin who owned The Rumble Booking Agency but he wasn't getting any dates for his band so he called Wayne and Skinny to help him out by booking the band through Music Factory. They agreed but when Danniels went to pick up his contact book Peter and Mark refused to give it to him and Danniels was told that this was the agency's property. Danniels told Wayne what had happened and Wayne, Danniels and a couple of biker friends of Mainline's Mendelson Joe showed up at the office. I have it from two sources that a fight ensued and Ray was thrown down the stairs getting a little banged up and escaped across the street to wait for the outcome. Needless to say Wayne and the bikers left with the book in hand.

I met with Wayne and Skinny to discuss them joining us and offered them $250 a week each to start with Concept and see where we go from here. They were very happy with that and very calmly JUMPED AT IT! It didn't take long however and then there were problems. The guys didn't like Fillion, didn't like the way he operated and talked to them, thought was mostly bullshit and lies, so they decided enough was enough and started making plans to move on. Should have talked to me. I thought they liked and respected me from the conversations we had. Unknown to them I was ready to buy Fillion out. When we started booking the schools for the fall season the two of them started bypassing the company booking system and hiding booking sheets in their desks mostly for the schools they had been booking before we got together. Both swear that they did not touch Concept's contacts but Fillion found the booking sheets in Skinny's desk. He told me he had seen Skinny leaving the office with files and figured they had only joined us so they could steal all our information and re-open Music Factory. One good point about Fillion he was very protective when it came to the agency. Based on what I was told and saw I had no choice but to let them go. I was pissed off at everybody. I had some interesting thoughts about where we could have taken the company together. An opportunity lost or maybe not. That old hindsight thing. I changed the locks, called my lawyer to make sure my ass was covered and that was that. Well not quite. A couple of days later Wayne showed up one night at the office with a couple of biker friends of Mendelson

Joe (sound familiar?) He was looking for Terry who, fortunately, wasn't there so nothing happened. This is funny for a couple of reasons. For a short time as I had mentioned previously about my misspent youth I rode with the Black Diamond Riders Motorcycle Club. I had also studied Judo with Canadian champion Frank Hatashita at his dojo on the second floor of a building on the southwest corner of Queen and Jarvis. Never made black belt but I was pretty good. I learned not to fight but could if I had to. Frank taught me not to get angry, get even and, if possible, gently. Good advice. Hard to impress me with a couple of bikers. The fact that my lawyer and one of my best friends, Sheldon (Shelly) Vanek, still represented a number of the Hell's Angels and Satin's Choice members and other questionable characters was a phone call away. Not sure where all this would have gone if Fillion had been there. Just another story in the world of music. Now here is another bit of a twist. Thompson doesn't remember being there so it comes down to another your side, my side and the truth. I'm going with the truth which is my side.

Unlike other cities there were now numerous rock music agencies in the Toronto market each grabbing a piece of the pie. Gil Moore independent, Sami Joe with Top Ten, Wayne & Skinny with Music Factory, Pete Rumble with The Rumble Agency, Eddy with Fredrick Lewis, Danniels and Scribner, my biggest competition, with Music Shoppe and that's just the higher profile ones. There was still Billy O'Conner, Bud Matton, Harold Kudlets, Bert Metcalfe, and people like Gino Empry, one of the best known promotion people in the business who handled all the bookings for The Royal York Hotel Imperial Room, which booked a lot of the upscale jazz artists and international performers. Gino was a funny little guy who pulled a lot of power in Toronto and in the entertainment business generally. He really wasn't an agent. He was a promotion person, one of the first in Toronto, to work with the print media. A very intelligent and shrewd person. He was also gay and when we first met he hit on me a few times until I warned him, sort of joking, to cool it or I would seriously hurt him. He stopped and we became good friends. He was the one that got me an invite to meet and greet The Happy Hooker, Zavery Hollander, when she arrived in Toronto. Quite a stellar event with the who's who of the Toronto elite showing up including the mayor. I got the introduction even shook hands with her and did the "Good to meet you" thing. That was about all of my involvement and interest in that evening but it didn't hurt to be seen.

Outside of Toronto the competition factor was considerably less. Most agents were using our bands because we had the best and we booked some of theirs under our banner. Dan Mombourquette's Dram Agency in Kitchener was the most well known in Southern Ontario with Copper Penny and Major Hoople's Boarding House. Others were Ron Metcalfe in St. Catherines, who had the dance club "The Castle", and recorded the hit single "Baby Elephant Walk", written by Henry Mancini, which became a huge hit. Then there was Herb Loch in Hamilton. There was, as always, some bands booking themselves. Across the country there were usually one or sometimes two agencies in each major market from Halifax to Vancouver. It was a credit to my people that we held the number one spot in the country. I finally hired a business manager, Paul Simmons, who tried to keep me on the straight and narrow financially. I guess he liked a challenge. He also worked with Catherine McKinnon, Don Heron and some other actors and actresses and was the exclusive agent for The Skyline Hotel chain in Canada. His partner was Andy Anka, Paul Anka's uncle, who was the one that talked Anka into going to New York against the family's wishes to become a huge artist with hit records like "Diana" and "I Did It My Way". For old guys Simmons and Andy were pretty cool. Lawrence Schurman's wife Bonnie worked in Simmons's office.

TID BITS

Unknown fact. Paul Simmons real name was Paul Somanski. I guess that was a show biz thing. The question you should be asking here is "Who cared" besides Paul!

We now had our own weekly bulletin that reported about what was going on in Toronto with the industry and our agency. It was "THE CONCEPT GREASE SHEET" well received and widely read. Shawn had been constantly on my case to give her a job in the agency but I didn't want her working in the office so giving her the Grease Sheet was a perfect solution. She did a good job. It was more like a gossip column then a trade paper. Later we changed the name to "THE CONCEPT HYPE HERALD" I liked the name Grease Sheet better but it was Shawn's project to run. We never competed with the trade publications in town but it was well read mostly for the gossip and news about where the bands were playing and what was going on behind the scenes. The circulation was very impressive for what the sheet was reaching across Canada and into U.S.A.

It was about this time I met 19 year old George Meek promoter extraordinaire! The reason I mention George is that he set the bar for concert promotions in Durham which was a model for the national tours. He called to meet. I agreed and we met in my office. He wanted to book The Rogues and Little Caesar and The Consuls in the Whitby arena just east of Toronto. We made the deal $350 for each band. Hard to believe the prices were so low. In his younger years George had been hit in the head with a baseball bat so his brain was kinda addled but not when it came to promoting a show or counting money He also took excellent care of the bands. The night of the show it sold out. 5000 people at $5 a head. A cool $25,000. I remember after the show Jerry McCarthy and I walked Meek home carrying 3 or 4 paper shopping bags full of cash. A few months later he booked the same two bands again this time in the Ajax Arena. Lesson learned. Once bitten twice shy. The bands picked up $1500 each. George still cleaned up. He kept at it for a couple of years and did well although I did change the deal to a guarantee versus a percentage of the gross instead of the flat fee. Our bands did very well and so did George. At one point he was running 2 or 3 shows a week using no less than 2 bands per show. I liked George and we became friends of a sort. He would only book through me. A few years later he was committed to The Whitby Psychiatric Hospital where he died shortly after. His epitaph should read "MEEK IN NAME BUT NOT IN DEED!"

At this point Concept was now solidly entrenched as the number one booking agency in Canada and was making a lot of money. I was re- thinking what I was doing. All along the way I had worked my butt off to build something but kept getting off track Duh me! More drama! I was going to buy Terry out but before I could he just up and left one day? Word was that it had something to do with defrauding the King Edward Hotel of a healthy amount of money. He and a partner had owned a spa in the hotel so that's where the alleged scandalous deed was perpetrated. I think, only a guess, Terry was charged with fraud but before anything could happen he split to parts unknown. Detroit was mentioned. Total conjecture on my part. I never heard from him again and that left me owning the agency exclusively. He never showed up to ask for a buyout. Later I found why.

He didn't put any money in originally so that explained why he wasn't around looking for a payout although we were doing great financially. He did surface again in 1974 under his old company name Canadian General Artists working with Robbie Tustin, local agent, and still managing Sea Dog but I never ran into him.

CHAPTER 22

I'm a manager?

was now spending a lot of time in recording studios around Toronto. All of them were busy. Everybody was recording. Re-enter Jack Richardson. He had made a deal for two of the bands that we were working with, the Guess Who and the Staccatos, to make promotion albums for Coke. At this point both bands had strong names in Canada. I started dropping around Nimbus 9, Jack's new studio in Yorkville, where I met soon to be legend Bob Ezrin and promotion man personified, Gary Muth. They were busy recording Alice Cooper who I was doing some dates for through his manager Shep Gordon. Also some great times hanging out in the studio with the Guess Who and meeting a lot of people. They had their first big hit in the states in 1968, The Wheatfield Soul album with the huge single "These Eyes" When These Eyes took off we had the band playing a week for $2000 at The Electric Circus Nightclub at 99 Queen St. W in Toronto, co-owned by Stan Freeman, American Music Corporation, and Moses Znaimer, CITY-TV owner, who was considered a visionary in the world of television. You will remember Stan from back in Bigland days when he was managing the Sparrows and tried to buy Bigland. When "These Eyes`` hit the charts in the U.S.A. The Guess Who`s concert fee went up dramatically. We had them out doing a Canadian tour before they took off to the States. The guys still loved hanging out in Toronto and the best was yet to come. As an aside Jack Richardson owned all the publishing for the Guess Who music as well as many other artists. He was fast becoming "The Godfather of the Canadian Music Recording Industry".

Then there was Joey Cee who played many roles in the business. At one point he was music director at CKFH. He was in and around the business since the early sixties. We had used him as a dj at the dances we were booking. He was also promoting his own shows. Our involment became more active when Joey got interested in the Stampeders and started promoting them and their records. Same thing with the Guess Who when "These Eyes" hit. He published a Canadian weekly trade paper, Record Week, where our bands were featured regularly and later another publication called Hot Toronto Magazine hit the stands and is still being published and circulated today. Joey was instrumental in getting a lot of the bands national recognition. He is another one of those people that it would be easier to list what he hasn't done rather than what he has. He has been just about everything in the business. Singer, songwriter, producer, publisher, writer, editor, promoter, dj, film, television and the list goes on. Joey Cee's biography, when he writes it, will be definite read should he share all his adventures with his many friends among the rich and famous. Glad to be able to call him a friend.

From 1968 on the business exploded, and I will have to jump back and forward with what was going on during this time with Canadian music nationally and internationally.

In 1968 I decided to get into the management business which begs the question, "What the hell were you thinking Tommy?" I honestly don't know what possessed me. I was working with some of the best managers in the business in Canada and the USA. All of my agents were managing somebody. I should have known better and stuck at with what I knew which was being a facilitator, great at putting things together, opening the doors, getting things lined up and then turn the artist over to a real manager, one that could provide the personal attention that is inevitably required. Once again hindsight is a wonderful thing. Along with the legendary Toronto vocalist Wally Zwolinski aka Wally Soul we put together a great five piece band. We named it Brutus. There was a rumour being bantered around that I had named the band Brutus to get revenge on Caesar. I could never understand the reasoning behind that one. Revenge for what? Caesar is what got me started in the business and, along with my own abilities, to where I was! Whoever thought that one up was badly misinformed and possibly in need of serious therapy. Maybe it was someone that I had slighted sometime in the past. BEWARE THE IDES OF MARCH! In realty I just thought Brutus was a great name to use as a follow up to my years with Caesar.

Wally and the guys were fun to work with all be it a little bizarre. No actually; fucking crazy would be a better fit, but great guys, musicians, and performers. We got them working locally quickly and appearing as the opening act for top bands such as the Guess Who and Chicago. We took Brutus into the studio in 1970 to record a single record, "Funky Roller Skates" on which I was the producer. Stop here! Let me repeat. I was the producer! First time for me. What a rush! Jack Richardson look out! I made a deal with Quality records to put the single out. It got strong regional play on radio and hit #7 on the R.P.M. Top 100 Chart. You can listen to it on Youtube. We released one more not so memorable single on Quality and then headed to Yorkville Records and more recording. I could see this wasn't going to work for me. It was taking up too much time and wasn't moving ahead fast enough. Like most of the bands in Toronto the line up of musicians that have passed through Brutus since is impressive. We had a lot of changes in members so it was difficult to get any momentum. Brutus was a sign of times to come for me. Management was not my forte. We did keep the name front and centre so the band was working but the recording side was not getting the attention that we needed to break out. At one point we changed the name of the band to Strange and added Maureen Murphy a great blues vocalist who was formerly with Sugar & Spice from Winnipeg. When Maureen sang it made the hair on my arms stand up! So good! That didn't work and the band split up in 1971. Later, in 1973, George Elms, my top agent, took over management of a reformed Brutus. George did a great job helping the band get organized and that included getting them recorded by Ralph Murphy, April Wine's producer. They had some decent hits but ran into the same brick wall. They never broke in the states.

I first met Jerry Doucette when he was playing guitar with The Reefers from Kitchener. Great guitar player, writer and performer. We brought him in to Toronto to join Brutus but that didn't last long. The personalities didn't work out. I talked to him about doing his own thing and suggested he contact my friend Shelly Siegal at Mushroom Records in Vancouver. He did and managed to knock off some great hits in Canada but not much in the States. Unfortunately Mushroom ran into financial problems and closed down. Jerry managed a few more hits but got lost in the shuffle when the market changed.

This was also the year that I had my first contact with Greg Brown and Janice Morgan who pretty well dominated my life for the next five years. Their band was Leather & Lace a soft rock band mostly playing bars in Northern Ontario as well as some American clubs through Harold Kudlets. They had checked out the agencies in Toronto and decided that Concept 376 was the agency they wanted to be with. They called me to meet and discuss our working together. I saw them for the first time at the Friar's Tavern on Yonge St. and liked what I saw and heard. We talked about what they wanted to do. Recording mostly. They'd be quite happy to stay in the studio and forget playing live. We agreed that wouldn't work as it doesn't pay the bills. We did however agree to work together. I called Bill Gilliland at Yorkville Records and arranged for us to get together with Janice and Greg to talk about recording opportunities. Bill heard them at the Friar's and he was interested and wanted to record them. We moved ahead and got the contracts signed. We folded Leather & Lace. Greg and I formed a management company, WBM (Wilson Brown Management.) Pretty creative Eh? Not! We started looking for new players. Dave Tamblyn, guitar player, came on board as well as Jeff Jones on bass. He had just left Rush after only one performance. Jeff is one of my favourite people and a hell of a bass player. We added Chuck Slater on drums

In 1969 one of the problems we were facing with the band was that Gilliland was distracted not only with other artists on Yorkville but he was considering Arc opening offices in the USA and working with MCA and Neil Bogart from Kama Sutra. The deal died because of the escalation of the Vietnam War. Can't say I was disappointed. He was also starting to get involved with English artists. We were moving ahead regardless. Meanwhile, for some reason, Johnny Mitchell, a dj from CHUM, got involved with us and started hanging around. I don't remember how or why or who brought him into our circle. I do know we didn't need him for anything. Those questions are yet to be answered. Mostly he was a nice guy. Greg thinks it was Bill that got Mitchell involved. Bill says no. I don't care. I know Mitchell was trying to do something with Yorkville so maybe that was the connection. I heard he was supposed to be a player/ singer and had a band named Balazar out of Detroit that he was grooming to blow Grand Funk Railroad out of the water. Might check the drug level there. Like that was going to happen! According to Bill he tried a couple of things with Mitchell, but there was nothing going on.

Greg informed me that the band had decided to call themselves "OCEAN". In retrospect we would have been better to call the band anything but. Actually we should have kept the original name Leather & Lace. Fit the times, the group, the image, and the music much better than Ocean which ended up labelling the group as a Gospel rock band. I believe that was partially because of the name plus the choice of the first record. It's amazing how smart I am now Eh? The band had rented a house in Agincourt so they could be together and rehearse anytime. Janice spent some of the time at my place with Shawn and me just to get away from 'The Man Cave". Gilliland and Greg started looking at material to record for an album. Lo and behold the winning single was "Put Your Hand In The Hand" that they picked off an Anne Murray album and written by none other than Gene McClellan (Caesar Alumnus). Greg wasn't happy with the lyrics in the second verse so he re-wrote them. After the record was released and Capitol heard it they were upset with the change and threatened to sue. Peter Stiemetz was Capitol's lawyer. Capitol backed off when Greg agreed to waive any writing royalties from the song. I think it was also an egg in the face thing with Capitol when it did become a huge hit. We heard that Anne Murray was not happy about it either. Would have been a great follow up to her previous hit "Snowbird". Once it was recorded there was a rumour that Mitchell had done the final remix on "Put You Hand In The Hand". I don't think so. If he did I never heard it nor did anybody else. We started avoiding him after that. I did listen to the final mix done by Bill and Greg and it was fine. Larry Leblanc met with Greg and Janice in my office to listen to the final mix. He also thought it was good. The band went to work recording their first album that had a song, "Stones I Throw" written by another Caesar Alumnus, Robbie Robertson. Thank you Caesar. Bill and Greg never did hit it off. It was a difficult situation. Bad karma I guess but for the most part it didn't interfere with what had to be done. Enter Randy Barber, a friend of Greg's, and great addition to the WBM team. We had stolen him from the Bank of Montreal. He was funny, intelligent, and well organized so he took some of the load off my "two hat situation" as the manager of Ocean and also the agent. I had been neglecting my Concept 376 Agency and needed to get back involved.

CHAPTER 23

Concept 376 In control

Back at the agency a couple of things were going on. Let's start with some questionably bad news. Ross White had decided to split and go on his own taking Edward Bear and a couple of other acts with him. Oops! Forgot to tell me he was leaving! Interestingly enough we continued to do dates on Edward Bear as did most other agencies in town. So Ross moves on and opens The White Agency in Oakville representing Edward Bear. Didn't last long. Shortly after he moved in with my biggest competitor Ron Scribner at Music Shoppe. I thought Ross would have been the perfect match for Larry. He wasn't very creative but he was very organized and would usually follow instructions.

TID BITS

In 1970 Terry Fillion and I both bought new lime green Opel Sports cars. Mine was a lemon and I hated it. A couple of months later I was stopped at a light on the Spadina overpass at Front St. and a transport truck rear-ended me drove me into the car in front and I had an instant Opel accordion that didn't play worth a damn. I was not unhappy about its demise.

It was around this time I first met another good friend, Peter Foldy, a multi-talented performer that had success in recording, photography and films. Originally from Budapest, Hungary his family had fled the country to get away from the communist regime and relocated to Australia. There Peter spent a lot of time growing up and hanging out with The Gibb brothers who would become international stars as the Bee Gees which is probably what inspired Peter to start writing music. He was already a performer doing some live appearances as well as television commercials around Sidney. The family moved to Toronto in December 1965. When they arrived we were in the middle of a huge snow storm, typical for Toronto at this time of the year, but Peter thought they had landed in Siberia He got right to it attending film school and continuing to write. He put a rock cover band together which is where I came in. He showed up at Concept in 1969 looking to get bookings for his band Sand Castle who were house band at The Place Pigalle on Avenue Rd. That was the start of a friendship that has lasted fifty plus years. Later, in 1971, they were house band at The Famous Door on Yonge, a topless bar. In 1972 He signed a recording contract with Kanata Records, a local independent label, and kept working live shows around his recording schedule. We did some dates for his band mostly in Toronto. Peter was a good live performer even though it was basically just a copy band.

His first record release was in 1973 called "Bondi Junction" and it took off". Peter was on his way, picking up number one in RPM as well as being featured on the cover, garnering a couple of Juno Award nominations. He had a national hit on his hands! He was also getting noticed in the U.S.A. We sent him out on a tour of The Maritimes in 1974 as opening act for Abraham's Children who were managed by Jack Morrow. I think Morrow was also the promoter. There was a problem with Peter getting paid. His manager at the time was none other than Jack Thomson who was, as far as I knew, still working for John Barry. The management company was the Agency for The Creative Arts which I thought was owned by Barry. After talking to Peter it would appear Jack was doing this on his own with a local musician Doug Spears and unknown to Barry. I suspect Barry found out which would explain why Thomson who, up to this time , had being promoting the hell out of Peter in the U.S.A. suddenly dropped Foldy from the management company. Ah. What a tangled web we weave.

Peter signed with Capitol-EMI in 1975 and had two more hits "Roxanne" and "Julie-Ann". Surprisingly all this record success did nothing for his draw power on the live circuit which was disappointing. He eventually decided to re-locate to Los Angeles and I gave him some names of people to contact. One that turned out to be a solid contact for him was Wayne Thompson who was well connected in the Los Angeles film and music business. Thompson's dad was a well known producer director. Wayne hooked him up with some of his contacts in the film community and that helped him get his start in that business along with his own initiatives. It didn't take him long to get back into recording with some decent results. Foldy signed with Free Flight Records that had been started as a sub label by RCA Records in Los Angeles and he had a great run with them until, suddenly, the label closed its doors which motivated Foldy to pay more attention to the film business and produce a number of successful films. Can't keep a good man down. He is also an excellent photographer and has taken some great candid shots of some of the stars such as Paul McCartney, Dennis Hopper, Ronald Reagan, Audrey Hepburn, Bette Davis, and Bob Hope. He has continued to release records and films and has been very successful living in Los Angeles. He still returns to Canada quite often to do some business and visit with his mom in Toronto.

Then came the legendary Crowbar. At this point they were still working with Hawkins but there was talk of a split in 1970 at which time we could try to sign them up with Concept. I spent a lot of time at Bad Manors, their farmhouse, in Ancaster. It was a semi throwback to pioneer times, pretty rustic and badly in need of repair. A lot of people living and passing through. Great vibe. Very 1960's. We used to go tobogganing, smoked a lot of doobies and consumed a lot of booze. The guys played a lot of music. It was a very layback place. Great family feeling and ideal for just hanging out. Cheaper than a therapist. I was waiting for Hawkins to fire them so I could start booking the band. Finally he did citing "Irreconcilable differences". Shortly after we got the news I had left the office late one afternoon but was coming back to do a booking signing ceremony with the band. While I was gone Lawrence Schurman took a call from a guy with a heavy accent asking if we could book a Chimpanzee. Lawrence took it in stride and invited him to the office for an audition. Lo and behold the guy shows up and is for real. The chimp wrote with a pencil, smoked cigarettes, along with some other tricks, like riding a bike. Later, as the chimp and his owner were on the way out, Crowbar arrived in limos to meet with me and sign the exclusive booking contract. Kelly Jay was still in the back seat of one of the limos and to everyone's surprise the chimp climbed in beside him. I think he may have been looking for an autograph or maybe a date with Kelly! Not sure which. No harm done and it made the evening even more memorable. I was booking some of their dates locally but they also still had some of their own dates. *I* remember one that I went to at The Royal York Hotel in the Imperial Ballroom for a fund raising function for the Pierre Trudeau's election campaign tour to promote his run as prime minister of Canada. His wife, Margaret Trudeau, had suggested they hire the band to do the whole fund raising tour. Kelly with his usual audacity went up to Pierre Trudeau introduced himself as from Crowbar then slipped Pierre a doobie. Trudeau kept it. Pretty cool.

In 1971 Crowbar signed with Daffodil Records and the first recording they did for the label was a live performance at Massey Hall in Toronto which was well documented by the media. Everybody that was anybody was there. What a fabulous night! Marty Onrot was the promoter along with CHUM. I had been working with Marty on some shows since 1964. We became friends and still are. Marty and I were born on the same date, February 8, a year apart. I'm the older one. Marty was promoting and managing some very talented artists and bands. James Leroy, Ray Materick, rock bands Barefoot and Scrubaloe Caine. Later he managed Crowbar as well as Domenic Troiano for a short while all of which Concept booked regularly.

Shawn had become good friends with Barbara Onrot and we were spending more time with Barbara and Marty at their home in the Forest Hill area of Toronto and socially around town. We drank, ate, smoked doobies, snorted coke, and had a good old time. One night among many stands out. Marty had booked George Carlin, the world famous comedian, at Massey Hall. George had just finished the very successful show. It was lay back time. We all went to Marty and Barbara's house to mellow out sitting on the floor in the living room. We had been fed, wined, drugged and were very happy. George entertained us with his stories and opinions, and we went back at him with ours. What a great night!

In 1970 I met Frank Davies who owned Daffodil Records. He had just gone into partnership with Ronnie Hawkins and John Finlay, Hawkins lawyer, (not to be confused with Jon Finley the performer) On the other hand lawyers are performers aren't they? Frank had arrived in Toronto in 1969 from England. The partnership with Hawkins and John Finlay didn't last long. Frank bought them out for $10,000 within a year. He was a very busy well connected guy. We were dealing with many of the same artists and people even though we didn't cross paths very often. I do know the bands were starting to make a lot more money because of Frank's promotions. His lawyer was the renowned Peter Steinmetz. In 1973, Frank, on the brink of bankruptcy, joined up with Bill Ballard and his partners Michael Cohl and Myron Wolfe. Myron's family owned, among many other things, The Oshawa Group, huge in the Canadian wholesale food business. As the saying goes, "the rest is history". Frank was and is definitely a great addition to the Canadian record business and a great boost for Canadian artists. Unfortunately Frank's problems were not dissimilar to many talented people in the music business. Financial control or lack thereof.

We were both dealing with Capitol Records. I had worked with a number of artists on Capitol since the early 1960's including the Beach Boys, Dave Clark Five, the Esquires, the Staccatos, Jim Croce, Edward Bear and Little River Band. In addition we had artists on Aquarius owned by Terry Fludd and Don Tarlton and distributed by Capitol with artists April Wine and Mashmakan. When Capitol picked up Daffodil we were booking a lot of the artists that were on that label. Crowbar, King Biscuit Boy, A Foot In Coldwater, Fludd and Hunt. That's when Dave Mazmanian was hired by Capitol as staff assistant to Paul White and the label manager for Daffodil 1971 to 1975. A most interesting guy. Originally operations manager at CKLB in Oshawa then operations at CHUM in Toronto and later as consultant for the opening of the new Toronto FM station Q107. We became friends, and shared the odd lunch at the Spadina Hotel enjoying the renowned fish and chips and the conversations. We have stayed friends over the years. Dave was a great connection for me with Capitol and Daffodil. He was one of the most liked and respected people in the media business. This is also where I re-connected with Deane Cameron. I met many people through the seventies but none more impressive then Deane. I first met him around 1971 when he was performing as the drummer with vocalist Tom Cochrane, in a folk rock band called Harvest. We were booking some dates on the band who had built an impressive following around Toronto. The only recordings they did were some demos for Capitol with Wayne Patton special projects manager. They were never were released. Once again. No manager. At the time Deane was working at Capitol-EMI Records in the warehouse. I only mention this because Paul White, myself and others started the same way which qualified record company warehouses a hell of an entry level job. Deane left there and landed

172 • I AM TOMMY

a job with Daffodil in 1972 as product manager. Later Deane moved over to GRT Records this time as new release coordination marketing working under Ross Reynolds., the president. In 1977 Deane returned to Capitol EMI under president Arnold Gosewich. Arnold was partners, 1956, with Harvey Glatt as owners of the Treble Clef Record Stores in Ottawa. Arnold became president of Capitol in 1969. Dean's new position was as manager of talent acquisition and was quickly promoted to vp responsible for the company's A&R department working with Paul White, Graham Thorpe and Eddie Colaro who was now Canadian special projects manager promoting Nickelback, Anne Murray, Buffy Sainte-Marie, Glass Tiger, Tom Cochrane, Stompin' Tom Connors, the Rankin Family, Johnny Reid and Serena Ryder. Arnold left the company in 1977 and, in 1982, moved to CBS as C.E.O. Deane made president of Capitol in 1988.

TID BITS

Recently, in September 2015, Deane was appointed President & Chief Executive Officer of the Corporation of Massey Hall and Roy Thomson Hall in Toronto. What a great career he has had.

1972. Good news! Myles Goodwyn, leader of April Wine called me to meet. He wanted to relocate the band business to Toronto in order to work closer with Concept. We had been doing most of their booking. I assigned George Elms to work closely with them and take care of business. They were one of the top bands in the country.

Speaking of GRT. Segue! In 1972 they were distributing the Axe Records and Tuesday Records labels both owned by another amazing guy Greg Hambleton. I always called him Mr. Kitchener because that was where most of the artists on his labels were from. There and Hamilton. We were again booking most of the artists on an arrangement with our associate the Dram Booking Agency who represented Thundermug, Steel River, Gary and Dave, Major Hoople's Boarding House, Fergus, and Rain with Charity Brown. All very strong in the local markets. Both George Elms and I worked very closely with Ross Reynolds, the President of GRT. Elms specifically with Greaseball Boogie Band which he managed. Great band that included my friend Maureen Murphy on vocals for a while. A very strong kick at the can but they never broke out despite being involved with some of the best musicians and producers in the country They finally disbanded in 1980. Other artists with GRT that we were working with included Dan Hill, Ian Thomas, Downchild Blues Band and Lighthouse. GRT was also distributing ABC Records and Dunhill who had, in addition to Steppenwolf, Jack Scott and other artists such as Danny & the Juniors, The Royal Teens and Bobby Vinton all of whom Caesar had performed with at one time or another and that I had booked.

When Marty Onrot picked up Crowbar for management, opportunity knocked. Clive Davis president of Colombia Records in The USA and a well known producer expressed interest in signing the band. Marty wouldn't make the deal. Couldn't agree on the terms of the contract. It was rumoured that the main problem was a lack of original material. It seems to me there may have been a shot at negotiating further and provide Crowbar with material that suited their sound. After all it was Clive Davis. That didn't happen and the band continued performing on the circuit until they finally split up in 1976.

Questionably bad news in 1972. My brother Jimmy called. He had been contacted by the police to inform him that our father had died in a flophouse on Jarvis St. and Jimmy would need to identify the body at the city morgue and pick up his belongings from the flophouse. Jimmy wanted nothing to do with any of this and told me to take care of it. I went to the flophouse on Jarvis. There were rows of beds some with men sleeping on them. The guy in charge led me to one with a shoebox on it which I opened. Inside there was an ID card and that was about it. His shoes and clothes and anything else personal were gone. From there I went to the morgue where I identified dad's body. When they asked how we wanted to dispose of the body as I had agreed with Jimmy I told them we didn't care and wanted nothing to do with it. The attendant said that since we didn't want to claim the body it would be buried by the city. That was it. I left. I called Jimmy to let him know what had happened and he just said "Good. It's over."

One of my favourite artists was Jim Croce one of the most talented and gentle people I ever met. He wasn't with us for long. I had Brutus on a couple shows with him which was a strange mix but it worked. We all did a TV shot in Montreal. Croce was on ABC Records and had some great hits the most notable "You don't Mess Around With Jim" and, my favourite, "Time in A Bottle", Also the catchy "Bad, Bad Leroy Brown" that hit number one on the American charts in July 1973. He was one of the easiest artists to work with and we were looking to do a lot more with him as he gained international recognition. In the times I was around him he was a great story teller and comedian but most of all we talked about his family, the most important thing in his life. If he had his way he wouldn't be performing on the road. He would be home with his family. On September 20, 1973 he died in a plane crash taking off in a charted airplane which hit a tree and everyone on board died. Croce was only 30 years old, the same age as me. The really sad part was that he was planning on giving up the music business.

CHAPTER 24

Moving on up

In Yorkville, I had become an infrequent visitor to The Riverboat Coffee House owned by Bernie Fiedler, one of the famous Three Bernie's in Toronto. There you rubbed elbows with the best. Gordon Lightfoot, Joni Mitchell, Neil Young, Bruce Colbourne, Murray McLaughlin, Dan Hill, Ian and Sylvia, Bob Dylan and many of the music business personalities behind the scenes. Bernie Solomon the entertainment lawyer who could have inspired the song "Bernie The Attorney". As well, Bernie Finklestein. I met this Bernie first at the El patio Cafe when we had to deal with the Stampeders problem back in 1966 and when he had just started managing The Paupers, one of the bands we booked. I want to say here that I was really disappointed when The Paupers didn't go all the way to the top. I thought they would be the next Beatles especially after they went with two drummers. Awesome! So Close! The leader, Skip Prokop, later joined up with Paul Hoffert to create one of my favourite bands. "Lighthouse"! In 1969 Bernie Finklestein had started True North Records which became one of the best indie labels in Canada. He is a great example of handling the financial part of the business properly. He managed Bruce Colborne, Dan Hill and Murray McLaughlin, two of whom were former residents at the Alvin Munch Hotel. One thing I love about Finklestein he was and is a rare commodity in the business. He respected his artists, put his ass on the line for them, told them the truth and earned their respect and friendship. We have remained friends over the years. One of my favourite guys. You should read his book True North If you want to get the real feel of what Yorkville was all about written by a person who lived it. Another great read. The Three Bernie's got together and set up a one call does it all collaboration including pretty well all phases of the business. I would have loved to be a fly on the wall to hear some of the discussions that went on at their board meetings.

Now I could stroll thru Yorkville and see one of the bands we Concept was working with in just about every cafe and coffee house in Yorkville Village. The same with the live talent venues on Yonge St., around Toronto, and Ontario. Most important our concert circuit was booming. I started hanging out with the "guys" at a local watering hole just south of CHUM on Yonge St. the Ports of Call was a hotel bar and restaurant. If you wanted to eat The Tiki Room had great food. We met in the Baton Rouge Bar on whenever Fridays or Saturdays we had the time available. The usuals, off and on, were Bill Ballard, Thor Eaton, John Basset and Bill Gilliland. All very accomplished drinkers and good fun guys. When we got happy enough some of us would hit the stage and sing along with the band who were very tolerant guys and a more than decent bar band. Fortunately everybody was having a great time including the band and we always took care of them. Sometimes, after closing time, Bill and I would split to his apartment, hang out, drink and talk for hours. Bill made friends easily. What you see is what you get. He got me gold season tickets for the Toronto Maple Leafs games and talked me into joining the Hot Stove Lounge, the Gardens private club, where I met the amazing maître d' Nick and thanks to Nick everybody that was anybody. Hockey was the magnet. On any given night you could meet the top stars and the power people.

Ballard was legendary for how much food he could put away at a sitting. I watched in awe. He never gained an ounce. He introduced me to his dad Harold Ballard. Not a lot to say about Harold. He was already a legend. Turned out we knew a lot of the same people and not surprisingly he knew my friend John Barry. Barry never ceased to amaze me. Also met Peter Larsen who was a great guy and fun to be around contrary to rumours. His official title was attractions manager for The Gardens, but he was involved in everything as far as I could tell. He was everywhere taking care of business.

CHAPTER 25

Concept 376 Time to Rock & Roll

R andy Bachman left The Guess Who in 1970 after a performance in New York and put a new band together. Brave Belt, who, although we did book some dates for them, were struggling as far as career success was concerned. Even with Bruce Allen as their manager it was also very hard for the band to get a record deal with an American label. They were turned down at least 20 or more times but Randy persevered. Finally, after changing the name to Bachman Turner Overdrive, Randy got a deal with Mercury Records and B.T.O. became an amazingly successful band. We all remember the iconic song "Taking Care of Business". Still hear it today in commercials and television sitcoms. We booked a few dates with them but it was all Bruce Allen at that point. I flew to a couple of dates out west. I remember, before the shows, we all had to clear out of backstage so that Randy could meet The Elders from the local Mormon Church in private. Also no smoking backstage. A touch unusual but welcome to rock & roll. Nothing is unusual. I suggested to Bruce Allen that he put the band into The PNE in Vancouver but he didn't think they would draw that well in the hometown. Eventually, like Don Hunter with the Guess Who, he took my advice and put them in. SOLD OUT! The one thing you can say about Randy he is impossible to keep down and continues to come up a winner despite some serious setbacks.

In the middle of all this Mel Shaw showed up in the office to discuss the lack of dates the Stampeders were getting from us. This was a new situation. We had kept them working steadily since they came to Toronto in 1966 with Bigland and through all the changes since. Mel met with Ross White first and his explanation was that the phones were not ringing for the band! I guess working the phones and selling was a foreign concept. Tim Cottini's response was even better or worse depending on your point of view. "Don't care. Nobody wants the band". Nice. Just what I needed. I'm hard to piss off but Tim managed. I told him to do it! "I want the fucking band working!" I spoke to agents in the office about the problem. It straightened out quickly and the band started getting dates again. Interesting situation that I hadn't noticed before but should have expected. The guys were making decisions on who worked, and who didn't without consulting me. Not a good situation. It wasn't long after in the same year that The Stampeders single, "Sweet City Woman," hit number one across the country as well as on CHUM. Even better it hit number eight on the charts in the States so not only did the band work more, they made more money. It also passed a message to the agents. You never know.

Both Mel and I had been working the American agencies, Mel for The Stampeders, me for Canadian representation for their acts in Canada as well as placing some of our own in the states. I already had the connection with Peter Golden at William Morris Agency as well as Leber and Krebs in their New York office whose big acts were The Rolling Stones and Aerosmith. My foot in the door was the work we did with the opening acts on The Stones, and other shows in Canada plus the rising interest in home grown artists breaking out of Canada. Got nowhere with Steve Leber. Word was out you if you were a Canadian band you could sign with Leber at William Morris worldwide if you didn't want to play anywhere in the world lol. Obviously Steve Leber wasn't high on Canadians.

One American agent who was pro-Canadian was Frank Barcelona owner of Premier Talent Agency in New York. I was referred to him by Sid Bernstein. Frank's door was always open and he always answered my phone calls. He set me up to talk to some of the promoters and even did some of the introductions.

TID BITS

Frank Barcelona is the only booking agent ever to be inducted into The American Rock & Roll Hall of Fame.

He wanted to do the same thing in the U.S.A. that we had done in Canada. Develop a national tour circuit with promoters coast to coast. He set up a conference in New York with all of the strong regional promoters across the U.S.A. including Bill Graham from San Francisco, Don Law in Boston, Barry Fey in Colorado and two of the top guys from Canada Martin Onrot, Toronto and Donald K Donald, Montreal. He wanted to form a network that would offer new artists an opportunity to tour nationally in America and Canada with everybody working together. The promoters, the media, the agents, the artists, mangers and record companies. He did it and it worked for a lot of years.

Frank booked the Mandala on some dates and, through Frank, we hooked up with Fred Petty a local agent in Boston who booked, among other venues, a great club, Lucifers in Boston, where we could showcase bands. George Olliver told me it was a great place to play. the Mandala and Grant Smith and The Power both played the club. In a discussion with Grant I got an interesting take on agents and managers. Fred Petty booked Grant's dates around Massachusetts and New York States and became a good friend. In Canada Grant booked his bar dates through Bud Matton Agency who also put him into Las Vegas. Grant's principal agent at Matton's was Brian Ayers, who also played in the band and booked the one-nighters. Sound familiar? Brian got 5 percent for his work but with the understanding that Grant was in charge. Brian forgot that a couple of times which was not a good idea. Grant Smith was brought up in a military family so there was not a lot of gray in his life. He very organized. For a short time Grant was pseudo managed by Murry Campbell who owned the Avenue Road Club and the Devils Den, both in Yorkville, and who was well connected in the drug world in Toronto to the point that Campbell felt it was necessary to carry a gun most of the time.

TID BITS

Grant had a shoulder holder custom made for Campbell's gun as a present. Campbell loved it!

Murry Campbell opened a lot of doors for the band through his contacts. For one nighters Grant depended on Ayers to deal with all the agents to deliver dates. Both Concept and Music Shoppe delivered most of the jobs in Canada.

Grant shared one story about performing in Vegas. Charley Mather, Matton's man in Vegas, knew everybody and was more of a power broker than an agent. Charley got Grant an invitation to meet Tom Jones and to attend an after hour's party that the famous actress, Connie Stevens, was throwing for the staff at the hotel she was working in. Connie was noted for being a wonderful person and a great performer. From the stage she introduced some celebrities that were in the crowd and she did special intro for Tom Jones who stood up and did the wave thing. The gesture was almost dismissive, bordering on rude, not really acknowledging the applause he received. It was also the same way he was treating his girlfriend. Connie then announced that there was another special guest in the audience; an amazingly talented young singer/performer. A newcomer from Canada. Grant Smith. Grant stood up amazed and embarrassed. He accepted the accolade from the crowd and he noticed the sour look on Tom Jones's face at this surprise announcement. Ego abounds! Some insulting remarks were exchanged between the two. Grant finally directed a fuck off exit line at Jones and left the club. Really! Some people! Grant lucked out and got a date at The Flamingo Hotel replacing Wayne Cochrane who had to cancel. Mather was not happy with the exchange between Grant and Jones who was his major artist. Back in Toronto Bud was livid. Nobody seemed to give a damn about the kind of person Jones was or that he instigated the scene.

Grant did a lot of recording. Starting in Art Snider's Studio as well as Newbury Sound on Eglinton Ave. in Toronto. A single was released on Boo records, one of the indies. Grant was surprised when he got a call that "Keep On Running", one of the songs he had just recorded, was being played on CHUM. He had thought they were just doing scratch tracks and was not happy with the unfinished tracks being released. The band went back in to finish the tracks. Later, when they were playing a date in New York City, Tony Orlando, Teen recording star and a&r person for MGM Records, met with Grant and offered him a deal to record with MGM. The deal was signed and the single "Thinkin About You" was released in the U.S.A. Nothing happened. Grant returned to Toronto. Back home Grant Smith and The Power opened for Spanky & The Gang and the Hollies at The O'Keefe Centre. With a constant change of personal that included some of the top players in Toronto they finally split up in 1970. To sum up: Grant was not comfortable with management but, for the most part, respected agents for the work they had to do. Grant would have been up there with the best but, in his own words, "Family was more important".

CHAPTER 26

Beetle Magazine- The Billy Arnold incident

We had a new tenant leasing our second floor office. Beetle Magazine. The newest music business magazine in Toronto run by owner/ publisher Moe Wortzman and Editor Darcy Barrett. This was my first contact with Linda Dawe, a new, young writer for the magazine, fresh in from Sault St. Marie and knock down get the hell out of the way good looking. She rivalled Gloria. I was well aware of her sexuality but she didn't appeal to me that way. I thought she was an interesting person that could become a good friend, despite my reputation that dictated otherwise. Poor Vic Wilson could hardly control himself when we first met her in my office. She became a regular fixture doing interviews with the bands passing through daily. Within a year she was assistant editor and responsible for much of the success of the magazine hiring people like writer and future Grammy award winner Rob Bowman. This is where Linda first met Scott Richards, former bass player for David Clayton Thomas and the Shays. Scott, after leaving the Shays, had a very successful career on the business side of music ending up as president of MCA Records Canada. Another crossover. Unknown to Linda it was love at first sight for Scott. He eventually joined Linda's promotion company Music Solutions. You can read all about them in her book "First True Love". A great love story and worth the read. Linda moved on to CBS Records to join Gary Muth and Carolyn Conner as part of the a&r group under president John Williams, who had just signed Mashmakan, one of our top groups, managed by Terry Fludd and Don Tarleton in Montreal. After CBS, in 1974, Linda moved to MCA Records with Scott

Richards and, alongside promotion man Jeff Burns. Linda worked promotions with Dolly Parton, Oscar Peterson, the Good Brothers, and Jefferson Starship among others. In 1976 Linda was hired by Ed Preston, vice- president and general Manager of RCA Records Canada, to work with Andy Nagy in promotions. Linda was the first female promotion manager in Canada working with the likes of Bob Marley, Hall & Oates, and Elton John. No dust on this lady. You Go Girl! She was and is great fun to know and work with and has been a great friend. One of the top promotion people in the business and a great looking broad. When is the last time you heard that expression? We did many promotions together as she worked with a lot of our bands.

As previously mentioned Marty Melhuish was the editor of Beetle for the first couple of issues of the magazine. In addition he was also involved with Ritchie Yorke, who became a world famous music journalist and writer, in the creation of Pop Magazine, Grapevine and Rainbow, all music industry trade publications. Rainbow had one nude centrefold of the rock band Fludd that blew the biz people away. Marty was associated with just about every music magazine in Toronto as well as being the Canadian correspondent with Billboard Magazine and writing great books about the people in the business. Fifteen to date. like Larry LeBlanc Marty did some incredible interviews. Melhuish remains as one of the most knowledgeable people in the music business. LeBlanc joined him as co-editor on the second issue of Beetle which gives me another story to share.

A true story as told by Larry, Marty, and me I call it "The Billy Arnold Incident." Billy was a local writer/columnist writing a column for Beetle Magazine.

Larry: "The artist in the Billy Arnold incident was Gary U.S. Bonds who had some great hit records like "New Orleans "and "Quarter To Three". I'm pretty sure the year was 1971. The incident took place on the lawn of 289 Davisville Ave. in Toronto where my wife Karen and I, were living. Marty Melhuish and I were the co-editors of Beetle Magazine, going into the second issue. Marty had done the first issue on his own and brought me in to help him with the second, as co-editor. There was no real money and neither of us could do it full time. In the first issue Billy Arnold had done a column on black music in Toronto. Marty had told him we were dropping the column for the second issue because of lack of response. Shortly after that Billy turned up at my house with American star singer Gary U.S. Bonds in tow, shouting, banging on the door because he was pissed off that his column had been dumped. We lived in the second floor. I wasn't there but Karen was, alone, and she was scared. She called you (Tommy) and somehow you got a hold of me and I raced to get home. Not sure whose car I was in because I don't remember having a car in those days. I think I may have, by coincidence, called you from nearby the house. When I arrived there were 3 police cars and 5 or 6 cops on the front steps and lawn. I got out of the car and Gary US Bonds said, hands rising in the air over his head, "I ain't got anything to do with any of this." The police asked if I wanted to press charges against Billy which was kind of silly because he hadn't really done anything other than yell and bang on the door. But he was a huge black guy and known to be violent, and well, outright scary. He had scared the hell out of Karen. She didn't know many people in the music biz and we were closest to you (Tommy and Shawn) in those days. Sharon thought she had seen a gun. "Yes, there was a gun involved which explains why so many police arrived. I remember Karen said that he threatened that he'd shoot someone which is why she called you (Tommy). In the end the police took Billy away and Gary US Bonds quietly left on his own".

Marty told basically, the same story, with a couple of differences. He was at the house already with Karen waiting for Larry when Billy showed up. He didn't see the gun.

My Story: About the same. I drove over to the house after getting the call from Karen. I talked to Billy and he calmed down which wasn't that hard to do as by then the police had arrived. They took him away. The gun had mysteriously disappeared. I don't know if they charged him or not. I don't think so but I do know he was deported later on some other criminal related charges.

When Marty and Larry left Beetle Magazine after the second edition Moe hired Elaine Banks, a hustler in the nicest meaning of the word, as Editor, She really got things happening and put them on the map. They were catering to the current rock market public, contrary to RPM, which was totally industry oriented. For us it was a great relationship as we were a handy source for news with our line up of artists and contacts. They were as tuned into Yorkville and the music business as you could get. As for Concept we got a lot of free mileage out of the relationship for the agency and our bands.

TID BITS

The drinking age in Toronto was lowered from 21 to 19 in 1971 and that changed the face of the business drastically, specifically in the high school and university business. The kids could now get in the bars.

Michael Cole had been around the music business since 1968. In his early years, among other things, he took a shot at managing a band called Icarius (aka Dixie Rump Roast) in partnership with Bob Ezrin from Nimbus and like me was lousy at it. He moved on to Cymba, his first production company. There is an excellent interview online that he did with Larry LeBlanc in Celebrity Access that will tell you everything you want to know about the man who became, and still is, one of the top promoters in the world. Can't help but like the guy. He didn't have much money available when he started but he was so totally tuned in to the business including making all the usual mistakes. As the saying goes you can make as many mistakes as you like. It's the wins that count. In 1973 Michael, with Bill Ballard and his other partners opened Concert Productions International, CPI. A dark cloud on the horizon for me and a few other people but great for Canada and the world..

CHAPTER 27

Put Your Hand in The Hand

first met Len Rambeau when we started doing some dates around Ontario for John Allan Cameron an up and coming folk singer. Len was one of those people that you instantly liked and trusted. Len had just got on board with Balmur Ltd., Anne Murray's management company. Anne was a hot item thanks to Snowbird, a Gene McClellan tune. Len had left a job in Halifax that was paying him really well but he was a friend of Anne's and someone she could trust. I hit it off with him right away and over the next few years we stayed in touch. I never booked Anne. I have no idea why not other than she was always represented by American agents. Up until Len got involved with Balmur I had only spoken to Brian O'Hern, Anne's producer, who I knew from the Arc Records days. He married Emmy Lou Harris, an amazing country singer. When we released Ocean's "Put Your Hand in The Hand" on Yorkville there was some real flack flying around. I think Capitol had passed on the song as a single for Anne because it was too religious and, when Ocean's version hit the top of the charts, Anne was justifiably pissed off. To compound the problem we had taken it off her album. The conflict didn't interfere with my relationship with Capitol since I was working with so many of their artists. Len and I never discussed it. Gene McClellan, who was friends with both Anne and myself, stayed neutral but did thank me for Ocean recording his song. The same neutrality continued when Greg Brown changed some of the lyrics in the song and talk of a lawsuit loomed but fortunately died when he agreed not to take a writer's royalty.

Balmur changed Anne's American manager Nick Savano who was also managing Frank Sinatra and Glenn Campbell and was Anne's good friend. It was no secret that Savano had strong contacts with the Mafia which was another motivation to cut the ties. They hooked Anne up with a new American manger, Shep Gordon manager of Alice Cooper, who I was involved with booking some dates on Alice Cooper in Canada. Small world.

Thanks to the dates we were doing with John Allan Cameron Len and I stayed in touch and both of us were happy to exchange information on various situations of interest to both of us. We often would see each other in Los Angeles and do the "Hi what's new" thing over coffee exchanging contacts and catching up stuff. I learned a lot from him. I was really happy for him when he took over the exclusive management of Anne in 1977 and bought Paul White from Capitol Records on board.

In 1971, thanks to everybody's input, Ocean's record took off and was running up the charts. Bill Gilliland had CHUM on side. Both of us were talking to stations across the country and getting co- operation from Rosemary Trombley who had put CKLW in Windsor on the map as a huge station for breaking Canadian records rock and rhythm and blues in the U.S.A. as well as Canada. One thing about Bill he was well known by somebody at every radio station in the country. Thanks to Roy Hennessy in Vancouver, a good friend of Bill's and who was doing the same as Rosemary only on the west coast and thanks to all the stations in between. The band pitched in getting all of their friends to call in to request the record on the Maple Leaf Radio System a group of 22 stations that were supporting Canadian records and got the record a guaranteed 2 week rotation on the A List. The same people that had helped get Caesar on the map did the same for us with Ocean. With everything under control with the band for the time being I flew to New York to meet Neil Bogart who had Ocean's record on the Kama Sutra label, in the U.S.A. and had made the deal for them overseas with Polygram Records. Huge reputation in the business and doing a fantastic job promoting Ocean's record. He told me that he loved it and it would go to the top of the chart. Good meeting with Neil, short to the point. We didn't have a lot to say. He was very friendly positive guy motivated to achieve by whatever means necessary to get the hit. Pure promotion, bullshit baffles brains attitude, and money was no problem. His parties were legendary. I think Bill took a few pages from Neil's manual for his promotions back in Canada. I left New York feeling very positive. The chart numbers was great but I was told we were not generating the expected sales. Weird and no explanation was forth coming even as the record continued to climb the charts worldwide.

Funny thing happened. It was reported in Billboard magazine in October, 1971 that I had left Concept to work full time with Ocean. Not sure where that one came from. It's true I did put Ross White in charge of the agency as general manager but he reported every activity to me so I knew what was going on and could step in anytime if I needed to. It was a fact though that I was spending a lot of time on Ocean.

One of the artists that Caesar backed up in the sixties was Freddy Cannon (Mr. Turn up the volume till you can't hear yourself think). He was a big hit through the sixties. Freddy was a great showman which worked for him. His first hit, "Tallahassee Lassie", was apparently written by Freddy and his mother. Dick Clark liked the song and it got Freddy an appearance on American Bandstand. A couple of more accolades for him before I move on to the reason I mention him here. "Tallahassee Lassie" was covered by The Rolling Stones. "Palisades' Park" hit #3 on the Billboard 100 chart. All in all he had 22 hits on the Top 100 in Billboard and he appeared on American Bandstand a record 109 times. Guess who was the promotion person from Kama Sutra working on Ocean's records? Rhetorical question. Of course it was Freddy Cannon. I met with him in Los Angeles and I swear he hadn't changed a bit. Still as gung ho and loud as always talking about going back on the road performing which he eventually did. Somewhere in there he mentioned that he really liked "Put Your Hand In The Hand". I never saw him again after that one time and I don't know what he did for us as far as the record.

I often wonder what Gilliland said about Neil Bogart in the unpublished book he wrote. An expose' on payola and kickbacks in the record business in Canada and the U.S.A. Somebody suggested that it was a large American record label that paid Bill $150,000 not to publish and imposed a lifetime gag order so we will never know what's in that book. Too bad. Let's guess. Payola, favours and kickbacks for sure. Mafia maybe? All speculation but all probably true. As much as I pumped him he wouldn't tell me a thing until he recently told me that he he doing a rewrite taking out the objectionable material that had caused the gag order.

According to the information available, the "Put Your Hand In The Hand" single never did sell a million units. It was top five or ten on most charts in the world and, #2 on Billboard's Top 100. It was #26 in the top 100 for the year on Billboard. I'm told it sold 680,000 units. I find that hard to believe. So few sales? The guesses range from over a million to 2 million. My guess would have been at least a million. No gold record, no nothing. Same story in Canada. Go figure. That's another "we'll never know" moment. Somewhere in there somebody made lot of money but I don't know who. Sure wasn't Ocean or me.

Despite all the drama, at this point Concept was now solidly entrenched in Canada and I was re- thinking what I was doing. All along the way I worked my butt off to build something and kept getting off track. Duh me! Natural conclusion. No partners. More drama. I tried to buy Terry out but before I could even talk to him about it he just disappeared one day? Word was it had something to do with defrauding the King Edward Hotel of a healthy amount of money? He and a partner had owned a spa in the hotel. That's where the alleged scandalous deed was perpetrated. I think, only a guess, Terry was charged with fraud but, before anything could happen, he split to parts unknown. Total conjecture on my part. No one ever talked to me about it. There were rumours he was in Detroit but then later I heard that he was back doing stuff around Toronto. I never ran into him. That left me owning the agency on my own. He never showed up to ask for a buyout. Later I found he didn't put any money in originally so maybe that explains it. He did surface again in 1974 under his old company name Canadian General Artists, working with Robbie Tustin local agent, and still managing Sea Dog but I never had any contact with him. Let sleeping dogs lie!

CHAPTER 28

Ocean Live in Los Angeles!

The agency was cooking right along so I started making plans to put Ocean on tour. Some time back I had made contact with "the master"; Bert Jacobs at Reb Foster Management in Los Angeles. I was booking a lot of dates in Canada for Steppenwolf, one of the bands Bert managed, as well as John Mayall and Three Dog Night. I was also talking to Jerry Edmonton (Jerry McCrohan), now in Steppenwolfe, and Jerry's brother Mars Bonfire (Dennis McCrohan), the guys who used to check out Caesar at the Jubilee Pavilion in Oshawa, back when I was new in the business. Although Bert and I hadn't met in person we talked often on the phone and had developed a great relationship.

When Ocean's "Put Your Hand in the Hand" was released in the U.S.A., it went viral, quickly hitting number two on the *Billboard* chart just behind Three Dog Night's number one "Joy to the World." Bert and I had started a competitive running commentary: "Hey, Tom. I'm number one in Japan." "Hey Bert, I'm number one in Italy." We went around the world that way. Riding high we behaved, at times, worse than a couple of cocky kids.

Bert had the world by the ass but he still had time to help an up-and-comer like me. He was The Man—the guy first to put rock concerts in baseball and football stadiums. One of the music industry's great managers, he had a storied past and was very connected. Originally a bookmaker in New York, according to the word on the street, Bert got permission to relocate to Los Angeles to move into personal management of artists. Bert swore he was the guy behind a number of big point-shaving betting deals in New York which allegedly was why he had to skip town. Was I going to argue?

I called Bert to let him know I was coming to Los Angeles to try to set up some dates for Ocean. Finally we would meet in person. I flew down the next day. First on my agenda was a sit-down with Jerry Heller the Guess who's American agent and, thanks to their manager Don Hunter, Ocean's new American agent. Jerry was fun to be around and his credentials were impressive. He was an aggressive guy and already successful even though his agency, Heller-Fischel, had just opened. I usually hung out with Jerry when I was in Los Angeles and we had a lot of fun doing the clubs and shows.

Jerry's partner, Don Fischel, was well connected in the television business and the exact opposite of Jerry. An unassuming guy who did everything quietly, unlike Jerry, who was like a bull in a china shop. The first year they grossed almost $2 million and within four years they were pulling in over $7 million. Jerry had originally worked for the Chartwell Agency as the agent responsible for the Guess Who that, at the time, were just breaking into the U.S.A. market. When he left Chartwell and opened Heller-Fischel, he bought the Guess Who contract from Chartwell for $150,000.

Jerry worked with many other artists. He brought in Elton John and Pink Floyd for their first major American tours. He also represented Journey, Marvin Gaye, Joan Armatrading, Van Morrison, War, the Average White Band, ELO, Eric Burdon, Crosby, Stills and Nash, Ike and Tina Turner, Creedence Clearwater Revival, Otis Redding, the Who, Grand Funk Railroad, Black Sabbath, Humble Pie, Styx, REO Speed wagon, the Four Tops, Jose Feliciano, the Grass Roots, and others. Later he worked with some of the top rap and hip hop artists in the world and ended up with a personal net worth of more than $20 million—not too shabby!

Jerry was a wizard at booking but he didn't know what to do with Ocean. The band had been labelled a gospel rock band which it wasn't but the ID stuck. That was the real problem, and it was too late to do anything about it. As I sat in the meeting sizing up Jerry, I thought, "I'm five foot six and a little bit and Jerry is about six two or so, and I'd say 200 pounds plus." I felt he was not the right agent for Ocean but I needed dates. Setting my size worries aside I just had to go for it. I blurted out, "No dates, Jerry. What a huge fucking drag! This is bull and you need to do something!" My heart was pumping overtime—I was actually waiting for my face to be rearranged. Instead he burst out laughing, did the Jerry hug thing, and said he would see what he could do to "get some dates together." To say I was sceptical would be an understatement. I was hoping to get something from Bert that would motivate Jerry.

I left Jerry's office, called Bert Jacobs, and went straight to his office. Once through the door I felt like I had landed on music's Mount Rushmore. On almost every inch of wall space were gold and platinum records as well as other awards. "Hi, Tom this way," said the secretary. Just following her down the hall was worth the trip to Los Angeles. Even the hallway was laden with gold and platinum. We reached Bert's office. The door was open, the lady stepped aside, and I walked in.

"Hey Tom. I'm number one in the world. What do you say now?" "Bert, give me a break. I'm working on it," was my reply. Dumb stuff, but we both laughed. Bert had Coke-bottle lens glasses and wore a wig that looked like he was having a really bad hair day. I tried hard not to stare at it.

I got straight to the point. "Bert, what I need is a high-profile date in a major city soon, while the record is hot--- Jerry's not doing anything."

He sat there for about a minute, saying nothing. Then he leaned forward and opened the humidor on his desk. I figured he was going to offer me a smoke. He was noted for the constant flow of doobies in his office. I leaned forward to look at the goodies. The contents were white and powdery. That humidor was about three-quarters full of cocaine. "Help yourself," he said. So I did a line, well two, well, never mind.

While I was indulging myself, he picked up the phone and dialled. "Bert Jacobs for Golden." There was a short pause. Then he said, "Peter, I need to put another band on the Forum show. Ocean." Another bit of silence ensued. "Put Your Hand in the Hand". Yeah, that one." Bert looked at me and asked, "How much?" I replied, "Five thousand plus expenses, and I'll need some equipment." He repeated that into the phone, said, "Okay," and hung up. "Done. Opening act July 17 in the Forum with John Mayall and Steppenwolf." He told me to call Peter Golden at William Morris Agency to make the arrangements and then broke up laughing. "Peter is really pissed. He hates changes. Call him and he will take care of whatever you need Tom." What to say? "Thanks, Bert. Love ya, man!" I called Jerry and told him to call Golden and take care of the business.

I decided to deal with another problem while I was in Los Angeles. Bill had hired Bob Gibson from the Gibson Stromberg Agency, one of the top public relations companies in the United States. They represented artists such as the Rolling Stones, Elton John, Pink Floyd, the Doors, the Pointer Sisters, Barbra Streisand, Neil Diamond, Jethro Tull, Steely Dan, Earth Wind and Fire, the New Kids on the Block, Crosby Stills and Nash and Ray Charles. Gibson's job was to promote Ocean and their records in America in conjunction with what Bogart was doing. Gibson was supposed to get press coverage for the band, and that meant all media, including newspapers and consumer and trade magazines but nothing was happening.

Gibson was a nice guy. I liked him and he was really well connected in Los Angeles. and generally in the business so the lack of activity didn't make sense. I asked him outright, "What's up?" He made it clear that it was all about the money. "Bill paid me a thousand dollars up front and nothing since, so no money, no deal." Bobby and I talked about the problems and I told him that Bert Jacobs was helping me get some dates for Ocean. After that conversation he became a lot more cooperative and actually did a few things for us for free. Unfortunately, he never got the rest of the money. The problems just kept stacking up.

There was one positive I could count on with Bobby. Front-row seats at any show whenever I was in Los Angeles. He had the best booths and tables in all the bars and restaurants. We went to the Whisky a Go Go on Sunset Strip, where he had his own booth, where we met and then watched Johnny Winter and his brother Edgar perform live. Outstanding! A couple of months later I saw Crowbar there also compliments of Gibson. Also Outstanding! At the Troubadour I got to meet the owner, Doug Weston, and Neil Diamond, who was performing that night. Bobby knew everybody.

While I was on the Coast I also met with Dick Clark's assistant Peggy to see if we could grab a date on American Bandstand for Ocean and the Stampeders. Mel Shaw had referred me. He apparently had a great relationship with Peggy. Dick Clark was partial to Canadian artists and had done his *Caravan of Stars* show in Canada a few times featuring Canadian bands such as the Mid-Knights, the Staccatos, and the Esquires with guest Andy Kim, but so far no date on the show for Ocean or the Stampeders. We never did get one. Mmmm.

We eventually did some television appearances in Toronto including one on CFTO with guest stars Mel Torme, Lionel Hampton, and my old friend Gene McClellan. In the station green room Gene and I spent most of the time catching up from the last time we had seen each other. It was one of those relationships where, even though we hadn't talked for ages, as soon as we got together it was like we'd seen each other just the day before.

The tour organizer for Ocean in Europe, Japan, and Australia was Barry Authors, a Canadian working in London, England and a long-time friend of Gilliland's. The first time I met with him was in Toronto, in Bill's office, to discuss the dates for the tours and what we would be doing. Bill had met him in the early 1960s when Barry was managing an act called the Mexicans (should I have been worried?). He had wanted Bill to record the band but that never happened. Barry made a living booking them on cruise ships and at resort hotels around the world. He managed to get a deal for them with Polydor in the U.K. and that had ushered him into the British music scene. This was beginning to look like a disaster in the making.

Bill had set up a company with Barry to manage two highly touted English bands, Parrish & Gurvitz and Roger Cook's Blue Mink. This deal led to Ocean's getting to record Roger's songs "We've Got a Dream" and "One More Chance" on their first album, plus another one on the second. They were great tunes. Wonderful for the co-writers and the publisher but they didn't do much for Ocean's record sales. Bill Gilliland admitted to me. "I took my eye off the ball, as far as Ocean was concerned, when I got involved with Beatles producer George Martin and the British duo Parrish & Gurvitz. The Beatles had broken up and the British press began calling Parrish & Gurvitz the next Beatles. I thought I'd found the pot of gold!" To say he was distracted would be an understatement.

I asked Bill if we could get George Martin to come to Toronto to work with Ocean or if we could send the band to England. I was thinking. *Just imagine!* I asked more than once but my request was going in one ear and out the other As Bill admits he was distracted. I thought it would be a great marriage. George Martin was somebody Greg Brown could work with. As an enticement I even tried to make a deal to bring Parrish & Gurvitz and Blue Mink over to tour Canada. That didn't happen either.

It was time to get Ocean to Los Angeles. I thought Gilliland was flying out with us but that was a no-go. I flew out on July 15 and the band followed the next day. Pretty well everything was provided so there wasn't a lot of setup to worry about. We stayed at the Sunset Hotel on the Strip because that's where most Canadians entertainers stayed. As soon as I arrived in Los Angeles I had spoke to Peter Golden and Bert Jacobs Thanks, guys!

At The Forum we got a real dressing room and catering plus beck-and-call people. Jerry Heller showed up and had to ask permission to get into the dressing room. Ha!

Ocean was finally onstage ready to play to 17,000 people. The show was sold out and the hall packed to the rafters. The lighting and sound were fantastic. The band was wired, although it took a little time for them to get it together and for the crowd to respond. After a couple of songs there was modest applause and some cheers. I was watching the clock knowing they had only 30 minutes to make an impression. Then the magic moment came. They started the song "Helplessly Hoping" with its amazing acappella harmonies. To this day I choke up when I relive the memory. You could have heard a pin drop all through the song, and when they finished, silence. Then pandemonium as the place went crazy! They received a standing ovation! We would have done an encore if we hadn't been first on the bill. That was an amazing night; I knew that in my soul, having seen some of the world's best shows this was a magic moment. I wish we had taped or filmed it—one of my big regrets. What a promotion piece that would have been. When I saw Jerry, all I could do was shrug: What's the problem?

Janice Morgan, the group's lead vocalist, remembers that night very well for more than the reaction to the show. Jerry Heller had dropped by the dressing room. In her own words:

"Oh wow, do I ever remember that dressing room, the real deal! Jerry and I exchanged some not-so-complimentary words after he grabbed/swatted my ass. Right after that move he grinned and then pulled me towards him, giving me a big hug while laughing his head off. Called me the Ice Queen because I didn't think an ass-grab was what I needed! But the night ended well, with us hanging out. Some dude from *Rolling Stone* magazine was there and he said he'd never seen that much reaction for an opening act before. I always wondered, after that gig, why things didn't start to happen like better gigs, etc. I'm beginning to understand there was a whole lot of stuff going on that I never knew about!"

With the show over and everybody still on a high we left the next morning and did one non-memorable festival date in Minneapolis. The site was in a farmer's field just outside the city. There were a couple of other acts on the show getting ready to perform on a stage that was actually a truck trailer. There were not a lot of people, maybe a couple of thousand, if that. Everybody thought the band was a folksy gospel act. The promoter came over and suggested that we, meaning me, head to his portable office. Knowing what he wanted to talk about I told the roadies to stop setting up until they heard from me. We discussed why we didn't draw a bigger crowd and why he thought we needed to renegotiate the fee. My reply, "I didn't hire the band and I didn't screw up the promotion. I just showed up with the group ready to perform." The discussion got a little heated and more than a bit tense. I offered a simple solution. "No pay, no play", and got up to leave. All's well that ends well. He was pissed off more at himself than me I think. Anyway I got the money and the band performed. We then went back to Toronto to get ready for The European Tour in September.

CHAPTER 29

Bands, Managers and Agents

At Concept, we were now grossing a lot of money and we were growing. Agency competition was, well, competitive but still polite, for the most part. We had a lot of control over the live market and we had earned it. I could count on a hand and a half the Canadian bands we weren't representing or working with. Things were running pretty smoothly as far as I could tell.

As previously mentioned, Elms took over the management of Brutus. He was an aggressive guy. He did a lot for his bands. He had the contacts. Then there was Chris Somerton, (Mr. Corporate). He had a personality that was made for the local business types. He had exclusive clients including Rael Bramer that owned The Gas Works on Yonge St, The Coal Bin club downtown on Adelaide St. and The Generator at Yonge & Eglinton, all of which were high profile and profitable. Great locations to break new acts in. One such band was Scrubaloe Caine who we had brought in from Calgary in 1971 featuring Henry Small vocalist and violin player. They were managed by Don Hunter and were already gathering interest wherever they played. Jimmy Kale, who had just split from The Guess Who under not so congenial circumstances, had been scouting the band for Hunter when they were playing at The Electric Circus Club in Quebec City. Jimmy really liked what he saw. Even better he was asked to play bass for them to which he agreed. One of the most exciting bands I have ever worked with. Scrubaloe was an amazing group that got caught up in the politics between Hunter and RCA. As well I heard Burton Cummings wasn't happy with the time Don was spending with Scrubaloe. Probably had something to do with Jimmy being in the band. In 1973 they released their debut album, Round One, on RCA, which they had recorded in the RCA Music Centre of The World Studio in Los Angeles. Produced by David Kirshenbaum one of the top producers in the business. The sessions were engineered by Brian Christian from Nimbus 9 studio. RCA released a couple of singles off the album with no success and that was about it. A second album was scrapped. Somewhere in there Hunter dropped the band for management. Martin Onrot picked them up for a short time.

Clive Davis from Arista Records in New York and one of the most knowledgeable executives and record producers in the business with a track record that was the envy of the music world had expressed interest in signing Scrubaloe and flew to Toronto to meet with new manager Martin Onrot. I attended the meeting as I knew Clive and I was very involved with the band and Marty. Over coffee in a restaurant we discussed the band but for some reason Marty turned the offer down saying that he felt the band wasn't ready to record yet. Baffled the hell out of me. Clive too. Scrubaloe Caine was one of the best bands I had ever worked with. Lack of material wasn't a problem. Clive could easily handled that but Marty was adamant so no deal. Almost identical to the Crowbar story.

With nothing going on the band split up in 1976 and in debt.

I knew all the guys well.It was another one of my favourite bands and, of course, Jimmy was a good friend. I wasn't involved in the recording side but I should have questioned why the band wasn't hooked up with Jack Richardson or Terry Brown and record in Toronto. Great studios, producers and some strong material available. In hindsight it was a mistake for Hunter or Onrot to manage the band. . Should have made a deal with Bruce Allan in Vancouver. He would have known what to do. After the breakup. Paul Dean, guitar player, headed back to Calgary and ende3d up with Streethearh that morphed into Loverboy. Henry Small, vocalist, formed a new band, Small Wonder, in Toronto and did a couple of moderate successful albums with CBS and then joined Burton Cummings touring band. I stayed in touch with Al Foreman, keyboards, who moved back to Vancouver to write and do studio sessions with Jim Vallance and working with Shelly Siegal at Mushroom Records.Scrubaloe was another disappointing"What if"

My guys were all top agents, well known and respected in the business, and very good at what they did. We were working closely with all the record companies that we had artists and bands with. That is part of the explanation of how we managed to get to where we were at the top of the market. Lawrence Schurman was, probably, next to George, the best agent in the office even though he was always so quiet. Along with Chris Somerton all three stayed with methrough the next five years and were the core of our business. Others such as John Sinclair, road manger for Flying Circus from Australia, Ross White, Fred White's older brotheras my general manger, another unique character that had formerly worked as the on air operator for Duff Roman at CKEY and, as I mentioned, left to form his own angency eventually merging with Music Shoppe. More agents. Larry Cuthbertson from Kitchener who worked with Elmes putting together Abernathy Shagnaster's Wash and Wear Band together with Gil Moore on drums. I thought the name was very creative. Then there was Gary Comier who, with Gary Topp his partner, was also a promter bringing in artits such as The Ramones, The Police with Sting, and Carole Pope. Comier was and is still on of my favfourite people.

At this point I decided to move Concept to bigger offices at 57 Spadina on the Southeast corner of King St. I made a deal with the gas station next door so we now had real parking spaces instead of two in front of our old office and otherwise all over the street collecting a multitude of parking tickets. I was travelling a lot and George was pretty well running the agents. I hired three more assistants. Linda Mouldy, who was involved with Tim Cottini, Rosemary Perruzza and Martha Harron, Don Harron and Catherine McKinnon's daughter, who married Gary Cormier. Can't say our office wasn't friendly. At this point I thought we were getting into a strong enough position to consider expanding. I had built the best team of agents in the country along with a stellar administration staff that was envied by just about everybody which is why most of them eventually ended up in important jobs in other areas of the business. These were the women that kept our ass out of the fire. Huge thanks to them. Everything was working great and the market was hot. Good time to expand. Wouldn't you know Revenue Canada shows up to do an audit? First time ever for me. A pushy little bastard that was rude and obnoxious. We opened up everything for him to review. He kept up a running commentary that was bordering on insolent regarding dead beat musicians, suspected money laundering, dope dealing, downing the music business generally and on and on. I finally had enough. I jammed his stuff into his briefcase and threw it down the stairs. I threatened to do the same with him if he didn't get out. He did. I got a call from Revenue Canada a couple of days later enquiring as to what had happened. I explained and also told them what I thought of the jerk.

Turned out this guy had a record of this kind of behaviour so they would put him in front of the civil service disciplinary committee. They were actually apologizing and said they would send another auditor to my office and that was that. The government doing something right. An oxymoron if I ever heard one. Go figure!

CHAPTER 30

Concept Expands

I saw this quote somewhere and it fit where I was going now. "If you are just maintaining it's the same as standing still". It had been on my mind that if I could establish offices in some major cities in the Central and Eastern Canadian markets that would give us more control on what was going on. The cross Canada market was going ballistic. If I could set some deals that would put our foot in the middle of it all then why not? After some preliminary discussions with people in Halifax, Montreal and Ottawa I climbed on a plane. First stop Halifax to make a deal with Skippy Yorke of The Skippy York Agency. Not a lot of creativity there but he did have a big chunk of the market due in part to Concept's bands. We had been dealing with Skippy for a few years and could always count on him to deliver when we needed it. He was "The Agent in The Maritimes" for rock & roll. A former truck driver and very aggressive in business. We had hit it off from day one. Tough as nails and always ready to make a deal. We sat down and hammered out the details to buy him out and open Concept East. This was done by attending a few establishments that served alcohol beverages and just so you know, I held my own, but barely. I can tell you Maritimers do know how to drink. Somewhere in that alcoholic and drug induced haze we made the deal. Skippy would get a draw plus bonuses on performance. It was a good arrangement for both of us. Win win. In addition, as part of the deal, at my cost, he would ship a box of live lobsters to Toronto every couple of weeks. Yeh!!

There were other promoters/agents who were active in the market in The Maritimes. Brookes Diamond and his wife Fiona were big in the folk and country artists business and were well known and respected. Although I knew Brookes well there was not a lot of that we could do together since my interest was rock. I was also tried to tie Doug and Joan Kirby, another husband /wife team, into the deal They were very strong in the college and university market and acting more as promoters than agents but still booking some of our acts. Mashmakan, April Wine, the Stampeders, and the Guess Who and Downchild Blues Band. Doug was pretty tight with Donald Tarlton in Montreal. He was working closer with Scribner then with me so I couldn't make the deal with them. They also wouldn't work with Skippy. Two so very different personalities so everything stayed status quo which was working fine. I told him about the new deal with Skippy and he was okay with it but would continue to work direct with Toronto. The Kirbys later relocated to Toronto at first to work in Scribner's office and then out on their own doing universities.

Next stop Montreal. Don Tarleton one of the top promoters in Canada with his partner Terry Flood was operating a booking agency for the artists and bands he managed. Tarlton is another one of those that what you see is what you get people who were so easy to work with. Ditto for Terry. Donald was always there. Nice guy but a hardnosed business man who knew how to get creative when he had to. It gets redundant but another one of my favourite people. I spent a lot of time in his office on D'Youville St. in historic Old Montreal as well as hanging out in the bars on Crescent St. where Don and Terry were really well known and celebrities in their own right. We were already booking the bands they managed, notably April Wine and Mashmakan, both very hot acts that we easily kept very busy. As well we had JB & The Playboys, Gino Vannelli and Mahogany Rush. We made the deal for Concept to take over their booking office. There was no money involved. Besides the fact that the agency was losing money The Montreal Musicians Union had told Donald that they were going to revoke his booking license for conflict of interest being a promoter, etc. So I was doing him and Terry a favour. This merger was a definite benefit to both sides. I kept their agent Skippy Snair. He wasn't the world's best booking agent but everybody liked him. He was more of a PR guy, party all night long, and a lot of drugs. He was a character and drove a dune buggy! His job was to keep visitors to the DKD office happy and be available to do anything as needed. He was very good at it. We added Concept to the mix. Donald was already spending more time at our office in Toronto these days. He enjoyed hanging around and all of the ladies liked him. Teddy Bear comes to mind. Interesting point here. Even with the office in Montreal we never penetrated the Quebec market. It was like a foreign country with its own artists and stars. We could do dates in The Montreal Forum and some of the local Montreal clubs; The Moustache, The Wrong Number, The Esquire, Snoopy's, and a few in Quebec City like the Electric Circle bar and we did have a couple of Quebec and Northern Ontario bars on the circuit that were bi-lingual border towns. Rouyn, Noranda and Clottier. That was about it. On the Ontario side just about every town was bi-lingual. On the Quebec side, Not so many and me half French Canadian who couldn't speak French. Shame on my father!

Next off to Ottawa to touch base with Harvey Glatt the Ottawa promoter who owned that market. What to say about Harvey and his wife Louis. Wonderful people who did and do so much for the Canadian artists and what they have contributed to the Ottawa culture. Harvey is another one of those people that it would be easier to list what he hasn't done rather than what he has. My first contact with him goes way back unknown to Harvey. Surprise! Flashback back to 1958 when I was working at CBS Records of Canada as the warehouse supervisor. Harvey and Arnold Gosewich, his partner, had just opened their first Treble Clef Music retail store. The first stand alone music and record store in Ottawa We were shipping records to them from CBS. A few times I had to call the store regarding shipments and returns and probably talked to both of them at one time or another. Who knew? They eventually grew to 15 stores. Arnold left in 1969 and went on to be president of Capitol EMI Records and later chairman of board for CBS Records Canada.

If anything was happening with entertainment in Ottawa good bet Harvey was involved initially with folk acts like Pete Seeger, Peter, Paul and Mary who he booked through Sam Guesser in Montreal, then dance companies and Broadway musicals. Eventually, when Tarlton took over booking rock and roll in Montreal from Guesser, Harvey moved into the rock world co-operating with Tarlton to produce shows for everybody from The Rolling Stones, the Beach Boys, and Led Zeppelin and away we go. Like Tarlton he also had his own record label. We were providing some of the opening acts for Harvey's bigger shows promoting the Guess Who, Stampeders, April Wine, and Mashmakan, Downchild and all our top artists and bands. I set up the Concept Ottawa office with two local agents. Tim Cottini, a former drummer with Marshmellow Soup Group, an up and coming band from Kingston, and Leonard Alexander who had worked with me at Alvin Munch. My thought was that local reps could increase what we were doing along the whole corridor from Toronto, Oshawa, Peterbourgh, Belleville, Kingston, Ottawa, and Montreal and then to the Maritimes.. We were already working with a couple of Ottawa bands. The Children and The Soul Searchers featuring some of the top players from Toronto. Steve Kennedy, William "Smitty"Smith and Dianne Brooks. We worked with the Esquires and the Staccatos who later, changed their name to the Five Man Electrical Band, and had some great hits. "Signs "and "I'm a Stranger Here", both big hits in the U.S.A. With Ottawa in place that very much established us in Eastern Canada. We did continue to work with other agents and promoters in all the markets as well as booking the high schools and universities. The agencies were smaller then Concept but very important links in the chain. Notably Dram in Kitchener, Larry Cuthbertson with Crossroads Talent Agency in Toronto, Herb Loch in Hamilton, Ron Metcalfe in St. Catherines and Jim Skarratt who was the promoter for McMaster University. When I got back to Toronto I got a call from Eddy Schmiel who owned Montreal Talent Associates in Montreal. He had heard about my taking over Tarleton's booking agency. He was interested in selling me his agency. He had been approached by Donald a year before but had turned him down because the money wasn't as good as he could do on his own. He was making great money split-booking Tarleton's acts as well as booking his own. He had just spoken to Donald who told him that he had sold his company to Concept in Toronto. I asked Eddy. "Why would I want to buy another Montreal agency"? His reply got my interest. "Wouldn't you like to buy one that's profitable?" Good attitude. I discussed the proposal with Paul Simmons, my business manager, told him to contact Eddy and make the deal. Simmons flew to Montreal and met Eddy at The Skyline Hotel. The agreement was that Eddy would close Montreal Talent and take over the Concept Montreal office. His draw would be $350 a week plus a bonus on performance plus a $5000 buyout for closing his office. Good deal for both of us. Eddy told me later, when word got out, he had a call from Scribner who flew to Montreal to talk to him face to face and offered to beat any offer that Concept made. Eddie's choice. Work with the number one agency in Canada or number two? No contest.

TID BITS

Quote: Eddie's comment. "With my $5,000 bonus, I went and bought myself a brand new 1973 Ford Mustang. My first new car. I was 21 at the time, felt quite successful, and on the road to bigger and better things. Dreams do come true."

The Western Canadian companies were all strong in their markets so my trip west was mostly a goodwill tour to reinforce our relationships. We were working closely with Bruce Allen on the coast. Had been since 1967 but It wasn't until Concept in 1972, that we made an exclusive deal to work each other's artists and Sam Feldman came on the scene as Bruce's partner. It was a great arrangement other than Bruce and Sam constantly bitching about the difference in the prices of the bands. They would book ours in Vancouver for $2500 a week or better, while we were getting theirs just $1000 to $1500. It was a draw power value problem, plus Ontario was a larger, far more competitive market. We had to work hard to improve the image of the western artists. Eventually, the prices started to level out as their bands got better known. That gave us access to Brave Belt who became BTO, Streetheart, later, Lover Boy, Doug & the Slugs, Trooper, The Powder Blues Band, former Montreal native Jerry Doucette, the Poppy Family's Susan and Terry Jacks, Stonebolt, Chilliwack, Valdy, Bim and The Hometown Band. The Seattle immigrants Heart as well Nick Gilder's Sweeney Todd who was dominating the charts with No.1 single "Roxy Roller". Bruce's market was mainly Vancouver but he was now also doing a lot in the western circuit through to Winnipeg as well as working with DKD.

Bruce and Sam are great examples of agents being managers. Bruce was and still is one of the best in the business that made the transition from being an agent to an outstanding manager while Sam, who was previously more management then agent oriented, would become the predominate agent in the business in Canada while still maintaining a management office. Of course, they stayed partners with the required separate offices to avoid any friction between them that has been duly noted by both guys. They were like Frick & Frack. A key person in their organization was Ingrid McDougal, Bruce's office manager, a constant mediator between the two. Lou Blair owner of The Refinery bar in Calgary later tied in with Bruce & Sam to co- managing Lover Boy.

Now that we were working closely with the Guess Who manager Don Hunter a lot of doors had opened for us in the U.S.A. with booking agencies, promoters, managers, and record labels. We spent a lot of time in each other's cities. Our agents were now household names in the Canadian business. Most of the bands were recording and working more regularly. We were either representing, or working with, just about everybody that was anybody with few exceptions.

CHAPTER 31

The Concept Ladies Alias The Strumpets.

Back in Toronto come on down Ms. Joni Wall aka Joni Elms Concept's new public relations person. The blonde bombshell formerly with a four piece all girls band called Eight of a Kind. Cute play on words. She was also formerly George Elm's wife. She was multi talented. This lady taught me to have a more open mind and a truly liberal outlook in life. Moral judgement was not an issue. In addition to public relations she took over as our bookkeeper which made my business manager, Paul Simmons, a very happy man. He never did take a liking to Ross White. She gave artist relations a whole new meaning. Enter Burton Cummings Burton and Joni. They met at the Nimbus 9 studio where the Guess Who was recording. They very quickly became an item. I remember one night Joni was supposed to pick up Burton at The Inn on The Park and deliver him to the El Macombo where the band was performing. They arrived late. Apparently they had lost track of time. We were all really pissed off and I had to have a conversation with Joni about priorities. In one ear and out the other! I am sure Hunter said nothing to Burton. I was getting calls from Burton at 2-3 in the morning, asking for her phone number. Not sure why he didn't write it down. Joni also had a short relationship with Gary Peterson, drummer for the Guess Who, around the same time. I think it may have been a mother thing. Joni was and is still a most favourite friend who never ceases to amaze and amuse me.

In 1971 enter the amazing Pegi Cecconi, our first female agent, who blossomed in the music business. Originally from Sudbury, Ontario, she was the rep booking the bands for the Rollin Richards High School. She desperately wanted out of Sudbury so Lawrence Schurman, who was booking the school for us, talked to me about hiring her. He was really high on her abilities so we agreed he could tell her that she should come to Toronto to work with Concept. Pegi jumped at the chance. She fit in right away and became a member of our slightly warped family. As with all new agents we gave her the dead file contacts. She actually made it work and booked quite a few dates. She did mention a remark that Lawrence had said. "Women can't be agents". Hello? It was his idea to bring her in? Lawrence. Chauvinist? Hard to believe but Pegi doesn't lie. As she started to succeed she says he also tried to steal her contacts. Truly family spirit. Besides becoming successful as an agent Pegi was another one of those who became a good friend. Love Pegi. She was and is the kind of person that, if she was your friend, would walk through fire for you. Once again. What you see is what you get and that is considerable. She, Joni, Barb Onrot, Shawn, Martha Smith and Gale Moss who was a friend of Bill Ballard, would get together and show up at the bars around town on a regular basis where our bands were performing and would literally take over the room. Great looking ladies, great public relations, slightly intimidating. Shawn came up with the name "The Strumpets" (Another term for whore first used by Shakespeare to describe loose women.) That said it all, tongue in cheek, and the ladies loved it. They even had the own room every year at The Juno Awards where they carried on with their fun and frolic and drinking their brains out along with the drugs and becoming a legend.

Pegi left Concept in 1975 to work with Ray Danniel's Music Shoppe and Ron Scribner, I admit I was disappointed. She did a good job until Ray fired her. She then tried to do some booking on her own with Downchild until Vic Wilson took the band away from her. Pegi told me at this point she was so disillusioned and did the right thing. Retreated back home to mom and the womb. She was nineteen. Her mother told her she had to get her butt back out there and get a job. No mercy! In 1976 She landed a job when Bernie Solomon called her and asked her to come to work with him. It would have been a challenge but it was the place to be to learn all about the music business beyond being an agent including exposure to publishing, sub-publishing, master recordings and licensing, and oh yeah, law, all of which would be invaluable in her future. She knew zip when she started but Solomon let her do everything and she was a quick study literally inhaling it all. She got to travel all over Europe first class and staying at five star hotels meeting some of the heavy hitters in the business there as well as the U.S.A. and many other countries around the world. By the time she left Solomon she finally got what she wanted. The opportunity to bring all her new skills and knowledge to the table and in 1978 joined Ray Danniels this time in SRO Management managing all the affairs of the company and the now very successful band Rush. Solomon pushed her to get Ray, the company, and the band to sign with him as clients but instead they went with Bob Farmer who had formerly worked for Bernie. Great move! Pegi was appointed vice-president of the company and as far as I know, along with Danniels and Sheila Posner she runs the place. One of her favourite lines "My greatest skill is that I screw up everything, but I only screw it up once."

TID BITS

Norm Amadio legendary jazz pianist who became a well-known figure from coast-to-coast in Canada as Musical Director for the weekly Music Hop show on CBC Television for five years as well as performing with Stan Getz, Carmen McRae, Peggy Lee, Coleman Hawkins, Flip Phillips and Chet Baker Joe Williams, and Lester Young is Pegi's uncle.

Sheila Posner was another one of those exceptional people. I called her "The Lady" however she was later renamed "The Dragon Lady." Sheila was and is one of the more beautiful and intelligent women I have known. I first met her when she was working for Eddie Glinnert's Fredrick Lewis Agency and Wayne Thompson. She worked with us only for a year then joined Music Shoppe, then SRO, and today manages the all the financial operations for Rush.

TID BITS

For a while there I started to feel that I was running a training school for agents and administration staff. On the bright side most of my "graduates" went on to very successful careers in the business.

If I were to gauge when the music business in Canada turned a corner it would be 1968. By 1971 I was managing Ocean and Brutus, The Guess Who had broken out in the U.S.A. with "These Eyes" and, April Wine, Mashmakan, Crowbar and The Stampeders were all hot in The Canadian Market and starting to make noise in America. Everybody was recording. Lighthouse had just formed and started their amazing rise in the business. I already knew and was friends with Skip Prokop formerly The Paupers. I got to know Paul Hoffert co-founder of the band with Skip and a brilliant musician very well. They were and still are one of my favourite bands. Loved the music and the whole big band concept. The road manager was Bruce Bell. He and I worked on a lot of dates for the band over the years. I First met him when he had an office in the same building as Glinnert and then, later, moved to The Thunder Sound studio on Davenport. The band was instrumental in opening a lot of doors for me just by association.

A big plus for me was Vinnie Fusco from Albert Grossman's office. I had worked with a few of Grossman's artists, Gord Lightfoot, Jessie Winchester, John Lee Hooker, and the Paupers of course, as well as knowing Bernie Finklestein and the guys in The Band including former Caesar Robbie Robertson. All that sure didn't hurt. Working with Vinnie was a bonus and meant more contacts for Concept. Our bands were now playing in every nook and cranny available. Live rock music was the predominate music everywhere. One of the movers & shakers was Terry Brown who I met in 1970 at The Toronto Sound Studio not far from the musician's union office. This was Toronto's first 16 track studio that Terry and his brother owned. Busy, busy. Working with many of the artists and bands that we were booking. Ian Thomas, Thundermug, Motherlode, Dr. Music, April Wine, the Stampeders, and with a track record that included Jimi Hendrix, Sonny and Cher, Kenny Rogers, Traffic, Joe Cocker, the Who, the Dave Clark Five, Rush, Procol Harum, The Troggs, Rough Trade, The Moody Blues, Small Faces, Manfred Mann, Barbra Streisand, Marianne Faithfull, Spencer Davis Group, Donovan, and, as usual, the list goes on.

The bands were making good money. So were the agents, managers and everybody else, especially the drug dealers. Business was booming! Lawrence Cuthbertson and George Elms partnered on a new band, Abernathy Shagnasters Wash & Wear Band, which I thought was a really creative name. The leader was Gil Moore, a local independent agent, who would later, along with Mike Levine and Rik Emmet, created Triumph one of Canada's most successful bands internationally. Truth was I really wanted to have Gill involved with Concept as an agent. He was good. It would have been an interesting merger.

About this time Cliff Hunt showed up looking for a job. Cliff had played in Brass Union, a great horn band from Hamilton that worked regularly from the time they started in 1962 till they folded in 1972. A very impressive run. His father was Colonel Hunt, musical director for The C.N.E., in Toronto. Cliff Jr. was at Concept for a while at our Spadina office. I put him to work as an agent with the Dead File, that famous list of high schools, and other contacts that almost never booked bands. I put him in an office with Pegi. Give him credit. He worked his ass off and did actually get some dates going. Working with Pegi didn't hurt. One short story He got a Thursday date at a local high school for Breathless, one of the bands we working with. It was an off day, which was always considered a "found money bonus date". In comes George Elms, my right arm, who also managed Manchild, formerly Five Shy, and Greaseball Boogie Band. Elms saw the paperwork and asked Cliff what he was doing putting Breathless on a date when Greaseball was open? Needless to say the date went to Greaseball. Sum it up to the pecking order. Not fair but an unwritten policy. Elms was the top producer in the company. Greaseball was making Elms and Concept a lot of money. A lot more than Cliff or Breathless. This was common practice in most agencies with a large roster and agents managing bands. It did, eventually, become a conflict of interest problem. Not only was Concept the number one booking agency we were also the largest with a staff of 10 or more people depending on any given day. We were making a lot of money but I can say that, for the most part, the egos never became a problem. I guess working with musicians helped. When I heard what happened I felt sorry for Cliff but had to let it pass. Give him credit. He hung in but his heart was never in it and finally, a year later, I did him a favour and fired him. It was a good thing for him. We became friends and still are today. Thanks to his dad, Colonel Hunt at The C.N.E and Billy O'Conner he immediately tied in with Billy's son Gary O'Conner to run the shows on the C.N.E. Band Shell stage plus working with his dad on the Grandstand Shows for the next couple of years eventually as an assistant producer working with artists like Johnny Cash and June Carter, Ray Charles, Red Skelton, Charlie Pride, the Beach Boys, Alice Cooper, the Band and Linda Ronstadt. They used mostly Concept bands on the band shell as well as some of the support acts on The Grandstand. All's well that ends well. There were a few problems with the band shell shows. Colonel Hunt had difficulty with the new wave music artists. His background was in the military as head of all music for the newly formed combined military forces. The problem started with Murray McLaughlin, remembering that Murray is a folk/country artist and not exactly controversial. Colonel Hunt had confused McLaughlin with the McLean Brothers, a toilet rock act, very controversial. A not even close misconception! Bernie Finklestein, Murray's manager, took it to the press and surprise! Colonel Hunt had to do a public apology for his error. Another band, Tite Ass, had to change their name to Shazam to play the band shell. After all this time still fighting to be accepted by the older generation. Young Cliff Hunt went on to an amazing career with his company Yangaroo that revolutionized the music industry moving it into the digital world controlling the voting for The Juno Awards and The Grammys and expanding worldwide.

Another story I just remembered. George Elms and Chris Somerton shared an apartment for awhile on Finch Ave., near Yonge St. in Toronto. Skippy Yorke, in the Halifax office, was flying the lobsters in every couple of weeks as we had agreed. Some of us would get together at George and Chris's apartment and have a lobster fest with the usual recreational substances. We had our own suppliers. Wayne, a former RCMP cop, provided marijuana as well as huge slabs of hash and Bob, our other dealer, many ounces of cocaine and other fun chemicals. Great fun and good bonding which says a lot about our state of minds. One day, during one of our lobster fests, Somerton came up with a deal for us, through one of his clients, the rep at Mohawk College, in Hamilton. Brand new TV's at bargain prices. We all jumped in. Price was around $275 a set. That's when TV's were going for 6-700 dollars or more. Somerton took the money, passed it on to the contact, and arranged to meet in three hours to pick up the TVs. The contact called with directions to meet at the drop spot, a gas station in Thornhill. Somerton trailed the truck in a Diamond Cab towards the meeting place when the truck suddenly took off down an alley and disappeared. It was a scam! Everybody's money was gone just like that. The Mohawk rep was no help in locating the guy. In the end Chris ended up having to pay everybody back. Cost him around $3000. Hell of a lesson.

CHAPTER 32

My bad judgement bites me.

n late 1971 I brought Vic Wilson back from England. I needed somebody to run the agency as I got busier with Ocean and Brutus as well as working the American market trying to put some reciprocal deals together with the agents and managers. I had known Vic for years. He was originally a sax player with The Little Diane & the Starlights back in our Bigland years. The leader was Tony Crivaro who had started the band first as Ko Ko and the Vikings then changed the name to the Starlights and brought Vic on board. Vic and Tony used to come out to see Caesar a lot at Crang Plaza and Masaryk Hall. Tony was influenced to start his first band because of what they saw, heard, and liked about Caesar. In 1968 Vic joined Caesar. I left him in charge of Concept as the president. The things that come back to bite you in the ass! In retrospect I should have given the reins to Eddie Smeall. He was much more suited for the position. No hidden agenda and interested in growing the company. This is where we get a bit of a twist in the story. As it turned out hiring Vic was not the best decision I ever made. While a very sociable guy Vic was not good as an agent or president. Everybody was "Paley". He gave a couple of the guys nicknames. Chris was "Tits". No idea why. Vic's favourite word, "Ballox" (Australian slang.) Here is the twist. He did nothing. He was okay with public relations but about as loyal as, well, not at all. I couldn't believe it. He got a call from Ray Danniels to meet and talk about Vic going into partnership with him to manage Rush and a couple of other bands. Ray had his own agenda. He hoped that he could diminish the power of Concept by taking Vic to Music Shoppe. Always open to an opportunity Vic agreed. A good move for Vic and, under the circumstance, for me even though I didn't know it at the time. In retrospect I should have made a deal with Danniels and amalgamated our companies which would have given us everything. A combined agency with Concept and Music Shoppe. Name to be decided. We would have a record label, publishing, management and, of course, the agency. That does sound familiar? We would have to find a name for the agency. Little play on words there. Not only did Vic leave without telling me but he tried to get Lawrence Schurman to go with him. Lawrence declined because he didn't like Danniels. I was mostly disappointed with Vic because he didn't tell me about the deal or the move. Of course I wouldn't have been happy even if he had but I would have least understood. But that was Vic and it would take a lot more than that to break the bond of friendship we had however, later on, he actually accomplished that too.

Early 1973 Danniels and Vic formed S.R.O. as a management company for Rush. By 1975 Vic had worn out his welcome with Rush and the rumour was that Danniels was told that either Vic goes or the band would. He left with a very nice monetary settlement. Other than that small blip we had good people that were great at what they did. We can't forget Mr Tim Cottini, The Great Cotteen, who I re-located to Toronto and closed the offices in Ottawa and Montreal as they had turned out to be an exercise in futility. Leonard Alexander left the company and moved to B.C. He shows up again later. Skippy Snair went back to work with Don Tarlton in management.

I kept working with Skippy Yorke in Halifax but he was, once again, on his own. So much for my multiple office idea. Was I disappointed? Yes but, "nothing ventured nothing gained".

Back in Toronto. David Bluestein (Blue). He first showed up working at The Rockpile, in 1968 then, in 1970, he worked as a road manager for Michael Cole's company, Cymba Productions. I hired him because no one at else would. Nobody trusted him. He was an intelligent guy and had access to a lot of people. He wanted to be part of the group and fit in. He was driving the guys crazy to book King Pest, his band. He was the drummer. Finally enough. "Look", I said. I'll give you a desk, a phone and some high schools to call and you book the bands". Blue was happy. I assigned Lawrence to coach him. He was a handful for sure. He smoked dope all day, every day. First thing in the morning light up, last thing at night light up. It took forever but finally, one Friday, he landed his first booking. It was late. He and the school rep agreed that the rep would send a confirmation telex on Monday. Come Monday Blue came to Lawrence devastated. The rep he was dealing with had died over the weekend in a car crash. Quote from Blue "I can't believe the kid died".

I was now talking to a lot of American agents and managers looking for Canadian representation or the opening spot on their tours.

On the family side in 1971 we had moved out of the penthouse to 15 Litzgate Ave. a three bedroom 2 storey townhouse in a family complex at Leslie and Sheppard Ave. E. In North York. In April Shawn was pregnant again and I was getting Ocean's European tour organized.

CHAPTER 33

Ocean Disaster

I t was time to take Ocean on the European Tour. The band and I flew out of Toronto on September 6, 1972 to Paris, France. The Polydor Record rep met us at the airport and took us to the hotel they had booked for us. Paris was just a four day stay over. We didn't doing much. Met the record company people and sightsee. We ate and drank a lot. At least I did. I do remember we had to leave our passports at the front desk of the hotel. The people were nice enough, if a bit aloof. That could have been because I didn't speak French but with some arm waving and hand signals I got my point across. From Paris, on September 10 we flew to Hamburg, Germany on Luftstanza Airlines arriving early in the morning. Again we were met by a Polydor promo rep. This time, a great looking young lady with "that accent" was on hand to take care of us. Loved the German accent. Loved the German women and loved Germany. After we got settled at the hotel the lady picked us up and drove us to the record company head office to meet the president of Polydor Germany who introduced us to all the staff and gave us a tour of the city. We did a couple of interviews. All in all very efficient and organized as one would expect in Germany. Jeff and I tried hustling the promo rep who very nicely rebuffed our advances and even that was attractive. Oh well. I think we were there for 2 days and then flew to Milan, Italy on Air Italia. I swear the wings of the plane were flapping like a bird it was so old. Met by the promo rep at the airport and driven to the hotel to meet the president of Poydor Italy and his" WOW!" 18 year old daughter! A knockout! Jeff and I were in trouble again. We had two days to do some promo interviews and roam the city with the daughter as a guide. Strike two. Not from lack of trying. I felt I was losing my touch. Up to this point I was beginning to wonder what the hell we were doing here. I called Barry Authors and he tells me that we have to do this promo stuff with the record company before we could tour live. The idea didn't make sense to me but I let it go. That was a mistake. I had forgotten Barry's previous experience was booking his band on boat cruises.

The band flew to Venice in Italy while Paul the roadie and I drove in a rented Fiat station wagon. Top speed 80 miles an hour or 90 if you got going down a steep hill, loaded to the roof with luggage. Always thought it was just going to flip over on its side if I turned too fast. For those of you that have been on The Autostrade, the famous hi-speed highway, you will appreciate the lack of lunacy of driving this car on The Autostrade. If there is a speed limit I don't know what it was. I just kept my foot to the floor. Two lanes, one for passing and, in this car, you needed to be seriously disturbed to even try to pass, not that there was ever anyone in front of us. Through the rearview mirror you would see this little black dot coming up on you and then whooooooosh gone by at what felt like supersonic speed. I tried to watch as the Massarettas, Ferrari's, Mercedes and Lambergetis flew past like we were standing still, but the wind from their passing was like a jet stream, so I needed two hands on the wheel as the Fiat threatened to get blown away. I almost got out of the car to see if we were really moving. We arrived, unscathed, and abandoned the car, gladly, in the parking lot, boarded the boat to Venice and on to the Eurotel Lido Hotel where we were staying. I was feeling more like a tourist then a band on tour. Outstanding tourist attractions all over Venice. St Marks Basilica in San Marco piazza, the food, glass blowing, gondolas the women and pigeons, hundreds of them. You had to wade through them.

We didn't play live on any of the dates except one. September 15, the only "Live" performance and that was a lip-sync of "Put Your Hand in The Hand" on stage at The International Music Festival in Venice. It was televised all over Europe. That's it. September 17 we flew back to Toronto almost in time to celebrate my son Tommy's fourth birthday on September sixteen. Better late than never.

I am told the tour was successful but you could have fooled me. I kept waiting to hear the dates that were being set up for a real live tour in Europe and England. Good thing I didn't hold my breath.

On our return to Toronto, I kept the band busy playing. One show at Ontario Place that went well and a couple of other dates locally then a short tour out west starting in Winnipeg for The University of Manitoba.

I lucked out and did an overnight with a fitness instructor. That perked me up but I don't think Janice approved. The next day a two and half- three hour drive for a concert at Brandon University in Brandon, Manitoba. Getting there was the dullest drive; I'm sure, in Canada, until the amazing Aurora Borealis aka The Northern Lights showed up. We had to stop to watch. What an absolutely beautiful light show. That's when you learn the power of the universe and the value of good marijuana. If you haven't seen them on the bucket list! After Brandon on to Klondike Days in Edmonton. I was trying to generate as much press as could be had but wasn't getting as great a reaction as I hoped. Not that it was bad, just not exciting. That done back to Toronto and get ready for Japan.

TID BITS

On October 18, 1972 my son, Jeremy Ryan Wilson, was born at The North York General Hospital across the street from our townhouse. What a beautiful baby!

Ocean- The Far East Tour- March, 1973

The promoter for The Far East tour was Mr. Ohno in Tokyo. His representative was Daniel Neneshkis, a tall white Russian, younger guy, that flew to Toronto to meet with me to discuss the dates, conditions, arrangements, the fees, etc. and, of course, to meet the band. We ended up with all expenses paid including any instruments we needed, production costs, travelling and hotels plus a cash fee of $3000 per date... This excluded any personal expenses incurred. With that agreed we all looked forward to a great tour. We had decided that Randy Barber would accompany the band and, subject to scheduling; I would join them in Sidney, Australia for the Aussie tour. All of this on the strength of one single.

On March 17, 1973 Randy and the band, flew out of Toronto to Honolulu, Hawaii. The first concert dates on the tour. This time they were actually playing live. This would be another I blew it. Should have been there. That's what I was supposed to do, run things. Barber was great but he listened to Greg. I wouldn't have. I don't know if it would have changed things but I like to think so. Moving right along, the other dates were Tokyo, Yakama, Osaka, Taipei, Hiroshima, Okinawa, Taiwan, and on to the Philippines. At Clark Air Force Base in Manila, where they had to stop the show while a squadron of B52's flew over so loud you couldn't hear yourself talk. Remember the Vietnam War was happening. There was almost an incident when Greg refused to play "Put Your Hand In The Hand" because the piano was so out of tune not to mention badly in need of repair. Not to play was not a good idea with so many weapons in plain view in the hands young edgy soldiers. The band almost got beat up. Fortunately clearer heads prevailed. Things were very tense. The band nearly broke up right there. It just keeps on coming! On to Subic NB, south of Manila, the last date on the tour. The band was supposed to go on to Australia but I had a call from Barry Authors, the tour co-ordinator, that we had a glitch. Surprise! There would have to be a three week layover in Tokyo before the first date in Australia or the band could fly to Sidney and park in a hotel. Neither the band or me could afford to do that. Barry Authors couldn't get Polydor to foot the bill and no way was Gilliland fronting any money so the band returned to Tokyo. I spoke with Ohno and Daniel, as did Randy, but they couldn't or wouldn't do anything, despite the success of the tour and promised return dates, everybody was out of money. Left with no choice I cancelled the Australia tour. Randy had to use his credit cards to get the band back to Toronto. It took a long time for him to get the money back. None of us were very happy and that was, I believe, the turning point in the future of the band. Absolutely no co-operation from the record company for touring or anything else and, most important, no financial support. What should have been an amazing opportunity turned out to be a failure. In June, Gilliland, on Yorkville's dime, rented a cottage for Ocean on the shores of Lake Simcoe at $1500 per week for three weeks for the purpose of writing and arranging new material for the next album and to rehearse. I was told that they spent a lot of time stoned which was probably just as well. Total waste of time. The second album, "Give Tomorrow's Children One More Chance" went out to a disappointing reaction in Canada and The U.S.A. Nothing was happening. There was no motivation, no confidence. There was nothing left that I could do so I stopped working with the band in late 1973. It wasn't a formal parting. Sort of a drift away. We just stop talking. They continued to perform, played a couple of dates locally including a week at the Sapphire tavern and some dates out west and in the U.S.A. Greg Brown was back in charge. I believe Kevin Hunter, manager for Natalie Cole, picked them up and kept them working mostly in bars. Craig Nicholson from *Pizzazz Productions* also managed them for a short time. In 1975 they had a chance to sign with Jack Richardson at Nimbus 9 but, after a rehearsal run in the studio, Richardson wasn't happy and suggested some changes one of which was to have one lead singer only. Janice. He thought the male/female duo thing was long gone. The band turned the deal down. Richardson offered to sign Janice only. She passed opting to stay with the band? They folded shortly after. What a waste.

From 1976 to 1980 Barber was the talent agent for Holiday Inns in Canada and then went to work with Bud Matton Agency as an agent. Rehab time. Both he and Greg Brown ended up at Music Shoppe as agents. There are a lot of reasons that Ocean failed and you can't put the blame on any one person. Let's start with me. Should have made a deal with Albert Grossman to co-manage or manage the band. Albert was a huge Canadian artist fan and represented some of the best performers. The Band, Gordon Lightfoot and Ian and Sylvia as well as Americans Janis Joplin, Bob Dylan and Jessie Winchester. Ocean was a perfect fit. I met Albert in 1969 when I was doing my meet everybody thing spending a lot of time in New York. I was working with Jessie Winchester doing dates in Canada. Jessie was a draft dodger so it was a given that Albert wanted to keep him out of the U.S.A. for the time being. Tom you stupid person! Make a deal with Albert to work with Ocean. I was not thrilled with his twenty-five percent management fee plus a piece of the publishing. Never entered my mind. Next error. Going into partnership with Greg Brown on the management. Starting to feel really stupid. Greg was a control person. Me too. No karma. I knew everybody and had the contacts. I should have taken control but didn't and paid for it. Gilliland lost it because he was too busy with George Martin and the English connection as well as the other artists he was working with. I had seen the real thing in Los Angeles on the forum show. We never achieved that level again. I did chase my contacts in the U.S.A. looking for opening spots on tours but with only one hit and a gospel image that was wishful thinking and an exercise in futility.

Jeff Jones went on and did amazing things including touring with Tom Cochrane's Red Ryder and also tours with Burton Cummings as well as doing his own solo recordings The guitar player; Dave Tamblyn opened a business creating strings and bows for violins. Chuck Slater, the drummer had personal issues that pushed him to end his own life. Janice was apprehensive about everything. She didn't realize she was the star in the band. Imagine what could have happened if she had gone for the deal with Richardson. We will never know. So fault, in no particular order of degree of responsibility, me, Gilliland and Greg. Gilliland wasn't the only one that fumbled the ball. We were so close. For me lesson learned. I never managed again.

TID BITS

Randy moved on to become The Chairman of the LCBO, The Liquor Control Board of Ontario. Cool!

CHAPTER 34

Back to booking

So you ask. What the hell was going on with the agency while I was running around all over hell's half acre? In fact the company was operating normally and making money thanks to the guys taking care of business.

On August 31, 1972, I booked the Guess Who into The C.N.E. Grandstand for a guarantee versus a very large percentage of the gate. Great fun. The cash office was in the roof of the Grandstand way up there, 1800 feet in the air, overlooking The C.N.E. grounds. Like being in an adult toy store, watching the money counting machines riffling away on the bills. We walked away with the largest fee the band had made up to this date. Also Concept's largest single agent's fee. By now the Guess Who were huge, doing 60 sometimes up to 90 dates a year in Canada, and the U.S.A. I was hanging out a lot with Don Hunter and hitting some of their dates in both counties. One memorable one was in Chicago. I flew down on March 13, the day before the show, and hooked up with Hunter to see the concert the next day. This is where I first encountered the famous - infamous Plaster Caster, Cynthia Albritton, a young lady whose goal was to make plaster casts of the genitals of any rock person she could convince to co-operate. There were more than a few takers and the lady became well known on the rock concert circuit. Never had the opportunity to be immortalized myself.

A little trivia here. I had found what became my favourite restaurant where I held a lot of my private meetings. It was The Surfin N' Turf operated by Tommy Considine, an amazing Greek chef and his wife Sofia. It was on Yonge St. a couple of doors north of the old Bigland office. The front looked like a typical steakhouse as did the first room inside with all the heavy red drapes decor and dimmed lighting. Then there was a backroom that was bright and simply decorated, very comfortable and with a curtain between the two rooms so it was private. We took the kids there a lot and they loved it. Their favourite appetizer was escargot with a seven up to drink.

Hunter considered himself a gourmet and a connoisseur of fine wines so one night I took him to the restaurant and introduced him to Tommy and Sophie. A night to remember. He put Tommy to the test talking about foods and wines. He actually was very knowledgeable but not in Tommy's league who had everything he was asking for in both foods and wines. I just sat back and enjoyed the contest and the meal.

It was an expensive night but well worth it. Tommy later told me that after that night Hunter would show up every so often with other people and spend a lot of money. That's what you call a good promotion.

I had called Sid Bernstein at GAC in New York to discuss working with him booking dates for some of his artists in Canada and working with some of my artists in the States, in particular Ocean. I asked for a meeting. We had first met when the David Clayton Thomas and the Shays were booked on the Hullabaloo TV show in 1965. He agreed to meet so I flew to New York. Here is the strange part. Out of the blue he told me he wanted to write a book and asked me to help him with it. I have no idea why he would ask me. I told him I knew nothing about book writing or publishing. He replied, and I will never forget his words, "I trust you". We never did work that one out. I made a few calls but it just wasn't my thing. How ideas change. As far as Ocean he didn't have anything because they only had the one hit and it was history by now.

I had transferred Ed Smeall from Montreal to Toronto and had closed that office. In addition to himself, he brought Mahogany Rush and Frank Marino with him as the exclusive agent.

Eddie was far more valuable in Toronto then he had been in Montreal. He fit in very quickly. He and Lawrence ran the high school department, and had created their own system. I still had to see all contracts that went out to Buyers. A rule that saved my ass a few times. The high school kids loved to talk to the agents. I guess it was exciting to be involved in the music business, so the guys set up a game. Using an egg timer, they had to close the deal within six minutes or they had to pretend they had another call coming in so they had to get off the line. Sometimes, when they got bored, they would page each other just to impress the kids. "Mick Jagger on line 2, Yoko Ohno on line #3."

One time Eddie came to me with a problem. He had a band cancel a gig at an out of town high school, his first cancellation at Concept. He came to me for advice on how to handle it. It was a Wednesday. In those days, the smaller schools held their dances on week nights because they couldn't afford to pay the weekend prices. Eddie asked me, "What should I tell them?" He thought he had a great excuse, a lie, but one that they would believe. I said no. Just tell them the truth. They might not like the reason but at least you will never have to remember what you said. Eddie tells me that to this day he always remembers, and practices, that advice. Always tell the client the truth, buyer or artist. They may not like it but they have more respect for you in the long run. Almost always worked for me.

I was still away a lot travelling across Canada and in the U.S.A. When I was around, I was mostly doing the 9 to 6 thing because of my young family so George was pretty much in charge most of the time. There were a lot of drugs around the office, but mostly recreational. coke, hash, marijuana and acid, all of which served as promotional vehicles. I had just finished a Concept 376 Promotional Album. This was a first for a Canadian booking agency. It featured 12 songs by bands we represented, plus credits for another 38 that we were working with. I remember when we attended a Canadian College Conference in Kitchener in 1973 we had our own booth and hospitality suite. Our guys and girls went to work. We were very quickly the suite to be in for fun and frolic as well as the best talent available. It was difficult to see through the fog and there was a lot of snorting, coughing, and laughing. We dominated the conference and solidified our hold on the university market This album was an amazing promotional vehicle for us as it quickly became the collector's item at the convention.

As I mentioned earlier in 1973 Michel Cohl, Bill Ballard and David Wolylnski had opened CPI (Concert Productions International) with a five million dollar loan from investors that included Harold Ballard. C.P.I. grew to be one of the most successful concert production companies in the world. Michael, along with Don Tarlton, controlled the important live concert business in Canada along with their associates across the country One of their first moves. A lock on Maple Leaf Gardens for future concerts.

Marty Onrot had been the promoter for Elton John, in Toronto since 1968, and had brought him into Maple Gardens twice in 1972, September 2 and October 5. When he tried to book Elton in the Gardens again, in 1973, he was turned down. Michael had arrived, and shut the door for anyone else to run concerts in the Gardens and there is no question that was aimed directly at Marty who was, at the time, still the big promoter in town as far as number of shows. That was it for Marty for any future dates at the Gardens with any artist. Marty quickly shifted gears and put Elton into Massey Hall for two nights instead. Sold out both shows. That was my first time meeting Elton. Great Guy, very open and friendly. Great show. It was a little tougher way for Marty to go but it worked and the more intimate seating didn't hurt. The important thing to note is that CPI now had an exclusive home base with the most important event venue in Canada. It didn't take long before there was no competition.

The Tour that was but never was.

I booked a reunited Steppenwolf tour with Onrot. Four dates. Ottawa, Kingston, Hamilton, and London, through their new manager Bobbi Roberts who was a musician, producer, record executive and film producer. With partner Hal Linden, he had started his new label Mum Records and He had just signed the Steppenwolf for recording. To date the band had sold $45 million dollars worth of records worldwide. They had just released a new album so I thought we would do really well with Marty's dates. I first met Bobbi when Johnny Rivers played the Beverly Hills Hotel in Toronto, in 1964. He showed up as Johnny's agent. We hit it off right away and agreed to try and do some things together He had just founded Dunhill Productions which became Dunhill Records the following year. Bobbie also managed other performers such as The Mamas and Papas, Richard Pryor, Mort Sahl, Mama Cass Elliott, Paul Anka and Ann-Margaret. We had stayed in touch over the years and had a good relationship. He was aware of my relationship with Steppenwolf and CBS Records. Mum Records was distributed by CBS in Canada so it was like old home week for me. Marty paid a large guarantee plus a percentage over a break point. The first date was in

Ottawa. A very small crowd. A disaster financially but the band was great. The second date, in Kingston, was an even worse disaster. At this point Marty wanted to cancel the last two dates and settle. Roberts refused. It got pretty tense with lawsuits threatening from both sides. In the end Marty and Roberts settled and the remaining shows were cancelled. Now here is the catch. Very quirky. There is no record of this tour anywhere that I can find. I recently contacted Bruno Ceriotti, a knowledgeable historian of rock & roll and who is an expert on his favourite band, Steppenwolf. Bruno lives in Bari Italy. He writes for the Los Angeles Free Press, has a 60's Music Facebook page, and is a journalist, writer and radio host. His information on the band is extensive he has no record of the tour either. I spoke to Goldy from the band but he doesn't remember the dates The only rational I came up with was that it was only two isolated dates that didn't draw so nobody cared enough about it to notice.

As an aside Onrot had just hired Paul Simmons as his business manager. Not that it mattered, but Paul wasn't happy with either one of us after this tour. Shouldn't have had a problem with me, I got paid for all four dates 'by Roberts and Marty.

CHAPTER 35

Concept at The 1974 Juno Awards

Against my better judgement, I had agreed to put Bob McBride out on tour. He had been with Lighthouse since 1970 but was released from the band in 1973 after a pretty impressive run of hits and Juno awards. The reason given was because of a suicide attempt, the first of many apparently. Bob's personal life was a mess He was depressed, doing drugs, and it was showing on stage too many times. He had convinced me that he was okay and needed to do the tour to get back on track. I liked Bob as a person and a performer so I said yes. The agents worked their butts off putting the dates together in the Maritimes. Not an easy job. He wasn't Lighthouse, and the personal problems persisted. Then he dropped the hammer. Out of the blue, no reason given, he cancelled the tour. The cancelation was written up in Billboard but no reason given there either. Later we heard that he flew to England with Peter Sherwood, a Vancouver promoter/manager to arrange some deal. Never heard what it was. What a pissoff. Another waste of a great talent.

Sherwood shows up here and there in the business. I had met him a couple of times, neither one of them memorable. His big claim to fame was Reveen, a magician and Impossiblist He tied in on a CHUM Presents with Duff Roman at Massey Hall. Very successful. Who knew? Later, in 1977, Sherwood and Duff got together to promote the impossible dream: "THE CONCERT IN THE SKY". Billed as the world's largest rock festival to be broadcast from the top of the CN Tower. They spent a year promoting the concept but, in the end, couldn't figure out how to make it work and make money. They were going to use some of our bands thanks to Duff. Today it would be a no brainer. Give that one to Arthur Fogel so he could say no.

TID BITS

In 1974 Ted Woloshyn, the noted broadcaster on CFRB 1010 in Toronto started his career as a dj on CHIC Radio in Brampton. Ted's Grandfather was Rudi Vallee. America's first teen idol!

A big happening for the industry in 1974 was the opening of Attic Records in Toronto by Al Mair and his partner Tom Williams. They were flying high right out of the box. Hottest independent label in the country and dedicated to developing Canadian talent. They had great contacts in the U.S.A. and overseas. We were working with quite a few artists on the label. Fludd, Downchild Blues Band, Goddo, the Nylons, Teenage Head, the newly formed Triumph, Jesse Winchester and the Lincolns. There was a whole new load of promotions going on and an excitement in the market. We were not working exclusively with any of these bands but we were doing a lot of dates on them so this was a bonus for us and we had a new place to hang around a lot. I have known both Tom and Al since the early sixties when they were promo guys for various labels and Mair had worked as general manager with Early Morning Productions managing Gordon Lightfoot's career. I have followed and been impressed with them ever since. What an amazing impact they had on the industry.

Larry LeBlanc was spending a lot of time in my office and earlier in the year he and Shawn decided to put a promotion company together. A first of its kind in Canada in that they were concentrating on the print media while all of the competitors were concentrating on the radio and television media. The company name was Media Machine and the office was in Larry's house on Walmer Rd. In Toronto. It started out strong with the first client being EMI-Capitol Records. Arnold Gosewich, the President, gave them the corporate account as well as access to all the artists on the labels. That netted them Sylvia Tyson and Peter Donato on individual contracts. The contacts were all Larry's and Shawn was great at talking to people so it was a workable union. It, unfortunately, didn't last long, only a couple of weeks. I didn't know until much later why not. One day Larry walked into the office and Shawn was there with Juan Rodregas, the entertainment writer from The Montreal Gazette, sitting on his lap. He took one look at them and said "No Shawn. I can't do this" and walked out of the room. He did not tell me about this until many years later when it didn't matter anymore.

Meanwhile, back at the ranch, I thought things were going great for me. In February I had put an offer in on an elegant three story house in the Moore Park area at 7 Inglewood Drive near St. Clair and Mt. Pleasant Ave. in Toronto. This was a big step up for the family. It was such a rush. Ten foot ceilings on the main floor and more rooms then you could shake a stick at. We planned to move in after The Juno Awards in March.

March 25, 1974, for the first time, we attended the Juno Awards as a company. Concept had a suite at The Inn On The Park where the ceremony was being held in The Centennial Ballroom. Big night for us despite there being no award category for agents. We shared the success of the many of the artists we were working with who were either nominated or won in almost every category. Our suite was one of the busiest in the hotel as The Concept Team entertained artists and business friends in our usual fashion. Lots of booze and drugs. It was an over the top success for us and our artists. We were the only agency represented in full force at the convention. Oh Oh! Walking around the ballroom meeting and greeting people I spotted Shawn making out over in a corner with Juan Rodriguez! I had thought she was hanging out with her girlfriends in The Strumpets room. Whoops. My past came back to haunt me. I didn't confront them, just turned and walked away. Mixed emotions. I was embarrassed for me and angry at her for what she was doing but I was also relieved as our relationship had been deteriorating to the point we were arguing about everything almost constantly to the point that it was getting abusive. I learned to stay calm when she was verbally exploding at me. It made her angrier until one night she lost it, got physical and heaved a heavy crystal ashtray at me just missing my head. I retaliated by going into her closet took all her clothes out piled them on the floor and jumped up and down on them laughing like a fool. More fodder for a shrink. It was just a matter of time before something had to give. Enter Juan.

Fortunately I did not see her or him after that encounter. Later I was told she had split to Montreal with Juan and without saying goodbye to the kids. That was cold. I had become an instant single parent. I experienced the feelings that I'm sure Joanne did when I left her. Proves the theory that what goes around comes around. It certainly put a damper on my celebrating Concept's success at The Junos. Things were getting weird to say the least. I moved into the Inglewood house with the boys and quickly hired a nanny to take care of the house and help out with the boys. The amazing Sofalita. She had just arrived from Jamaica. She was a short, stout, wonderful black woman who loved children and my boys loved her back. She was so sweet and kind and had the tiniest voice. She fit right in. We had our new family and bonus; Lisa, my daughter, being around a lot more often now that Shawn was out of the picture. I had to work out schedules for everybody and got the boys enrolled in schools. Tommy in Deer Park Elementary and Jeremy in Montessori French Immersion. One of the perks of the house was a third floor room that I set up as a playroom and put in eclectic trains, Selectric racing cars, a helicopter that could fly around in circles and a ton of other toys. The rules were simple. The boys could do anything they wanted to in that room including crashing the cars into the train or any other havoc they could think up but, only in that room, nowhere else in the house. It worked although I winced whenever I saw the holes they had smashed in the walls. The house was a lot of fun for us. The boys shared a bedroom, Sofalita had her own room and I had the huge master bedroom with a fireplace. They were happy, Lisa was happy, I was happy, Sofalita was happy and we settled into a comfortable family routine.

CHAPTER 36

A great year for Concept

975 was a great year for Concept. There was an article in The Toronto Star that listed The Top Fifty powers behind Canadian pop music and I was one of them. One thing I had done all the way along, from Bigland to Concept, was develop a close relationship with Billboard magazine. I got lucky when I made connection with the top salesman in the Chicago office Steve Lapin. That got me introduced to Lee Zhito the publisher. Later Steve became the sales rep for Canada and eventually he also became a good friend. I spent a lot of money with him and Billboard but it paid off with all the free stuff we and our bands got. It wasn't always about the booking. Our biggest plus were guys like Marty Melhuish and Larry LeBlanc as Canadian Reps for Billboard plus contributing writers like Ritchie Yorke and David Farrell. The crown jewel for the year was when I was invited to head up a panel of experts from the Canadian Music Business to do an open discussion at the 1975 Billboard International Talent Forum, in Los Angeles, June 4 to 7. Great articles in Billboard about the panel mentioning The Top Fifty in Canada article. This was certainly one of the most important promotion opportunities I'd ever had. Everybody that was anybody in the business would be there from all over the world. Heads of all the record companies, publishing companies, the top agents, promoters, managers, the best, and the most powerful people in the business. Bill Graham, Dick Clark, Frank Barcelona, Clive Davis, David Geffen, Herb Alpert and well pretty well everybody that was anybody. My panel was made up of Al Mair, from the new star on the block, Attic Records, Alan Wood president the Toronto Musicians Union and

vice-president of the American Federation of Musicians, Bruce Allen Bruce Allen Talent manager of BTO and Lover Boy, Bill Ballard, Maple Leaf Gardens and CPI, John Murphy, ABC Records and Dave Garrick, general manager The Canadian National Exhibition in Toronto and a director on The Canadian Fair Association board of directors. Great press leading up to the conference. There was a talent showcase in the main convention room that held about 300 or 400 people. I had, as a favour to Burton Cummings and Don Hunter, booked Maclean & MacLean a singing comedy duo that they were working with. Concept was doing their booking in Eastern Canada. They did a toilet rock mix of rock and folk type humour that people loved. Their material was off the wall raw and bluntly offensive. I don't know what possessed me but I was concerned about the reaction of this crowd so spoke to the guys and asked if they could tone it down this one time just to play safe. They could be funny without the toilet material. Their theme song was a rendition of "Yada" titled "Fuck Ya" and another tune was 'Lickin' My Dick'. Get the picture? They were produced by Skip Prokop (Lighthouse) on a live album and Jack Richardson on a studio album with Burton singing a couple of songs. Quite a controversy with Burton's record label They didn't want him to do it. I crossed my fingers and hoped for the best. The other act I booked was Foot in Cold Water who ended up getting stranded in the Halifax Airport and couldn't make the show. Not batting a thousand here! Long story short McLean & McLean went on stage used the filthiest material they had and cleared the room within five minutes and I mean empty except for the Canadian group which were sitting there in total shock. That would teach me to try and tell artists what to do. How stupid was I? Needless to say a lot of flak on that one from, well, everybody. Most importantly from Lee Zhito, the Billboard publisher. I had the Mcleans at the airport on a plane back to Canada within an hour. Poor Marty Melhuish almost lost his job with Billboard over this mess.

Quote from Marty "If I hadn't delivered some large advertising-filled supplements to the magazine on Canada, Quebec, Gordon Lightfoot etc, I would have probably got the boot".

I had a great ally in the Chicago sales guy Steve Lapin who covered Canada and who was also embarrassed with this fiasco. Fortunately, on the positive side, my panel was a hit as one of the most controversial and heated discussions of the convention. Later in conversation with Lee Zhito we had a few laughs at the memory. Whew.

TID BITS

I bought my first Mercedes in 1975. Great car. Loved it. Shortly after Wayne Thompson told me he also bought one because his Dad told hi m that the Mercedes showed you had class. Then George Elms bought one and Tom Williams from Attic. Vic Wilson and Ronnie Hawkins bought Rolls Royce's. "Welcome to Hollywood North".

In February one of our most popular artists Gino Vannelli had appeared on Soul Train television show broadcast from The Apollo Theatre in New York to sing his latest A&M hit "People Gotta Move" becoming only the second white artist to perform on the show and he was spectacular. The song had made it to number 22 on the Billboard Top 100. His next single "I Just Wanna Stop" reached number 1 in Canada and number 4 in the USA earning him a Grammy Award. We tried a new idea. Gino's manager was Richard Burkhart who, over the years, also managed Canadian William Shatner as well as Chris de Burgh, The Carpenters and Herb Alpert, Gino's mentor, and president of A&M Records in the U.S.A. Alpert had signed Gino for the label as well as The Tijuana Brass, The Captain & Tennille, Prince, Pat Boone, Lou Rawls, and also managed Natalie Cole replacing her former manager Canadian Kevin Hunter. We booked Gino into Mike Lyon's Colonial Tavern on Yonge St., in Toronto. A&M was all over the date promotionally as were we and the media. It was reported in The Toronto Star, that for a two week run in July he drew over 7000 people, mostly women, and set a house record.

FYI. Forever Young News Flash February 16, 2015 (Darrell Dick/Toronto Star) "Gino Vannelli is pictured in July, 1975 at The Colonial Tavern in Toronto where he drew 7000 spectators over a two week run. He was described by The Star as a "pampered artist" who's body gyrates wildly to the beat of the music, it was reported that his sexuality has caused women to faint, most recently in New Orleans", but he feels being a sex symbol doesn't mean he can't be taken seriously". "I'm not into shaking my behind for the sake of shaking my behind" he insists. "I'm into singing my songs".

I booked Gordon Lightfoot and Liona Boyd into Edmonton's Klondike Days. First time since the early 60's that I had the opportunity to book Lightfoot because of his annual canoe trips on different rivers in Canada which were always in the summer when all the fairs were operating. Gord and I flew out together from Toronto. Out came the scotch and coke. We both carried our own. I love flying first class. The stewardess's looked the other way except when they asked for Gord's autograph. By the time we got to Edmonton we were in decently mellow shape. When we got to the arena Liona was having a stage fright thing going on. I thought she was going throw up. Women that beautiful and talented do not throw up. We all did our best to calm her down; after all it was only 16,000 people. She got it together. Just her on a chair, on stage, alone, and she blew them away. Gord went on did his show and he never missed a beat. Standing ovation. Great band with Red Shay on guitar. Worth the price of admission. Still in awe to this day. The man's consumption level was incredible but it would take its toll. Let me add here. Gord was and is, in my opinion, one of the most iconic artists and writers in the history of music folk, rock or otherwise and a Canadian Treasure. Also a fun guy.

The Guess Who Farewell Tour

October, 1975 and the last tour for the Guess Who. I can't speak for anybody else but for me it was not the happiest tour I had ever been on. A four city concert tour with opening acts Mike Quarto, a recording artist from Detroit who's sister, Susie Quatro, was a huge star. Starting in Toronto then to Hamilton with promoter Jim Skarrett and Ottawa with promoter Harvey Glatt. Bill Wallace, the bass player, apparently with some heavy stress issues going on, came close to a nervous breakdown in Ottawa. On to The Montreal Forum for Don Tarlton. This was the last show of the farewell tour. It didn't sell out. We had all piled on more promotion with the media and Larry was grabbing interviews a couple of weeks before the gig. The Guess Who was never that strong in Quebec. We ended up about three quarters sold. Nevertheless they played one hell of a show and gave the people that were there a memorable rock and roll experience. Burton was amazing and Dominic on guitar was outstanding.

Here's a story shared by Larry LeBlanc prior to the last date the Guess Who performed. RCA Records had set up an interview for Burton Cummings and Dominic Troiano with Juan Rodriguez the entertainment writer at The Montreal Gazette. Remember him? Burton didn't want to do it because Rodriguez had given him a bad review previously in Cream Magazine. It was a fuck you kind of review of the Guess Who album "Road Food".

LeBlanc set up the interview. Burton calls Larry (LeBlanc) at four o'clock in the morning and he's wasted. He wants Juan's phone number. Larry gives it to him. Burton calls Juan and says they talked for an hour and he told Juan what he thought of him and his article and was apparently quite abusive. Larry spoke to Juan later who told him not to worry about it. The interview was okay even though Burton was a dickhead and actually pretty funny. Burton told Larry about the conversation and said that this would fuck up the article he and Donny were about to do. Larry said no there would be no problem with Juan and bet Burton three sweaters that they had seen in clothing store in Montreal worth $100 bucks apiece There was no problem and Larry won the bet.

Juan Rodriguez's Rock 'n' Roll Life- Week 5 Special to The Gazette 02.14.2013; Quote Juan re Burton. "The Guess Who never had my blessings but a promo tour in 1975 brought us face to face. The group was on its last legs and I wore a brand new Guess Who T-shirt for the occasion. (I had no clean change of laundry, I swear). Politesse reigned during the Q&A. But at 5 a.m., my phone rang." If I woke you up, I'm glad!" It was Burton (Cummings) on a bender, seething over my review of the 1974 album Road Food, which I trashed song by song for Creem. "Do you know the harm that review did us?" he blathered wildly. "Why don't you go back where you came from, you wetback!" The interview got good space with no mention of the unfortunate call. His PR rep phoned, apologizing profusely. "It's nothing personal," I replied. "It never is: Some of the nicest people make the worst music and vice versa."

After the show at the Forum we all gathered together for an insane farewell party at the world famous Queen Elizabeth Hotel on René Lévesque Boulevard West, in the heart of Downtown Montreal.

TID BITS

The Queen Elizabeth Hotel is the hotel where former Beatle John Lennon and Yoko Ono conducted their world news Bed-In in 1969. "Give Peace a Chance" was recorded in their room by local producer Andre Perry and became an anthem of the American anti-war movement during the 1970s.

Everybody that had anything to do with the Guess Who was there. On the bedroom dresser a dinner plate brimming with cocaine, bags of marijuana, hash, booze galore and a ton of food. I'll spare you the details other than to say there were some hilarious incidents as evidenced by a lot of heavy duty hangovers that would be part of our immediate future. The next morning Larry LeBlanc and I flew back to Toronto to take care of business. The next day we flew out to Winnipeg for a special "Guess Who Day" where the band would receive the keys to the city from the Mayor. We were all still pretty messed up mentally and physically. Definitely challenged people. It's called stamina. Flying home to Toronto after another party was a quiet trip which for me was not only a good thing it was mentally and physically required. Shortly after this show and not necessarily relevant, other than the timing was suspicious. Almost everyone connected with the Guess Who were audited, That includes the band, the manager, the record company, the accountants, Larry LeBlanc the publicist and even the technical crew for suspected tax evasion but not me. I have no idea why not. This was all related to Hunter not paying tax on the band's income not just for 1974 but many previous years and it expanded from there. Hunter lasted another year running his company and by then it had been discovered how many bad investments he had made for the band. The big one. The Grand Prairie Shopping Centre in Grande Prairie, Alberta. Huge financial disaster. This all brings up the question. What the hell was he doing?

When I look back at what The Guess Who accomplished I have to wonder how much "right place right time" came into play for Hunter. Jack Richardson was doing all the recording and made all the deals with RCA. Jerry Heller loved the band and kept them booked whenever and wherever they wanted to be. At least 80 to 90 dates a year. As I previously mentioned he and his partner Don FIshel had left Chartwell back in 1970 and opened The Heller Fishel Agency in LA on Sunset. Jerry paid Chartwell $150,000 to release The Guess Who contract and moved them to his agency. He made his money back and then some in the two years. Jim Martin, Jumbo, the Road Manager, was handling everything as far as touring and taking care of the band on the road. In other words what was Don doing? Obviously one thing for sure, bad bookkeeping. I don't know what happened with him after all this. One story has him owning a chicken farm in B.C. He certainly never showed up again in the music business. Just sayin. Jimmy Kale later registered the name the Guess Who. Great move. He is still touring a band as the Guess Who.

More disappointing news. Crowbar was packing it in despite an amazing shot at success. Same old problem. Too many fingers in the pie and in trouble financially with mismanagement of their funds by their representatives. What a shame. Sound familiar? One of the great bands. We had a good run with them and I made some good friends, especially Sonnie Bernardi, The drummer. Another What If?

In 1975 one of the biggest moments in my life happened at The Ports of Call where I had continued hanging out but now only on Saturday nights when I could so everybody knew where to find me when I wasn't working. It was a great release. I didn't have to think and it was always busy. One night I saw Eddy Smiel, one of the agents that worked with me, coming through the door with a young lady in tow. Her name was Lucy Delima. She tells the story of our first meeting much better than I could so hear it is in Lucy's own words.

"I was doing volunteer work for a church youth group and Eddie was the agent who'd booked the band "Maiden Canada" for a dance at the church. It was a Saturday night. He came out to the gig to make sure everything was going well. After the dance, he came up to me and started telling me about his "boss." He couldn't say enough nice things about you and then asked me if I wanted to go meet you at the Ports of Call. I agreed to go with him. It was just the two of us. When we arrived he stood at the door looking around and then exclaimed "There he is!!" pointing at the stage. You were up there singing with the band. He spotted some co-workers at a table upstairs and we went up and sat with them. Upon leaving the stage you came upstairs and sat in a chair beside me with Eddie on the other side of me. As rude as it was on my part Eddie saw only my back for the rest of the evening. Once you and I started talking we didn't want to stop. When The Ports was closing you asked the gang if they wanted to go eat somewhere. Most said they did and you called Sai Wu's which was about to close. There were 8 of us; you, me and 6 of your staff members. (Don't know why I remember that number.) Magically, to me, Sai Wu's stayed open just so they could serve your party. We went there and sat eating and drinking until the wee hours of the morning. Eddie was long gone and you offered to drive me home. I invited you up and we talked for a couple more hours. At around 6:30am, I walked you to the door. You leaned in to kiss me and our front teeth clashed because I was smiling at the time. We both laughed at this. You gave me your business card and asked me to call you. On Monday afternoon, I called you. Your receptionist answered the phone and asked who it was. I told her, "It's Lucy." She repeated my name and this was followed by laughter throughout your office. I was embarrassed and almost hung up but you came on the phone and explained that she thought it was the lady from "Lucy's Open Kitchen," who was somewhat strange. Anyway, the rest is history."

I was thirty-six. Lucy was nineteen and born on December 21, the same day as Joanne, my first wife. I am not sure if that means anything as far as my choice of women. The next month or so was a complete dedication to pursuing and hopefully winning Lucy. I wined and dined her, sent roses to her office and did everything but stand on my head. (I would have done that if she asked). I took her with me to a pre-screening of the film JAWS that Scott Richards had invited me to. It was in The MGM Building on Victoria Park. They had a small movie theatre on the main floor. It was very crowded so Lucy had to sit on my lap. I wasn't complaining. This was all totally contrary to my usual approach. I was GOBSMACKED! (I always wanted to use that word.) I told her I was in love with her and got an "I love you too" back. We talked for hours on end and finally I asked her to stay over at my place to meet the boys and Lisa. I immediately assured her she would have a separate bedroom. She agreed and soon became a regular at the house and shortly moved in permanently. My personal life was wonderful. Lucy and I moved our relationship step by step to another levels. We both had a history. Layer by layer we learned from each other and began to heal. I had issues as did she. Hers were more physical and physiological while mine were all physiological. Lucy had been abused very badly but slowly and surely we drew it all out and discovered the joy of true love mentally; emotionally and physically. It was amazing!

CHAPTER 37

Nashville fun time

n late 1975, on the recommendation of Paul Simmons my business manager, I moved my offices to his building at 125 Dupont St., near Davenport. We took the 2nd and 3rd floors. Based on what transpired it would appear a couple of things were happening there. I was spending a lot of time on my personal life and not on the business. Paul stepped over the line and may have gone a bit too heavy on the guys about the issue of employer versus employee status. Not sure where his head was at. It was none of his business. I was unaware of this. I had always thought of all of us as a team and had never treated anybody as an employee. Paul's remarks may be why Chris Somerton resigned to work full time for Rael Bramer booking all his clubs. He went on Rael's payroll and off mine. He still used our bands though.

Business had started to slow down thanks to the Disco craze. The new dance groove was hurting the live market everywhere. I started looking for ways to cut expenses. We weren't broke. Just careful. I met with the agents and told them that everybody had to take a cut or I would have to let some people go. They all agreed to the cut. We ground out the next few months until things started to improve.

A lot was happening in 1975. Thanks to my friendship with Sol Holliff who had managed Johnny Cash. I had been negotiating with Waylon Jennings and Willie Nelson's people to represent them for touring in Canada and I had set up Larry LeBlanc to handle the PR for a proposed combined Canadian tour. He co-ordinated with Barry Hogan who was the promotion person from RCA Canada, Waylon's label at the time. They flew down south to meet with Waylon &

Willie at the Red Rock Amphitheatre just outside Denver, Colorado. Larry tells me Waylon was happy with the tour idea but wanted nothing to do with the press or interviews. Willie assured Larry he would handle anything Waylon wouldn't. I wasn't worried either way. Both artists could sell out on word of mouth.

I flew to Nashville to meet Waylon's people. George Dasinger, who worked closely with Waylon, set up the meeting. Dasinger was also the manager of Goose Creek Symphony The Number One Gravy Band an incredible southern rock band I was also booking in Canada. We were doing a Western Canada tour with them through Frank Wippert which was starting in Winnipeg a couple of days after I finished my meetings in Nashville. George picked me up at the airport and delivered me to The Spence Manor Hotel on Nashville's Music Row known for its party atmosphere and guitar-shaped pool. I had flashbacks about my Uncle Eddy who had built my first amp. I know he would have given up something precious to be where I was. I dropped off my luggage and then we went on to Waylon's office.

Talk about organized. His operation was like a well tuned machine. The office occupied a large room. A round table sat in the middle with phones spaced about every three feet. Four guys were on the phones co-ordinating dates for performances, recordings. Merchandising, the media and whatever. They all stood as they talked and everyone was pumped. The atmosphere was electric. If Hawkins had put it together like this he would have been a Superstar. I had thoughts of doing the same in my office but knew my people would likely reject the set up. It was like being the floor of The Stock Exchange.

After a tour of the office we sat down to discuss the deal to tour Waylon and Willie in Canada. We poured over the details for the next couple of hours. I thought it went well. George dropped me back at The Spence and told me they would have an answer for me the next day but to consider it a done deal. He said he would pick me up later in the day for a tour of Music Row and to some of the clubs around town. When he showed up that evening with a couple of the guys from the office he dived right into the first order of business. He promptly laid out a line of coke on the coffee table in the form of a question mark about 6 inches long including the curve. "Excuse me?" I said, "Who's first?" "Uh That's just for you Tom", was the reply.

That night we did the rounds. I met Hank Williams Jr. A big moment for me. I had been following his career with interest and had considered calling about doing a Canadian tour. What I didn't know is that just a year prior to our introduction he had almost OD'd on Darvon a very dangerous pain pill. Hank was three years old when his father died at age twenty-nine from a lethal combo of alcohol and speed. Hank Williams Sr. was an icon in country music. By the early 70's young Hank was following in his father's footsteps anaesthetizing himself with booze and painkillers. He had been pure country playing his dad's music till lately. Due to some of my family, including my uncle Eddy, I was brought up on country music as well as big band jazz, R&B, blues and rock & roll. Hank Jr. was just getting into the new sound that blended country with southern blues and rock. He was considered a junior member of the Outlaws an exclusive club created by Waylon, Willie and Johnny Cash to offer an alternative to the traditional Nashville template for country music.

No question, there was a lot of amazing and diversified music coming out of the south. Hank and I talked for quite a while and I asked him if he wanted to play up in Canada. He asked "Why" I told him "Well a lot of your friends went North to perform like Ronnie Hawkins, Levon Helms, Conway Twitty, Elvis, Waylon, Willy, Carl Perkins, Jerry Lee Lewis and they all loved playing in Canada." He knew them all. I got him excited about Canada and I knew, after seeing his show, he would knock them dead. I told him about the tour I was doing with Goose Creek Symphony. He knew the band and liked what they were doing. We agreed I would talk to him about a tour. Hey! Nothing ventured, nothing gained.

We arrived back at the hotel around three that morning. I think it needs to be said here that when it came to drinking and other recreational pursuits with these guys I was an amateur way out of my league. They were still talking and laughing while I was having difficulty even seeing. Totally blotto but still standing. I got through the side door of the hotel and out of sight immediately went down on my hands and knees. *I* found out later that's why there was a side door so you could enter the hotel and avoid the embarrassment of going through the lobby. Crawling to the elevator I hit the button for the second floor hoping to find my room. It was a good guess although finding the room number was a challenge. If you want to have some fun try opening a hotel room door when the key is bigger than the door. At this point I was laughing my head off at my ineptness. I somehow managed to get the door open and closed. I slept on the floor rather than tackle the bed which looked enormous and in my state would have been as challenging as mountain climbing.

Later that same day I met with the guys at the office who gave me a high five for still being able to function. Ha ha very funny. I had gotten my taste of southern hospitality and Lady Luck had helped me. I now had in my pocket the Waylon and Willie tour with the bonus of a possible Hank Jr. tour so I left town on a high, literally, very happy to fly directly to Winnipeg to kick off the Goose Creek Symphony tour with Frank Wippert and Larry LeBlanc. Awesome tour! Every date SOLD out or close to it. The band was incredible. The down home approach worked well. They liked Vancouver so much they decided to stay for a while and record an album.

TID BITS

Waylon was Buddy Holly's bass player and was supposed to be on the plane that crashed in Clear Lake, Iowa in 1959, killing the pilot as well as Buddy Holly, The Big Bopper and Ritchie Valens. Waylon had taken a bus instead.

From Vancouver I flew to Carmel, California to meet with Dan Weiner and Fred Bollander the owners of Monterey Peninsula Artists one of my favourite American agencies. Paul Goldman the agent I worked with was a great guy and we hit it off immediately. The agency was in a house just outside Carmel right on the ocean.

Once again my personal life became a problem. Shawn was back in Toronto and wanted to see the kids on a more regular basis. I agreed and the first couple of times went okay. I was the only one who answered the door when she picked them up and returned them. Then I got a call from Sofalita that Shawn had showed up and was in the living room with a couple of her friends laughing it up and smoking joints. I raced to get home and told all of them to get out and warned Shawn that if she wanted to keep seeing the kids she would not be allowed inside the house but wait outside until I brought them out. Same rule when she bought them back. Sofalita was very frightened and had hidden upstairs. I got her calmed down and told her in future she was not to open the door for Shawn when I was not home and to call me. Things settled down after that but unfortunately Sofalita never got over it and shortly informed me she was going back to Jamaica to get married. She told me about her cousin Nidia who had moved to Canada and was looking for a job so I met her and hired her as the new Nanny. We were all very sad when we said goodbye to Sofalita. We all loved her.

CHAPTER 38

Terry Dean. To Mob or not to Mob

My new agenda with the agency was a proposed partnership with Marty Onrot and Terry Dean, a new acquaintance who was, previously, in charge of running The Lakeshore Film Studios for John Barry. The concept was to operate three companies under one umbrella. Marty would be the promoter with his international contacts, venues, record companies, artists, managers and agents. Terry would handle all the film and television projects. I would be the agent. Marty and I were well documented as the saying goes, Terry not so much. Although he did have some heavyweight contacts he kept a low profile.

We agreed on the terms and I sent the proposal to my lawyer Shelly Vanek to draft. I got a call from him a couple of days later. "What's up?" I said. "Well", says Shelly, "You might want to check out Terry Dene some more before you put this deal together". "And why is that"? I asked. Shelly replied. "I have been talking to a few people I know and his name keeps coming up". That's close to verbatim. As I mentioned earlier in the book Shelly had some interesting and well connected, albeit questionable clients, so I trusted his instincts and advice.

I called a detective agency that he referred me to that he knew was discreet and experienced in this type of investigation. It cost me few bucks. Ten days later I received a hand delivered eight page report. I won't bore you with all the details however the report was a mind blower. Here is a condensed version and it's verifiable.

Terry was English. His mother and he migrated to the U.S.A. in 1957 and settled in Miami. He joined the United States Air Force in 1959. On leave in Daytona Beach in 1963, he was busted for disorderly conduct. Also, in 1963 he was court-marshalled for passing bad checks. He became an American citizen on April 14, 1964. That same year he showed up in Detroit working at The Playboy Club. Then, in partnership with Theodore Licavoli, he ran Ted-Terry Productions, an artist management and booking agency. The building where their office was located was owned by Peter Licavoli and Joe Bommarito. Dean was good friends with Peter Licavoli, identified as being one of the four controlling Dons of the Detroit crime family.

Dean spent a lot of time at the Licavoli ranch in Tucson, Arizona. Joseph Bommarito was named as a top echelon member of the Mafia. According to the report he also kept company with Joe Bonanno, identified as the head of one of the five Costra Nostra families in New York. Needless to say, I was more than just a tad concerned. Terry was, well, the wrong kind of connected. The list was impressive and scary as hell. One close associate, Anthony Giacalone, was in front of a Grand Jury in Detroit in the matter of the disappearance of Jimmy Hoffa.

Early in 1970, Terry moved to Oakville, Ontario where he was living with Tisa Farrow, actress Mia Farrow's sister. He took over the operation of The Lakeshore Film Studios on Lakeshore Blvd. West in Etobicoke. Dean was president until February 1973 when he was fired for mismanagement. I first met him through Jack Thompson and we developed a pretty good relationship. He was a tall, good looking guy who impressed the ladies. He was a guy's guy, a great talker, and he knew a lot of important people.

I had no choice. I called for a meeting and I got right to the point. "Terry you have a lot of friends that are a concern to Marty and me." Terry didn't deny his affiliations only to admit that he did intend to use his connections to get us some business that would be very helpful and profitable. What if we went ahead with the deal? No question it would open a lot of doors for us in America and elsewhere but could we live with it and what would be the cost and I don't mean financially.

After talking it over a few times Marty and I killed the deal and looked over our shoulders for quite awhile after. I heard later that Dean left town and headed back to Detroit, Tucson or New York. That was my last attempt at trying to partner up with anybody!

CHAPTER 39

The Exodus

My agents weren't happy. So what was the problem? Apparently it started with my cutting their draw temporarily and the new rule about no new management by agents. They could keep the artists they already had. I did restore everybody's draw but really what was I thinking? No management? On the other hand I had calls from a couple of managers complaining about running into my guys trying to pick up the management on the same bands that they were talking to. One complaint was from Bruce Bell manager of Lighthouse. He had run into Lawrence and Eddy talking to a band he was already negotiating with. Not good for the agency and that's why the rule. Around this same time I got some horrible news. Hank Williams Jr. had an accident on a mountain climbing trip. While scaling Ajax Peak in Montana the snow under Williams' feet gave way and he fell crashing face first into a boulder some feet below. His face was split open down the middle, hairline to chin as if struck with an axe. I felt so bad for him and I asked his rep to pass on my very best to him for a fast recovery As it turned out it took plastic surgeons two years to reconstruct the shattered bones and torn flesh; and another two years beyond that for Hank to rebuild his personal life and musical career. I hated to lose the tour but was so glad to hear that he was recovering.

I was spending a lot of money personally. I flew Lucy, my future wife, and her sister Mary to Los Vegas for a week. Neither one had been there before. I had hooked them up with Paul Anka through his uncle Andy to take care of them which he generously did while they were there. They had a great time. Stayed at the MGM Grand, got in to see all the shows, and met some celebrities. Like I said I was spending money.

On March 6, 1976 David Bluestein, unknown to me, had a meeting with all my agents out of the office. He told them about the great deal he had. An offer to open a new booking agency yet to be named and financed by Michael Cohl, Bill Ballard, Ray Daniels and David Wolylnski, and to be run by Bluestein. According to what I was told later they would all be twenty percent shareholders. Sounded like a hell of a deal. Apparently there was a long discussion on the name. Bluestein wanted to go with The Trillium Agency. Eddy came up with a name that Don Tarlton had used in a promotion in Montreal. "The Agency".

So the reply from the guys on the proposal. Cottini's response was, of course, "sounds good to me." A man of few words and straight to the point as usual. Lawrence and Eddie put their answer on hold until they could sit down and talk to me. The story was going to be they were all going into management. Really? I certainly would have believed that for about four and a half seconds. About a week after that meeting I left the office feeling pretty good and looking forward to new ways to expand our business. First one that left was George Elms who actually was supposed to be going full time into management so had one foot out the door to start with but he did end up working for the new agency. Everybody was busy on the phones, sending faxes to confirm dates; this was before emails and computers. The aroma of marijuana, nicotine and coffee was in the air. The guys were chain smoking and exchanging information with each other and clients. Irene, the office manager, had everything under control. Normal day. The next morning I got to the office around seven. When I opened the door I found a huge mess. Papers and files all over the floor and furniture all over the office. Bluestein and Cottini had split the night before taking all their files and some furniture. No warning. There were gouges and holes in the walls where they had smashed into it with furniture on their way down the stairs. They already had an office ready to go. It was a sub-lease from Moe Wortzman owner and publisher of Beetle magazine, who was in financial trouble so agreed to split his space at 913 Bathurst St. just north of Bloor. An auspicious start to the day. Later, around 11 am, Eddie and Lawrence came in to talk to me about what was going on and to resign. Thank God they didn't use the manager story. I honestly didn't hear a lot of what they said. I was a tad distracted. The only staff left was Irene the office manager. Joni had moved downstairs about a month previous to work full time with Simmons. I called Larry LeBlanc and told him what happened.

More to deal with. Vinnie Cinquimani showed up with his wife. He wanted her to see his new office and meet me. Great timing. Vinnie had been referred to me by Burton Cummings who had met Vinnie in New York shortly after he had left the Guess Who. Vinnie and his wife had been married six months when he decided to re-locate to Toronto primarily to be a musician with his duo GCB. I had booked him and his partner on a few dates. I had talked to him about becoming an agent which he finally agreed to do. I had just hired him a week previously and now here he was a little bewildered and confused. Welcome to my world. Vinnie asked "Where is everybody?" I explained what had happened. Poor Vinnie. A quote from him from an interview he did with Larry LeBlanc years later. "Concept was the biggest artist booking agency in Canada however the moment I joined everybody left the company to form The Agency?" I should have told Vinnie it was his fault. Only kidding.

It never rains but it pours. George Dasinger, Waylon's rep, called to tell me he was flying up to meet with me and showed up a couple of days later with more bad news. The Waylon, Willy tour wasn't going to happen in the near future. The reason? A drug bust at Waylon's studio in Nashville where the guys had hidden the drugs in the amplifiers and the feds got tipped off. Another problem turned up. On the last Canadian tour Ritchie Albright, the guitar player for Waylon, got into a punch-up with a Mountie and was tossed out of the country. Thanks for sharing George. Made my day. Dasinger did stay in contact with me providing gratefully received moral support. He assured me once they got their legal problems sorted out they would be in touch. Wasn't going to hold my breath on that one.

Steve Lapin from Billboard also showed up on his way through to Montreal. He offered to do whatever he could to help. At that point I was beyond help. Going to shock therapy was becoming an interesting alternative.

Hardly a ripple from anyone outside the company which was disappointing. Everyone knew what had happened but nobody was talking about it. Apparently I didn't have as many friends as I thought I had. It was a statement of how much I was out of touch with the staff. The agency business was in turmoil for a while with everybody jostling for position with the artists and managers. Included in the mass exodus were most of the bands which was a given as my agents had been working with them every day. The Stampeders stayed with me temporarily thanks to my friend Mel Shaw. Another exception was Mike Levine and Gil Moore with Triumph. I had them signed to an exclusive booking contract. We got together to discuss the situation. It was a no-brainer. They had to get on with their career which was on the brink of breaking out. Mike and Gil asked if I would release them from the contract. Of course I agreed. What was I going to do? At this point I didn't know if I even had a business. I thought that they were a class act and appreciated the way they handled their business with me. They went on to become a huge success in the business and made a ton of money. A short story told to me by Mike Levine. They had hired Eddie Glinnert to clean up their past business with promoters and other people that owed them money. Eddie sued everybody and collected every penny. He would have loved every moment of that. They took on Neil Dixon and Steve Propas as managers with the proviso that Neil and Steve had to drop all their other clients which they did. Later on Mike and Gill fired them. What fun! Steve and Neil sued for breach of contract. Mike tells me they all agreed to settle out of court at a business dinner at Barbarian's Steakhouse, the famous restaurant on Elm St. in downtown Toronto. It was one of my favourite hangouts and for the movers and shakers in the business world including the music business. The owner, Harry Barbarian, knew and was known by virtually everybody and a great guy to fill you in on the latest stories going around. Can't think of a better place to pull the plug. From that point on Mike and Gill managed their own affairs. One of the few bands to do so successfully.

Despite everything that had gone on I decided to go ahead with what was a big event for me. I asked Lucy to marry me and she said yes. September, 17, 1976, the day after my son Tommy's birthday. The wedding was one of the more entertaining parties of the year attended by a lot of the well known people in the business from everywhere. There was still nothing being talked about regarding my business problems. The reception was at Fantasy Farm, great name. A beautiful banquet facility in Toronto. The reception was in The Make Believe Ballroom. Batting a 1000 here. A fantasy in the truest sense of the word. My ushers were Gord Josie from The Friars, Fred White from CHUM, Bill Ballard, Maple Leaf Gardens and CPI, Marty Onrot, and my best man, my brother Jimmy.

Gord Lightfoot was one of the guests and decided he was going to write a song for Lucy and me. I had booked Little Caesar & The Consuls as the entertainment for the evening so Lightfoot got together with them and wrote the song on the spot. Gord and the band did one run through and it was ready to go. Gord graciously posed for a picture with Lucy. I did the same with my ushers and best man then Gord and I headed upstairs to the private suite reserved for hanging out before the reception. We shared a couple or more tumblers of scotch and then I left to start greeting the guests. It was a hell of a turnout. Everybody from Bernie Solomon to Catherine McKinnon, Lucy's family, my family, a lot of friends from all over Canada and The U.S.A. All in all around two hundred plus people. The bar was in a corner of the room and in order to get to it you had to cross a narrow bridge over a shallow moat. When the drinking had reached the right level. That would be mellow. The fun began. The bartender watched to see who misstepped on the bridge and ended up with at least one foot in the moat, sometimes two. First one in was Bernie Solomon.

Then it was time. Caesar is on stage and ready to play the first dance for the bride and groom. Can't find the groom who is back upstairs in the private room with Gord and the scotch. They finally found me and we got through the first dance. Moving right along it's time for Gord's song. He got up on stage with his guitar and they started to play. There was an immediate problem. Gord had decided, last minute, to re-write the song and was performing something entirely different than what the band was playing. May have had something to do with the scotch or just Gord's sense of humour. Somehow they worked their way through and ended the song at the same time. The crowd loved it, applauded, shouted and whistled. How could you not love Gordon Lightfoot and Caesar together on one stage?

Everybody had a great time and left happy. For our honeymoon Lucy and I flew to Florida where I ended up, on the second day, with a horrible sunburn from sitting out at the pool to long. Not a fun honeymoon but it was great to get away from everything for a short time and be one on one with Lucy.

CHAPTER 40

The Bay City Rollers, The Hollies and Roger Davies

Having recovered from the initial shock of the mutiny Vinnie and I started to re-group. Vinnie agreed to stay and we started to rebuild with what we had left of the agency which wasn't much. I wondered why Vinnie didn't go with the rest of the guys. I was told he didn't like Bluestein. At that point we shared the sentiment. In reality, I don't think he was asked. First tour that we were involved with is one I had started before Vinnie joined me. The Bay City Rollers from Scotland who had a Beatle like following in Canada and America. Their recordings were flying of the shelves. The promoter was Don Tarlton. I had put Caesar on the show as the opening act for the tour at $500 per night. They paid their own expenses. We did six dates starting in Ottawa with Beatles type mania and riots in every city. August 11, Thursday, Ottawa, On Friday, August 13, Toronto at Toronto City Hall Square. Huge crowd over 65,000 fans. Total bedlam with thousands of hysterical teenage girls sent into ecstasy and some even fainting when the Rollers stepped on stage. All the dates sold out except Edmonton that only had 9000 fans. A quote from Edmonton Journal music critic Joe Sorenberger's concert review of the show in Edmonton sums up the whole atmosphere on all the dates. "The Bay City Rollers, the five-man, tartan-clad rock band from Scotland, which tries very hard to be the new Beatles," he wrote. "Just fewer than 9,000 teenyboppers watched the show at the Northlands Coliseum in Edmonton were inspired by the Rollers to rush the stage. The Rollers played only about 40 minutes before leaving the stage twice when the crush of fans before them became too dangerous. The third time they reappeared Coliseum manager Don Clarke decided to put an end to it himself. When it was all over, when the screaming had faded, the smoke had cleared and the twenty-seven fainting, hysterical girls had been cared for, it was obvious that something had gone wrong." This was the way it was on every date of the tour and it gave Caesar a memory they will never forget. It was something to see and experience.

Back to work. Next up The Hollies tour. Interesting sidelight. Months previously, I was watching a television special from Australia starring Kenny Rogers with special guest Olivia Newton John and guest band Sherbet. Loved Sherbet! I got on the phone the next day and tracked down Roger Davis, their manager, in Australia and made the deal right there, on the phone, to bring them to Canada. Timing is everything. Roger had already been talking with Robin Brittan, The Hollies manager. As It turned out, Roger wanted to use Canada as a jump off point to get into the U.S.A. He was working on his connections, specifically, Robert Stigwood president of RSO who managed The Bee Gees, Eric Clapton and Andy Gibb. The label was, at one point, the hottest in the world with soundtracks to Fame, Grease and Saturday Night Fever. Roger made the record deal with RSO and we were off and running, we thought.

The music business in Australia was a very tight community. Everybody knew everybody with the Bee Gees, Olivia Newton John, and Helen Reddy being the forerunners. The guys in Sherbet and the Bee Gees were good friends as was Peter Foldy who often tells stories about his relationship with everybody. I had been talking to Glen Wheatly, the manager of Little River Band, long before they became a huge success and when he was still learning to be an agent in Australia and England, Another bass player/agent who just showed up in Toronto. We did a lot dates with the Little River Band in Canada in 76 -77. We also did dates on another Australian band Men at Work. Then there was Terry Wilkens and Flying Circus. When they first moved to Canada they did not have a manager. Terry was the spokesperson. While they were still in Australia Terry had seen Toronto band McKenna Mendelson Mainline, the band that Wayne Thompson was managing, at a concert in Sidney. Australia. Terry talked to the guys in the band and heard all about Canada and got interested in checking it out. The music business in Australia was a very tight community. Everybody knew everybody with the Bee Gees, Olivia Newton John, and Helen Reddy being the forerunners. The guys in Sherbet and the Bee Gees were good friends as was Peter Foldy who often tells stories about his relationship with everybody. I had been talking to Glen Wheatly, the manager of Little River Band, long before they became a huge success and when he was still learning to be an agent in Australia and England, Another bass player/agent who just showed up in Toronto. We did a lot dates with the Little River Band in Canada in 76 -77. We also did dates on another Australian band Men at Work. Then there was Terry Wilkens and Flying Circus. When they first moved to Canada they did not have a manager. Terry was the spokesperson. While they were still in Australia Terry had seen Toronto band McKenna Mendelson Mainline, the band that Wayne Thompson was managing, at a concert in Sidney. Australia. Terry talked to the guys in the band and heard all about Canada and got interested in checking it out. At first they worked with Wayne and Skinny at Music Factory. We were doing some dates with them. I remember one tour that kept the band on the road for two months before they headed back to Australia in 1971 and then returned a year later where they became a part of the Canadian music scene. They signed a deal with Capitol- EMI Records that was said to be worth a million dollars. They were picked up for management by HP&Bell, Paul Hoffert and Bruce Bell, from Lighthouse and, later by Grant Spence formerly a member of Lighthouse. At first they worked with Wayne and Skinny at Music Factory. We were doing some dates with them. I remember one tour that kept the band on the road for two months before they headed back to Australia in 1971 and then returned a year later where they became a part of the Canadian music scene. They signed a deal with Capitol- EMI Records that was said to be worth a million dollars. They were picked up for management by HP&Bell, Paul Hoffert and Bruce Bell, from Lighthouse and, later by Grant Spence formerly a member of Lighthouse.

Roger Davis and I hit it off immediately. Kindred spirits? I don't know, but we thought a lot alike and like me he was high on women as artists. He too had worked his way up through the ranks and became a partner in Australia's first National agency. The Let It Be Agency. The boys in the band loved Toronto and were finding it sort of Australianish. Another new word? The girls loved them. My wife Lucy was their tour guide and was a great public relations person so they got to meet a lot of women people as well as guys. As word got around who they were they started getting recognized on the street and in some of the clubs.

TID BITS

Roger started as a roadie and a bass player. Sound familiar?

First Canadian date. Massey Hall promoted by Marty Onrot. Great start. A knock them dead show by the Hollies and Sherbet including encores for both. Excellent reviews. From there it was Winnipeg, Regina, Saskatoon, Edmonton, Calgary and Vancouver. All great dates. All promoted by Frank Wippert out of Winnipeg. The bands got along really well. It was like a travelling frat house. Robin and Roger were good friends and we talked about future tours with this same package. While on this tour I spent a lot of time trying to explain what had happened to me back in Toronto Not a lot of wiggle room here so I told the truth. Both Roger and Robin expressed their disgust with the way I had been handled. They both said that they would work with me on future dates. That meant a lot to me. Problem was I wasn't sure I was going to be around to work with!

After the tour with the Hollies time for Sherbet to chase the American dream. Never happened. We kept them working but it was mostly going nowhere dates. Same thing was happening with dates in the States. They basically got cut off at the knees by RSO, their record company who, by that time, were having troubles of their own dealing with lawsuits by the Bee Gees, $200 million dollars worth, for mismanagement. Sherbet should have been a home run but RSO thought the name Sherbet wasn't tough enough. Hello? Australia. Number one! Where were their heads at? Not tough enough? Sherbet was the most successful Australian rock band of the 1970s. With 20 consecutive hit singles to their credit, 17 albums that yielded ten platinum and 40 gold disc awards Sherbet was the first domestic act to sell a million dollars worth of records in Australia. Under Roger's direction the band pioneered the concept of national rock tours travelling cross-country to play everywhere including the secondary markets. Put the band on stage anywhere and they nailed it. The same idea we had back in the sixties in Canada and what Frank Barcelano had done in The States. I'm not sure what happened but, after a couple of recordings that didn't fly, the label dropped the band. They should have come back to Canada and work with some of our people like Bob Ezrin or Terry Brown. I think Roger, as I did with Ocean, lost interest when there was no progress and he had other things to do. Sherbet, after banging their heads against the wall, were running around America and releasing records on a couple of different labels that never made it past the top 200. In Australia they had lost touch and were considered passé. Accomplishing nothing as far as a career, without record company support, or a manager, a couple of name changes that didn't help, they just faded away. After the Hollies tour Roger relocated to the U.S.A. permanently. He had made a deal to work for Lee Kramer who was managing Olivia Newton John. He later went on his own to manage Olvia, Tina Turner, Cher, and Janet Jackson. He was instrumental in Tina's and Olivia's career comeback in the Eighties. Where the hell was he when I was managing Ocean? We stayed in touch but there wasn't much we could do together at the time but I did so want to tour Tina Turner. She is just an amazing artist and one blistering hot lady.

CHAPTER 41

Running out of options

I n 1977 Vinnie was offered a job at Music Shoppe working for Ron Scribner. We had an amicable parting. While we weren't close friends we did respect and like each other. I couldn't fault him for accepting the opportunity. Our office was not the most exciting place to be these days. Irene had left about 3 or 4 weeks after the guys to go to work, where else, The Agency. The writing was on the wall as far as my future and Concept. With very little happening I closed the office on Dupont and started working out of home. I sold the Inglewood house and we rented the main floor of a two storey house at 2 Heathdale Road. It was not Inglewood but it was at least in a decent neighbourhood with good schools for the kids. Lucy and I were still having fun and enjoying each other. I was doing enough that it kept my name in the hat barely.

That same year Bluestein tried to make a deal with Scribner to merge their two agencies under the name Music Shoppe. Ron, thinking it was a done deal, jumped the gun and leaked the news of the merger to the media and articles started showing up all over the place. This was big news in the Canadian music business. One very well read article was in Billboard Magazine written by David Farrell. They had a few meetings to organize the merger but couldn't get some of the people to commit. In the end, Bluestein took a pass and stayed as The Agency. Within days after that, Vinnie, along with Scribner's longest associate Ralph Jolivet and long standing agent with Music Shoppe Mike Greggs, pulled the same exodus on Scribner that had been done to me. They left and formed Platinum Artists which took Scribner out of the business permanently. One thing you can say about the agency business loyalty knows no bounds. Eventually, in 1985, Platinum folded. Vinnie and Mike Greggs joined The Agency that was now to all appearances and thanks to the agents and staff, oops, mostly my former agents and staff, the top agency in the country working hand in hand with Sam Feldman and Bruce Allen on the coast. Much later, in 1993, Sam Feldman, with his partners, opened an office, S.L. Feldman & Associates Agency, in Toronto, and went head to head with The Agency which was losing money hand over fist. In the end The Agency ended up selling out to Feldman. Vinnie joined up as a vp. and then, later, as president of what is today, one of the largest and most successful booking agencies in the world of music. For me that was a kind of retribution and, at the same time, a compliment to Ron and me. What goes around comes around. It's like a legacy. I wasn't sure what happened to Ralph Jolivet until years later I found him retired in Thailand.

CHAPTER 42

Lisa Dalbello. The last dance

This all leads up to my next and last adventure in Canada. An interesting challenge for me. In 1978 I got a call from Elvio Del Zotto of the Tridel Corporation one of the largest real estate developers in Canada. He wanted to contract me to work with Lisa Dabello, a Toronto performer and writer. Her dad was president of Aluma, a sub company of Tridel, and had asked Elvio to help with his daughter's career which was having difficulties. Elvio agreed to help. She had released her first album of dance styled pop songs, "Lisa Dalbello" in 1977, produced by David Foster, which won her a "Most promising Female Vocalist" Juno award. A second album, Pretty Girls, in 1978, gave Lisa a "Best New Female Vocalist" Juno as well. She had a hit single, "Pretty Girls", the title track from the album.

Lisa was and is an amazing talent, writer, performer, hell of a voice, great looking woman and, for the most part, not at all interested in listening to anybody regarding her career. Here's Tommy again. At this point Lisa's career was at a real low point despite all the accolades. Bring in a gunslinger. That would be me. This wasn't management. It was more agent/facilitator. I met with Elvio, the first time, at the Woman's Bakery outlet west off Yonge St., near Summerhill, behind the main production facility for Hunt's Bakery and Woman's Bakery stores. Del Zotto's Tridel owned both the companies. He also financed Talisman Records which Lisa was signed to for recording & publishing. This was after the disaster with MCA Records when they dropped her from the label because her productions were too expensive. Short sighted I think. Lisa had also been working with

Jim Vallance from Vancouver who I got to know when he was working with Al Forman the keyboard player from Scrubaloe Caine. She did some amazing recordings with him. He knew how to work with an artist to get to most out of them. Unfortunately, that went south when she was signed to Capitol and changed producers. Elvio and I discussed what needed to be done, what the problems were, and what I could do to get things back on track. This was, in hindsight, an exercise in futility. We agreed on my contract which was fair and I moved into my own office at the Tridel Head Office on Keele St. north of Finch Ave. in Toronto. I also moved Lucy and the boys to an apartment on Steeles Ave. at Yonge St. which was ten minutes from the office. I had fired Nidia. Caught her smoking dope. We hired a new nanny, a young Chinese guy who was wonderful with the boys. Lucy went back to work. Shortly after I started the job I was invited to Elvio's house on the Bridle path, the most prestigious area in Toronto, for a social/business evening. I met his family and some of his business associates who I don't remember which may be just as well. I don't know how big the house was but it was big enough to have a full sized tennis court in the basement.

I knew Lisa from some of the shows I had done that she was on. She was the opening act on one Gino Vannelli tour. Lisa was also firmly entrenched in the music scene in Toronto working in the studios doing background vocals, commercials and appearances on music shows on television. With artists like Domenic Troiano, Shawn Jackson, Roy Kenner and Wayne St. John. I had the first meeting with Lisa's mom and dad and Lisa at the office. I thought it went okay. First order of business I set up a tour in Upper New York and Michigan states through some of my contacts like Frank Barcelona, Sid Bernstein and Fred Petty to promote the record in The States to see if we could get some momentum going. Interesting tour. I spent most of my time hauling everybody out of everybody else's room. Party time. I will say that onstage Lisa was dynamite. We did the usual radio and media interviews and appearances almost as an afterthought.

Behind the scenes was Roy Kenner one of my favourite people on earth. Booked him first with RK & The Associates, then with Domenic Troiano and the Mandala and eventually with the James Gang. He was Lisa's boyfriend and had spent a lot of time dealing with Delzotto and Lisa's parents before I came along. Kenner was certainly involved in launching Lisa's career. Her first single, "Don't Want To Stand in Your Way", was co-written by Kenner and Lisa, and is regarded as one of the strongest songs on her self-titled 1977 debut album.

I loved that song. Roy also set Lisa up with David Foster, a friend of his one of the best writers and producers ever in the music business and who worked with everyone from Natalie Cole, Celine Dion, Whitney Houston, Jennifer Lopez to Rod Stewart and Barbra Streisand. David has never forgiven Roy, tongue in cheek, but the situation was, apparently, difficult. The problem was a simple one. Lisa was very stubborn, knew what she wanted, and I guess David wasn't it. Roy was doing everything he could to get Lisa on track. I believe I could have convinced Lisa to listen and work with someone, not me, who would understand what she was looking for and had the knowledge to know what to do we would have been home free and she would have had an outstanding career probably managing herself. However and not for lack of trying I wasn't involved with any of the recording activities and was pretty well relegated to being a promotion man. I tried to make it happen but Lisa really wasn't interested in listening. She was so young. She had her own visions and path to follow so, in fact, it didn't matter what the people around her did or didn't do, including me. I hadn't thought of it at the time but I should have tried to set her up with Roger Davies. A couple of good things happened. Lucy met Lisa and her younger brother Stefan at a Variety Club function at Variety Village in Toronto that we attended. I was a member. Lucy and Stefan hit it off and she was able to help him out with his girl problems. He was only seventeen. They were good buddies. Elvio hired Lucy to do some promotion work with his Hunt's Bakery company. I had only been involved for a few months and was already realizing that this was not something that I could work with. I was pretty well blocked off. Anything I was willing to offer wouldn't be worth the powder to blow it to hell. I kept looking for a solution even though I knew what it was. Roadblock at every turn. That being realized, I met with Elvio, told him what I thought and resigned. Nothing in my contract said I had to be masochistic. As an aside, it turned out later, and nothing to do with me, Roger Davies did pick up the management on Lisa and ran with it. Enter Deane Cameron as A&R at Capitol Records working with Lisa first through Elvio then, later, with Roger Davies. Short lived. Roger had by this time worked with the best in the world and couldn't get Lisa's career on track. It is fascinating story. Whatever else she is an amazing talent that should be a superstar. You can't help but like and respect her as an artist, writer, producer and performer and person. She did, eventually, find a niche that worked for her and while not exactly Madonna or Mama Gaga, like a cat, she landed on her feet.

CHAPTER 43

It's over.

So that was it. A very long journey. Writing this book has been a catharsis for me. If you recall my remarks at the beginning of my life in the music business about managers, agent/managers, friends, record producers, radio people, lawyers, publishers, writers, arrangers, accountants and just about everybody I have come across in the Canadian music business all had high hopes when it came to management. The list shortens considerably when it comes to moving outside the comfort zone and up the ladder into the national and international markets, delivering the goods, and being successful. Bruce Allen, who I still like and respect in spite of himself, is one of the few that went the extra mile beyond the barriers to take his artists international where they deserved to go. No easy task with a lot of pitfalls and disappointments along the way. Bruce liked and respected his artists, had their interests at heart and, most important they trusted him with their careers and he delivered. Ray Danniels was another one that did the same thing with rock stars Rush. So many others, Some just totally inept, some with good intentions who were not equipped to deliver while others were just a-holes taking advantage of the artists for the almighty buck. So many different people so many different motives. People dealing with amazing talent but didn't take it to the top for many reasons not the least of which was that they just really didn't know how. Sometimes it was the artists themselves that fucked it up. What a huge waste of talent got left behind and there is no question the drugs, booze, life style and lack of knowledge took their toll. The good Canadian managers such as Bruce Allen, Ray Daniels, Bernie Finklestein,

Donald Tarlton and Terry Fludd, Len Rambeau, Mel Shaw, Warren Cosford and a short list of others, went all the way because they cared about their artists and took care of business.

So there you have it. That is my story. There was no longer a place for me in the business in Canada. It broke my heart that I couldn't take my family with me on the journey I was about to take to try and find myself.

Fortunately Shawn had cleaned up her act and was married to a pretty nice guy so I called her and we agreed that I would send Tom and Jeremy to live with her and her husband until I could get myself together. Lucy was okay with that. I told all that I would stay in touch and let them know when we could get back together. It broke my heart to say goodbye to the boys in the apartment and it was all I could do not breakdown in front of them. I did as soon as I closed the door behind me. It was like I had a hole in my heart. I had already spoken to my daughter Lisa who was living with her mother Joanne. The kids were justifiably confused about what was happening with me. I didn't speak with anyone in the business. What would be the point? I left Toronto on May 16, 1979. I bought a plane ticket to Los Angeles and got my ass the hell out of town. What happened to me after that is a sequel for another time. I should call it the continuing adventures of Tommy Wilson.

What a ride Scribner and I had from the very early days as pioneers in his basement to the amazing adventures through the 50's 60's and 70's. What we did can never be done again. The world has changed in so many ways. We, along with so many others, helped create a rock music industry in Canada that has grown to become the envy of the world and represents many billions of dollars added to the economy every year. It was a most exciting period in music business history both onstage and backstage and it doesn't get much better than that! The view I shared is a different from the usual. As an agent I worked with or was involved with so many people it boggles the mind and has made this a very difficult book to write. I apologize to all the people I have missed and/or left out. I had to force myself to stop or I would be writing for the next five years. You know who you are and you know what you did. May the journey never end

In 1982 Ron Scribner joined Marsh Realty a commercial real estate company in Toronto as an agent and had a very successful career I don't know if he was happy. I hope so. He was a good friend for many years until his death of a heart attack in 2000. I still miss him and Domenic Troiano.

As for me the best is yet to come. My life has been one adventure after another. Hope you enjoyed my journey. Thanks to all my friends and so many other people who have put up with my emails, phone calls, and meetings while I wrote this story. Special thanks to Vivian Risi who inspired me to start writing and I hope will write her own story that needs to be told.

Larry LeBlanc, Jerry McCarthy, Shawne Jackson Roy Kenner, Duff Roman, Marty Melhuish, Lawrence Schurman, Roger Ashby, Bill Gilliland, Pegi Cecconi and Lucy Wilson for all their help support and information. My son Jeremy who created the amazing cover for this book. Tom Jr. who helped with the editing. My big brother and my best friend Jimmy one the straightest people I know and who was unfortunate enough to share my journey and hung in through all of it. The women, the drugs, the booze, the wins, the losses and the lifestyle that was 180 degrees different than his. He never once judged me. He was invaluable in the editing with his knowledge of language, grammar and structure. Last but most important, thanks to my children Lisa, Tom, Jeremy and my grandsons Aleks and Booker who are my life and to my beautiful daughter-in laws Yvonne and Kate. Thank you for being. I love you all.

In the words of my friend Linda Dawe"As we both know, it's all about the journey" "Hang On Sloopy"The best is yet to come.

Tommy Wilson

TIDBIT

The story doesn't end there. As I said in the beginning my life has been a roller coaster ride with many ups and downs. That rule didn't change in 1979 and the best is yet to come. Funny , sad, exciting, scary a challenge but never a dull moment. I can hardly wait till I have finished writing the continuing story. After all

I AM TOMMY!

TOM WILSON HISTORY IN PICTURES

Dad & Jimmy 1938

Me & Santa Clause 1943

Mom, Dad, Jim & Me 1946 Port Dover

Me second on the right Central Tech, Junior Basketball Team 1952

Me 16 years old 1957

Original Consuls 1957

Little Caesar & The Consuls 1960

Joanne & Me June 3,1961

Ron Scribner Duff Roman & Caesar 1963

Joanne & Me 1964

Little Caesar & The Consuls 1965

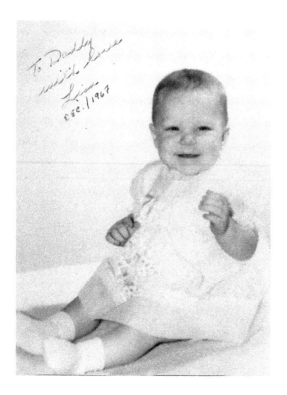

Lisa Kathleen Wilson Born April 10, 1967

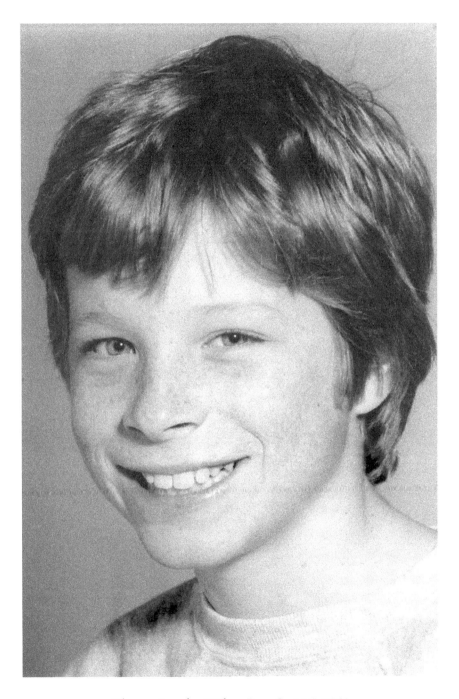

Thomas Brandon Wilson Born Sept.16, 1968

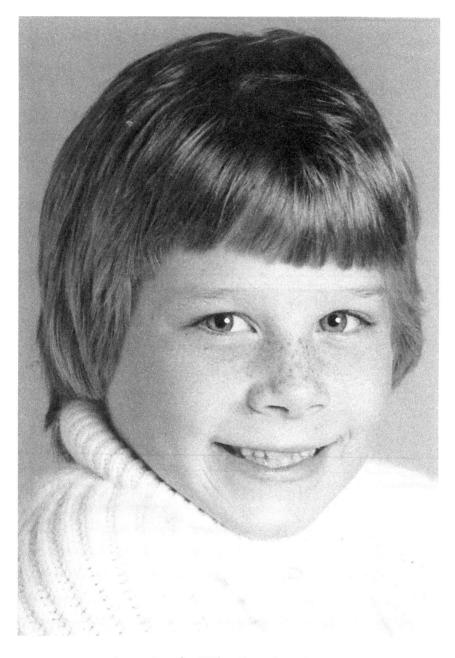

Jeremy Brandon Wilson Born Oct. 18, 1972

Ocean 1971

Me & Burton Cummings 1975

Tom Wilson. His Concept 376, with offices in Toronto and Montreal and connections all over the continent, likely makes Wilson our most powerful booking agent. Consequently, he's the man *Billboard* picked to head a panel discussion on Canadian music later this year in Los Angeles, and with Wilson persuading people like David Garrick, Bruce Allen and Al Mair to join him on the panel, it could very well make Wilson even more significant than he already is.

Me Toronto Star June 7, 1975

Lucy & Me Sept. 17, 1976

Gord Lightfoot & Lucy 1976

Gord Josie, Jim Wilson, Fred White, Me, Bill Ballard ,Martin Onrot
The groomsmen, my wedding Sept.17,1976

LITTLE CAESAR & THE CONSULS DISCOGRAPHY

Singles

1956 Runaway/ I'm Happy (Able Records)

1963 If...(I Found A New Girl)/Two Bits (Columbia)

1964 Troubles And Trials/Something's Funny, something's wrong

1965 **(My Girl) Sloopy/ Poison Ivy (Red Leaf)**

1965 You Really Got A Hold On Me/It's So Easy (Red Leaf)

1965 Shout/

1966 You Laugh Too Much /A Thousand Miles Away(Red Leaf)

1966 Mercy Mr. Perry/I'll Do The same Thing For You (Columbia)

1967 My Love For You/My love for you instrumental (Columbia)

1976 Hang On Sloopy

1965 Little Caesar & The Consuls (Red Leaf)

1993 The Original Little Caesar & The Consul Since 1956 (Attic Records)

Compilations/Other 1990 "(My Girl) Sloopy" on 'Made In Canada - Volume One: The Early Years' (BMG) - compilation

.

CPSIA information can be obtained
at www.ICGtesting.com
Printed in the USA
LVHW090509110219
607101LV00003B/12/P

9 781525 529078